CHARTISM IN ESSEX AND SUFFOLK

by
A. F. J. BROWN

ESSEX RECORD OFFICE &
SUFFOLK LIBRARIES AND ARCHIVES
1982

First published 1982
by the Essex Record Office,
County Hall,
Chelmsford
and the Suffolk Record Office
and Suffolk County Libraries Dept.,
County Hall,
Ipswich.

© Essex County Council and Suffolk County Council

Essex Record Office Publication No. 87

ISBN 0 900360 62 3

Printed by J.B. Offset, Marks Tey, Colchester

Chartism in Essex and Suffolk

Chartism in Essex and Suffolk

CONTENTS

Preface

1. **The Economic and Political Background**
   - *The local economy* — 9
   - *Early Reform movements* — 14
   - *Rural workers' movements* — 22
   - *Urban working-class movements* — 30

2. **Chartism, 1838-9**
   - *Foundations* — 39
   - *Chartist influence widens* — 46
   - *Into the countryside* — 50
   - *The wider conflict* — 56

3. **Years of Maturity, 1841-5** — 62

4. **Recovery and Final Decline, 1846-58** — 77

5. **Assessment**
   - *Chartist aims and methods* — 85
   - *The limitations of Essex and Suffolk Chartism* — 96
   - *The response of the Establishment* — 103

6. **The Legacy of Essex and Suffolk Chartism**
   - *Contribution to later Reform movements* — 110
   - *Influence on later working-class movements* — 117

7. **Conclusion** — 123

   Sources, Notes and References — 126

   Map: Major scenes of Chartist activity — 132

   Indexes — 133

Preface

This book originated over forty years ago in a conversation with my tutor, G. D. H. Cole, who believed that Chartism could not be fully known until it had been examined in its regional settings. The research and writing were carried out in 1939 and 1947 and the final revision in 1981-2. It is now offered as a contribution to the slowly growing body of regional Chartist studies, with two claims to possible usefulness. Firstly, though Chartism was at its most powerful in industrial areas and major urban centres, it did take root in some predominantly rural regions, too, and the sum of its support in the latter places constituted an appreciable part of its total national strength. In the absence of any survey known to me of one of these rural Chartist regions, Essex and Suffolk Chartism seemed a topic important enough to merit the completion of my earlier work upon it. Secondly, I hope that a service will have been done to Local History if working-class movements are shown to have exerted influence within local society; they have been largely ignored by local historians until recently.

I have limited myself to Essex and Suffolk for three reasons. Together they constituted one of Chartism's recognised regions in 1838-9, in 1848 and probably during the intervening years; to have included the adjacent county of Norfolk would have obliged me to give the major Chartist centre of Norwich a superficial treatment which its rich history did not deserve; and, finally, Essex and Suffolk contained few enough Chartist branches to permit a detailed study of at least some of them.

My thanks to a number of people for their advice and assistance, especially the following; Mr. Victor Gray and Mr. William Serjeant, the Essex and Suffolk County Archivists; the staffs of the Essex and Suffolk Record Offices; Mr. P. R. Gifford and the staff of the Essex Libraries, Local Studies Dept., at Colchester; and Mrs. Cynthia Bambrick of Lexden, Colchester.

Arthur Brown
September 1982

1

The Economic and Political Background

The local economy
During the 18th century the region's economy had been transformed by the decline of the woollen cloth industry and the expansion of agriculture. In 1700 the production of bays and says had so dominated north Essex and south Suffolk as to make them one of Britain's most industrialised regions. Its centres had been Colchester with 1,600 handloom weavers, Braintree and Bocking with 800, Sudbury and Long Melford also with 800, then Halstead, Coggeshall and a dozen other smaller centres. The 6,000 handloom weavers and the 2,000 combers, fullers, beaters and roughers were chiefly concentrated in the towns; the 60,000 domestic spinners were found all over the region, most of them in villages, producing yarn for Norfolk and London as well as for Essex and Suffolk. In its main areas the industry dominated local society, with the clothiers living in impressive houses and exerting considerable civic influence and with the textile population taking most of the produce of the neighbouring farms. From 1700, however, it was in constant decline, due mainly to its dependence on the Spanish and Portuguese markets from which the wars of the period so frequently cut it off. The Napoleonic Wars completed its extinction; by 1830 weaving had ceased and only a few hundred spinners were producing yarn for Norfolk.

As the cloth industry died out, the silk industry moved in from Spitalfields to take advantage of the unemployed textile labour, the low wage-rates and the proximity to London. It took root in Braintree and Bocking, Halstead, Coggeshall and Sudbury, but only to a small extent in Colchester; there were throwing mills also in a number of other places, though some had only a brief existence. The weavers all used handlooms, mostly in their own homes, until Samuel Courtauld in the 1830s began to employ hundreds of female weavers on power-looms in Halstead. The silk was thrown in water-mills and later in steam-mills. In 1851 there were about 1,500 male and female handloom weavers and 2,500 female throwsters, twisters and winders; in addition, Courtauld's Halstead factory employed several hundred female power-loom weavers. Silk proved an inadequate replacement for woollen cloth, employing far fewer workers; 600 or more villages, which once had spun woollen yarn, received no income at all from silk. Women's employment was thus badly affected. Except for silk and domestic service, there were now only three very minor occupations for the growing female population of the villages, straw-plaiting in the Halstead district, domestic tailoring for Colchester clothing firms and tambour-lace making in and near Coggeshall, but in 1830 these between them probably employed only 5,000 at the most. The silk industry itself proved insecure, except for Courtaulds, and its workers, male and female, sometimes had little or no work. There was always the danger, too, that London firms operating in the region would transfer their businesses elsewhere, leaving their workers here to persuade another firm to come in their place, not a situation that strengthened the workers' bargaining position.

While the cloth industry declined, agriculture expanded until by 1800 it dominated the economy. The proximity of London had long been a stimulus to Essex and Suffolk farming and after 1750 the capital's population growth encouraged further development here. Landowners, especially in Essex, having in many cases made their own fortunes in trade, were ready to favour enterprising and technically progressive tenants. Indeed, they themselves often took a lead in trying out new methods and using improved equipment. Farmers owning their own farms were also to the fore. Arthur Young, the agricultural journalist, wrote of those he met in Suffolk:

> "The most interesting circumstance is . . . the rich yeomanry, as they were once called, being very numerous, farmers occupying their own lands, of a value from £100 to £400 a year. A most valuable set of men, having the means and the most powerful inducements to good husbandry, carry agriculture to a high degree of perfection".[1]

There was therefore a general readiness to take up the new techniques from Norfolk and elsewhere and to adapt them to individual farms, though, as Young noted, the many small improvements made by the region's farmers on their own initiative added much to the general progress. By 1800 new rotations, systematic drainage and manuring, reclamation of coastal land, the grubbing up of unprofitable woodland, improved implements, more efficient farm buildings, experiments in stock-breeding and the first steps in drill-sowing were being reported from all over Essex and Suffolk, which had now come to be regarded as a particularly progressive region. Supporting services were improving. Most main roads to London were turnpiked, as were some of those to the ports, such as from Sudbury to Colchester and from Braintree to Maldon. Rivers were canalised or otherwise improved so as to carry farm produce cheaply to the ports for shipment to London, the Netherlands or north-east England. The Stour had been made navigable to Sudbury in 1706, the Blyth to Halesworth in 1756, and the Stort to Bishop's Stortford in 1769. The improvement of the Chelmer, so long discussed, was finally completed in 1797, though with Heybridge instead of Maldon as the starting-point. At almost the same time the 16-mile Gipping Navigation linked Ipswich to Stowmarket, costing £26,000 but halving transport costs for farmers and coal merchants. By 1800 improved equipment was being manufactured by Ransomes of Ipswich and Garretts of Leiston, though many farmers still relied on the village smith and wheelwright.

The Napoleonic Wars brought unprecedented prosperity to farmers and landowners. Wheat prices were doubled, sometimes trebled. The military camps offered a particularly convenient market. Some landowners and farmers, especially in west Suffolk, extended their estates and farms through enclosure, considered a patriotic policy in wartime and facilitated by new legislation. Under-used land and even good pasture were converted to arable cultivation, so that in north-west Essex dairy-farming almost ceased.[2] Technical progress was accelerated. However, the Peace brought two decades of depression. Optimism yielded to anxiety, as the Corn Laws came under attack, Reform threatened the agricultural hegemony, tenant-farmers quarrelled with landowners over rent, and labourers by strikes, riots and incendiarism gave the impression of getting completely out of hand. Reform came in 1832 but landowners and farmers remained masters of their villages, the labourers were contained, prices steadied, wages were kept down, while social security costs were reduced by the New Poor Law. Though small farmers, who had remained solvent during the high prices of wartime, struggled in the post-war depression, in the 1830s the substantial farmers began to recover, often with their holdings increased. They faced a constant struggle which they did not win every year, but by 1850 they found that they had survived Corn Law Repeal and were equipped to profit from the favourable prospects opening before them. The standard of farming was still improving, partly through the educational work of the agricultural societies, which by 1845 were active in every area of Suffolk and at Dunmow, Earls Colne, Braintree, the Oakleys, Witham and numerous other centres in Essex.[3] Surveys of Suffolk farming in the 1840s showed that the practices which in 1800 had been largely confined to a progressive minority, such as machine-threshing, drilling and systematic draining, were commonplace all over the county.[4] Meanwhile enclosure was still adding to the cultivated area; in 1816-40 there were 43 Acts for this purpose passed for Suffolk and a somewhat smaller number for Essex where the long-enclosed countryside offered less scope.[5]

Landowners and farmers dominated the whole region. The former constituted a powerful ruling group, overwhelmingly Tory and Anglican; the few surviving Whigs, on central issues like the Corn Laws, the containment of rural discontent or the Anglican establishment, did not dissent from the majority. Most landowning families, whatever their origins in commerce or the professions, had been long enough settled here to have acquired the assurance, experience and local knowledge needed to meet all challenges. They had always absorbed qualified newcomers to their ranks and they mixed with the larger farmers with easy condescension. They could be bigoted and reactionary, like 'Gaffer Gooch' of Benacre Hall, and over their rentals they behaved selfishly after 1815, but they gave way when they had to and most of them chose to facilitate the passage of the Reform Bill rather than risk a disruptive confrontation by opposing it. They remained rich throughout the depression. A number of families had bought land before the great rise in its price and, having raised rents in the War, they maintained these in the post-war depression without large reductions. With their wealth, social position and political power, their rule was as powerful as they cared to make it, especially in the absence of serious challenge from the middle class who in this region were too dependent upon agriculture to offer any. They provided Tory and Whig M.P.s for the counties and sometimes even for Ipswich, Colchester and Maldon, while Bury St. Edmunds, Eye, Aldeburgh, Orford and Dunwich were their pocket boroughs. At Quarter Sessions they could supervise their counties, at Petty Sessions control their immediate districts and, as individual Justices, check and direct parish officers. Any movement against their dominance of rural society had no prospect of even limited success.

Under the supervision of the landowners, the farmers ran the villages, proving equally successful in the prosperous years up to 1815 and in the period of uncertainty and depression after Waterloo. The more enterprising of them had mastered the new agricultural techniques and, with typical self-reliance, had modified these to suit their own soil. Through fluctuating prices, war-time labour problems and the post-war depression they had gone steadily ahead. As small farmers relinquished their holdings, those remaining increased their own acreages. In Little Baddow, with its 2,738 acres, 24 men had been farming in 1750, about half of them on less than 50 acres; by 1800 there were seventeen farmers, only one with under 50 acres; and by 1851 there were only ten, four of them with over 200 acres each and a fifth with some 700 acres.[6] Wheat output in Essex had increased to well over 500,000 quarters by 1820, of which little more than a third was consumed in the county, the remainder going to London, northeast England and the Netherlands. The 120,000 quarters of wheat and 140,000 sacks of flour, which reached London from Essex through the main corn factors, comprised 38 per cent of all the British wheat and 39 per cent of all the British flour sold in London through such channels; Suffolk supplied 21 per cent and 9 per cent respectively. Wheat and flour also reached London by channels other than these factors. Moreover, Essex wheat fetched higher prices in London than that from other counties.[7] So farmers here regarded London prices as something to which their local customers took second place, especially in times of scarcity when prices were even higher. By 1815, when farming had been completely commercialised, many farmers had become hard-headed businessmen for whom the village interdependence of earlier times was now no more than a memory. Until 1834 Poor Law administration remained their responsibility and served as a reminder of their obligation to the village poor, but then the New Poor Law broke their direct connection with such problems. Meanwhile they controlled the villages, making the parish Vestries into their instruments of government. Until the 1830s they took turns as Overseers of the Poor, through the Settlement Law they controlled migration in and out of the villages, and unofficially they decided at Vestry what wages to pay the labourers. When, after 1834, Boards of Guardians assumed the administration of poor relief, farmers usually had a majority on these. Meanwhile they still performed the other parish offices and still settled village affairs between themselves at the Vestry. They developed their own institutions, such as agricultural societies and associations to combat crime. They were capable of defending their interests even against clergy and landowners, as was made clear in 1829-32 when some Suffolk farmers diverted labourers' protests into a movement for lower tithes and rents, and many voted for Reform candidates in the hope that Reform would remedy their grievances on these two issues. Generally, however, landowner, clergyman and farmer worked together to run the villages.

Furthermore, even in the towns the influence of landowners and farmers had been considerable ever since the collapse of the cloth trade had removed from the urban economies the only important industry not dependent on agriculture and on rural customers. The relationship of town and countryside had thereby been reversed; whereas in 1700 local agriculture had served the textile towns of north Essex and south Suffolk by feeding their inhabitants, by 1830 most towns were ancillary to agriculture and tended to accept its leadership. Apart from silk manufacture, new industries had failed to develop. As late as 1830 the expansion of Ransomes lay in the future, while Garretts at Leiston, Smyths at Peasenhall and Bentalls at Heybridge remained modest undertakings, and all four of them were still producing farming machinery and equipment mainly for the Eastern Counties. The other minor industries, which were also in the main closely connected with agriculture, remained on a small scale. At Colchester in 1851 the largest tannery employed eighteen workers, the largest mill eight, the largest brewery six and the largest malting only two; the larger of the agricultural machinery foundries in the town employed eighteen and the smaller one four. The railway made an impression when it was opened, but, after the navvies left and the public houses became quieter places, the number of permanent railwaymen proved to be insignificant, except at Colchester and Ipswich. Though steam was used at scattered points in the economy, only in part of the silk industry did it concentrate many workers in single factories. This absence of industrialisation was reflected in the 1831 census figures:

Percentage of families chiefly dependent on different occupations

	Agriculture	Trade, manufactures and handicrafts	Other occupations or none
Great Britain	35	44	21
Suffolk	55	32	13
Essex	55	28	17

Most Essex and Suffolk towns were therefore not places where were to be found any substantial groups of industrialists or others whose interests were unconnected with agriculture. Most urban businesses were on the small scale, too, and in 1815-50 their owners experienced uncertainty and insecurity to an extent that made them not insensitive to the dangers of offending their valued rural customers; indeed, there is firm evidence that they had reason to fear the consequences of voting at municipal and Parliamentary elections in a way that displeased the agricultural interests. Chelmsford, with a population of about 7,000, had an economy fairly typical of the towns in the region.[8] It contained about 26 small concerns in milling, malting, brewing and other industries ancillary to agriculture. Many of its 200 workshops were producing goods and services for the population of the adjacent villages. As the county town, a market town and a transport stage, it contained 80 inns and beershops, 150 retail shops, 120 other commercial businesses and 90 professional firms, but not a single factory that was independent of agriculture. Colchester was very similar, with only a silk factory, a large wholesale tailoring firm and its fisheries unconnected with farming. Its population was double Chelmsford's. It contained 60 small industrial concerns closely connected with agriculture, 350 workshops, 130 inns and beerhouses, 330 shops, 100 other commercial establishments and 90 professional firms. Essentially, it was a large market town; a petition from its tradesmen asked for legislation to aid the farmers, since "your petitioners are entirely dependent on agriculture for support".[9] Bury St. Edmunds, a county town, had 75 inns and beerhouses, 420 retail shops and other commercial establishments and 80 professional firms; there were also 40 small industrial concerns of the market-town kind and 300 workshops. Ipswich, where the population grew from 11,277 to 24,423 in 1801-41, did contain Ransomes' agricultural machinery works which, though on a modest scale in 1840, was soon to move to a new site and by 1850 employ about a thousand workers.[10] Other industries were two shipyards, one counted a large one with its 75 workers; "an immense paper manufactory" with 200 or more employees, mostly female; and two other foundries. It was the largest port between the Thames and Yarmouth. Yet it was also quite the most important agricultural centre in Suffolk, handling a third of all wheat marketed in the county. As the 1851 census shows, most men worked in mills, maltings, workshops, inns, shops and other establishments of the market-town kind; a contemporary writer saw it as "this non-manufacturing town".

Not only were the region's towns closely dependent upon agriculture and its prosperity, but very few of them were of a size to develop the independence of outlook to be found in very large industrial towns elsewhere. The absence of industrial employment caused migration from the region far to exceed movement into it, as population figures show:

	1801	1831	1851	Increase, 1801-51
Great Britain	10,500,000	16,300,000	20,800,000	98%
Suffolk	214,000	296,000	337,000	57%
Essex	226,000	317,000	369,000	63%

Towns remained small. In 1831 Essex contained seven with more than 4,000 inhabitants and seven with between 2,001 and 4,000, Suffolk five and fourteen respectively.

In 1815-50 the urban economy remained depressed or stagnant, with confidence low. The former quiet prosperity of the market-towns in 1750-90 had yielded to a *malaise* which seemed to brood over the whole economy. "There is no heart in us for commencing large measures of improvement" was the *Essex Standard*'s explanation of Colchester's failure to reorganise its vital river facilities at the Hythe. From the 1830s agriculture did start edging forward again, but the almost complete absence of industry, outside Ipswich and the silk-weaving towns, denied full employment to the increasing population, sent many young people away from the region in search of work, kept wages low and intensified discontent. At the same time economic stagnation led to a social stagnation in which no significant group of enterprising industrialists or large mass of factory workers had come into existence to lead the region in new social or political directions.

Early Reform Movements

The Reform cause in Essex and Suffolk originated in Whig opposition to the growing power of the King and his Tory supporters. The influence of Wilkes was considerable; in 1763, for instance, Bamber Gascoigne, Treasury candidate at Maldon, reported that "ribbons with Liberty, Property and No Excise are the ornaments of my opponents' booths and carriages . . . Guineas and scraps of Northern Britons are scattered all over the town, and I can assure you that the opposition is founded by that ingenious gentleman Mr. Wilkes and his crew and is aimed more immediately at Government than me".[11] After Wilkes' exclusion from Parliament in 1769 a number of Essex Freeholders met at the Shire Hall, Chelmsford, "in support of the right of election" and launched a petition of protest. The case of Admiral Keppel was taken up by the Reformers as an opportunity to demonstrate against Royal power. His acquittal was celebrated by illuminations in Colchester, Chelmsford, Harwich and Braintree in Essex, and at Beccles, Bury and Sudbury in Suffolk. At Bungay the occasion was linked with support for Wilkes and a request for "a speedy peace with America".[12] The American War was as unpopular in Whig circles here as elsewhere. In 1776 five hundred "respectable signatures" were secured to a Colchester petition for "conciliatory measures" towards the Americans and in 1780 a much stronger Essex resolution condemned the War as having united France and Spain against Britain and threatened the nation with economic ruin; indeed the Essex cloth industry was almost at a standstill. Signed by Lords Dacre, Cavendish and Waltham and some sixty other Whig gentlemen, this resolution also included the county's earliest Reform programme, namely Annual Parliaments, a hundred extra Parliamentary seats for the counties and an end to rotten boroughs. The Suffolk Whigs held a County meeting and passed a similar resolution.[13] Sir Robert Smyth of Berechurch Hall, Colchester, went as a 'deputy' to a national convention for Peace and Reform and followed this with a petition that secured 258 Colchester signatures. At the 1784 election he won a seat at Colchester, while in the pocket borough of Bury St. Edmunds a leading Suffolk Reformer put himself forward as an advocate of "that constitutional reform in the House of Commons which the general voice of the people . . . so loudly and so justly demands". A distinct Reform movement was now developing, especially in Essex where the Whigs had the support of some County Freeholders, some borough voters and parts of the Colchester, Chelmsford and Harwich street crowds. Committees were formed in several towns and pro-Reform petitions went up to Parliament, including one from Braintree and Halstead which carried the signatures of an impressive number of clothiers.[14] Nor did the anti-Jacobin campaign after 1789 completely silence the movement. In 1795 a Colchester meeting opposed war with France and in 1797 Essex and Suffolk Whigs met to ask the King to dismiss the Government and replace it with a Reforming one.[15] Although these meetings, supported by "Ninety Noblemen and Gentlemen of the first respectability" in Suffolk and by a similar group in Essex, were not banned, but only ridiculed and ignored, plebeian Reformers met less indulgence. A nonconformist clothier of Colchester, Richard Patmore, was prosecuted for selling Tom Paine's works, while among poor people in trouble for "sedition" was a man who wanted the French to land in England soon because he could then help them cut George III's head off.[16] Reform societies existed in several places in Essex and Suffolk, though the Press usually denied the very existence of "Jacobin" sentiments here. Crabb Robinson, the diarist, then articled to a Colchester lawyer, avidly followed the trials of the English Reformers, Hardy, Tooke and Thelwall, and on reading of their acquittal, ran through the streets shouting "Not Guilty".[17] By 1798, however, well organised anti-Jacobinism had overwhelmed the dissidents and, without being completely crushed, Reform politics subsided for a decade or more.

In 1810 the movement revived, when an Essex Freeholders' Club was formed to oppose Parliamentary corruption, to end the coalition by which Whigs and Tories shared the two county seats and to seek electoral Reform and shorter Parliaments. Among the leaders were veteran Whigs like the rector of Stisted, who, looking back to the 1780s, rejoiced that "the fire that had then been raised had never been quite extinguished", and leading landowners such as Burgoyne, Honywood and Ducane. However, the Club made a new departure in seeking support among the commercial and professional classes.[18] One of their leaders was D. W. Harvey, radical lawyer of Kelvedon and future leader of Essex Reform. He now accepted an invitation from Colchester Whigs to contest a seat on a Reform programme and also made a tacit pact with Essex nonconformists to become their spokesman, thus enrolling a formidable middle-class body. By bribery at first and, when funds ran out, by fearless campaigning, he was elected in 1818 and, after an interval, was again returned in 1826. In Ipswich, too, a Reform group had re-emerged, which, like its counterparts at Bury St. Edmunds and Chelmsford, held a demonstration against the Peterloo Massacre; the presence of numerous "labouring men and lower order of mechanics" among the 1,500 crowd showed that the movement was now reaching the urban poor.[19] The latter point was re-emphasised in 1820 when Queen Caroline's acquittal on a charge of adultery, and the rebuff thus given to George IV, led the Whigs at Ipswich, now in control of the Corporation, to announce an official illumination which was supported in two-thirds of the houses and enjoyed by huge crowds roaming the brightly-lit streets. The town's Whigs met to congratulate the Queen, and their sons held their own meeting at which 600 "respectable" youths gave a display of oratorical talent while fathers, mothers and sisters listened with pride. It was a comfortable occasion and an impressive performance which showed that, in Ipswich at least, the middle class was already too assured to be denied electoral recognition for long. Among other addresses sent from Suffolk towns to the Queen was one from Framlingham, signed by 1,105 men and 1,084 women. At Colchester, where Tories controlled the Corporation, 150 Special Constables prevented public demonstrations, but a radical group issued handbills urging an illumination, which was supported in the poorer parts of the town. The organiser, a confectioner, was boycotted by several of his well-to-do customers. The Queen's cause had thus united the three sources of Reform support, the Whigs, the middle-class groups led by D. W. Harvey and plebeian elements like the four Colchester clubs which followed "the independent interest".[20] There was a renewal of feeling at the Queen's death in 1821. Her funeral procession attracted large crowds from Stratford to Chelmsford, where thousands slept in the streets in order to greet it. At Witham next day a huge demonstration marked its arrival and at Kelvedon Lord Western and Peter Du Cane at the head of their tenantry were waiting to escort it to Colchester, where the crowd protected a local cabinet-maker when the authorities tried to stop him fixing upon the coffin the inscription which Caroline had requested. Next day thousands walked with it to Harwich and watched the ship sail away with the coffin.[21] The whole affair revealed how widely disgust with Government had spread, and this was reflected in the elections. At Colchester the Whigs won a seat in 1818 with Harvey and in 1820 with another candidate and accomplished the almost impossible task of securing places on the Corporation. At Ipswich they won both Parliamentary seats in 1820 and gained municipal control, using it to stop an official celebration of George IV's coronation. An attempt by Tories there to have the Duke of Wellington elected High Steward led to his decisive rejection at the Poll. Next, in 1822-3, Reform was taken into agricultural politics when the Whig, Sir

Henry Bunbury, persuaded meetings of Suffolk farmers that only Reform could give them relief from agricultural depression.[22]

Despite these successes, the Reform cause did not yet constitute a serious challenge to the rulers of this agricultural region and in the comparative calm of the mid-1820s the movement seemed almost to have subsided. Yet this proved to be the decade when middle-class people, whose political involvement had been limited and sporadic, were moving quietly towards a more general pro-Reform position. To some extent this was the culmination of several decades of social change during which these shopkeepers, merchants, small industrialists, professional men and master artisans had been slowly developing into a separate social grouping, more numerous than in the past, somewhat more prosperous, better educated, sharing similar ambitions and values and, in this region at least, bound closely together by their nonconformist loyalties. This process was signalised and further developed by the emergence of a Liberal Press favourable to their aspirations, the *Suffolk Chronicle* and the *Essex Mercury*. Their growing coherence was not at first matched by a corresponding political unity. Many of them were held back by agricultural connections and their consequent reluctance to oppose the Corn Laws, as well as by their lingering respect for the power and the social standing of the rural establishment. Yet they did share the belief that financial corruption in public life, both national and municipal, caused high taxation and that Reform might usher in new prosperity and they complained bitterly of the disabilities and indignities suffered by nonconformists. They felt increasingly that their own economic standing merited some political privilege and they looked with resentment at the electoral situation in their own region.[23] They saw that in the two county constituencies they had no voice at all even if, like Samuel Courtauld at Braintree or Robert Garrett at Leiston, they were large employers and high ratepayers. They knew that in the borough of Harwich the two M.P.s were elected by the Corporation, a self-perpetuating and corrupt body of thirty-two men, most of whom had long been under some form of obligation to the Government. The Bury St. Edmunds electorate was so restricted that the Duke of Grafton and the Earl of Bristol always in effect chose one M.P. each. The voters were so few at Aldeburgh, Dunwich, Orford and Eye that their eight members were in effect nominated by five aristocratic families. At Maldon, Colchester, Ipswich and Sudbury, it is true, the electorates numbered 3,000, 1,100, 800 and 600 respectively, but few middle-class people were among them, since the franchise belonged to those serving an apprenticeship to an existing freeman and to their sons and grandsons and, at Maldon, also to those marrying a freeman's daughter. A number of these electors were workingmen, much poorer than the voteless middle class, and at Maldon about 700 of the freemen were labourers. Furthermore, since the franchise was inherited by sons and grandsons of those qualified by apprenticeship, many voters lived miles away from the boroughs, having migrated when the cloth industry declined or in order to get higher wages in London. In 1830 Colchester voters comprised 317 living in London, 487 in other places and only 304 in the borough itself, so that, to the resentment of the unenfranchised middle class, a majority of electors did not even pay rates in the town. Over half the Ipswich electorate lived outside the borough. By contrast, few middle-class men had the vote. At Ipswich only seven of the 50 leading merchants and industrialists did and only three out of 22 doctors. At Colchester five lawyers, a leading banker and the Headmaster of the Grammar School were excluded. Consequently, when during 1815-32 Reform groups were started in the main towns, they increasingly represented the excluded middle class. At Ipswich the leading Reformers, whose occupations can be identified, comprised seven professional men, five merchants or bankers, five shopkeepers, three industrialists, one publican, one postmaster and one gentleman. At Woodbridge the Bull Parliament, as the Reformers who met at the Bull were called, consisted of a banker, a brewer, two timber merchants, an ironmonger, a doctor and two publicans. Leading Colchester Reformers included three merchants with businesses at the Hythe, three small industrialists and two clothiers, two professional men, two nonconformist ministers, a banker and a grocer. By 1830 these leaders were at last receiving support from a majority of their own class. Ipswich's leading banker could claim:

"It was not those who were destitute of property who were now the advocates of a Reform of Parliament; it was men who were possessed of property who advocated Reform because they considered a Reformed Parliament could make their property more secure".[24]

Among farmers no organised Reform movement had yet developed but opposition was growing against the tithe system, State expenditure on sinecures and unmerited pensions, and also the high rents they had to pay for their farms in the post-war depression. The last of these grievances is several times voiced in the diary of a Southend doctor:

"Read of the death of Earl Winchelsea . . . . No loss, and had it taken place earlier, it would have been better for this part of the country. He owned farms in Foulness and has demanded such rents as to oblige the old tenants to leave them and will ruin those who have taken them.

The agricultural state of the county is as flat as possible. Rents are still excessive, but down they must come, however reluctantly on the part of the landlords, who appear, in general, regarding themselves only and their tenants as nothing".[25]

By 1821 farmers for the first time united with Reformers over the Queen Caroline issue. Leading farmers expressed sympathy for the Queen and in central Suffolk two hundred of the "respectable yeomanry" signed a letter supporting her. A Suffolk county meeting at Stowmarket petitioned for aid to agriculture, lower taxes, Parliamentary Reform and an end to public corruption. In 1822, amid unemployment and incendiary fires, Suffolk Whigs set out to link the farmers' protests with the urban Reform movement. At a meeting to discuss the depression, despite opposition from Government supporters, disgruntled farmers insisted on prolonging proceedings in order to pass a resolution for Reform. In 1823 a Reform meeting at Bury St. Edmunds successfully petitioned the High Sheriff for an official county meeting to discuss the subject, at which once again the farmers voted overwhelmingly for Reform. Many Tory farmers had absented themselves from this meeting, so that the vote gave a false impression of the strength of the movement among agriculturalists as a whole, but their very absence was a confession that opinion was fast turning against the Government. In Essex, where the Whigs were fewer, the Tories held their ground; when D. W. Harvey proposed to a farmers' meeting at Chelmsford that they should support Reform as the key to lower taxes, he was told "that there was a chance of having his patriotism cooled in the River Chelmer".[26]

With the return of depression in 1829, there was a renewal of meetings demanding relief in both counties. Though in many places rent and tithe were temporarily reduced, farmers became increasingly outspoken. One from Earl Stonham, after attacking the modern squire living in a fine house on the proceeds of his estate, wrote:

"All we ask is a fair rent. If we were to put on smock frocks, work from morning to night harder than any labourer, walk to market and live on skim milk and Suffolk cheese, all this would not enable us to pay rent and tithe disproportionate to the price of corn".[27]

Rent and tithe dominated a High Sheriff's meeting called at the insistence of the West Suffolk Grand Jury, and farmers barracked Sir Thomas Gooch and Sir Edward Kerrison when they tried to prevent discussion of these issues. "A large body of principal landowners and most respectable yeomanry" at a similar Essex meeting heard the Duke of Wellington denounced, Essex landowners openly criticised and the lowering of rents and Parliamentary Reform placed firmly on the agenda. One critic noted "the caution with which the subject of rent had been avoided" and proposed "that the first effort to relieve the difficulties under which we are labouring should be a permanent reduction of rents", adding that tithe should be reduced too. D. W. Harvey persuaded the meeting to petition Parliament for abolition of rotten boroughs, more frequent elections, lower taxes and Poor Law 'reform'. At the Nomination for a county by-election held outside Chelmsford's Shire Hall the largely farming audience pressed for lower rents, tithe abolition and Parliamentary Reform. By the time the Grey Government presented its Reform Bill, many Essex and Suffolk farmers already believed that a Reformed Parliament would abolish tithe and reduce taxes. A Suffolk contemporary recalled how "everyone believed that the kingdom of heaven was at hand. In ten years time, I heard people say, there would be no tithe to pay".[28] Though tenant-farmers did not possess the county franchise unless they were freeholders as well as tenants, all farmers paid tithe and taxes, so that many electors were now ready to rebel against the Whig-Tory coalitions which had long dominated Essex and Suffolk county elections. This new phenomenon of rural radicalism, ephemeral though it was to prove, coincided with the upsurge of Reform sentiments in the towns and with the publication of the 1830 Reform Bill. Without this largely unexpected reinforcement the Reform cause in Essex and Suffolk would have been far less impressive in size and far less influential in its consequences.

The prospects for Reform had never seemed so bright.[29] "The day is fast approaching", wrote the *Suffolk Chronicle*, "when the voice of the People will be heard". The response to the Reform Bill's publication showed that many farmers supported it, urban workers were enthusiastic and the middle-class public had thrown aside remaining reservations. Farmers were prominent among the 3,000 people at a Suffolk demonstration. Many Chelmsford workers turned out to hear D. W. Harvey and Wellesley, the Essex Reform leaders. Both workers and middle-class people thronged the meetings held in the towns, not least in the corrupt boroughs of Bury St. Edmunds, where 400 copies of the *Bury Post* containing details of the Bill were sold in an hour, and of Eye, where the borough-owner had made clear his intention to resist the Bill. Equally impressive were the demonstrations in smaller towns like Mildenhall, Southwold, Halesworth, Beccles and Bungay; at Laxfield "all the principal inhabitants" were present. "It is a glorious movement — a universal burst of patriotic feeling", proclaimed the *Suffolk Chronicle*. "Reform must come", wrote a veteran Suffolk radical, "and Reform will remove all grievances and satisfy all demands". Colchester, Maldon, Ipswich and Sudbury 'outvoters', living outside their boroughs and destined to lose their franchise under the Bill, were so swept along in the current optimism that they refused Tory invitations to resist the measure and save their franchise. At the election of May 1831, Colchester, Ipswich, Sudbury and the counties of Essex and Suffolk returned Reformers. The corrupt boroughs did not, though at Harwich 3,000 people from the town and nearby villages demonstrated against the two victorious Tories and prevented their chairing. There was some opposition to Reform. A petition against "the Jacobin Bill" was signed by the corrupt Essex Corporations and others whose reactions were equally predictable, and a new weekly paper, the *Essex Standard*, was started to oppose Reform since the *Colchester Gazette* had joined the Reformers. However, there were notable desertions from the anti-Reform camp, including the Dukes of Grafton and Norfolk and other leading landowners. An enthusiastic Essex Reformer wrote:

"For Reform: All the aristocracy of the county; about half of the country gentlemen of fortune; a small proportion of the squirelings and the clergy only; and the great bulk of the independent members of the professions, tradesmen and yeomanry, forming together an immense majority of the inhabitants.

Against Reform: Half of the country gentlemen of fortune; four-fifths of the squirelings; nineteen-twentieths of the clergy; all the corporations and such of the professional men, tradesmen and yeomen as are under the influence of the above".[30]

When the Lords, in October 1831, rejected the Bill, the Reformers were "stunned", but they quickly rallied, and all the more effectively because they could now count on support from organised Reform Committees in all the main towns and a number of villages. At Bury the Reformers flew a black flag from the church, held an indignation meeting of 4,000 people and renewed their petitions. At Ipswich, while Tories rang church bells and fired cannons, 2,500 Reformers held a protest meeting. "Inflammatory handbills" circulated in Colchester. To regulate public anger, the Dukes of Grafton and Norfolk, the Earl of Gosfield and Lord Huntingfield, part-owner of the borough of Dunwich, summoned a Reform meeting which immense crowds attended. When 1,580 gentlemen, farmers and tradesmen failed to persuade the High Sheriff of Essex to call a similar meeting, the Whigs called their own, passing a resolution rebuking the Lords for irresponsibility and predicting that such obduracy could have "consequences dangerous, if not fatal, to the dearest interests of the country". The Bill's next defeat, in May 1832, set off a further round of protests, but by now almost everyone of influence, both locally and nationally, was ready to accept the *Chelmsford Chronicle*'s warning that "in the hour when popular fury is triumphant, all classes are in jeopardy". So the Bill's final passage was assured and it was greeted with rapture. As coaches brought the London papers, crowds thronged the streets to read the news, processions were formed, bands paraded the streets and cannons were fired. At Ipswich the effigy of a Bishop was burnt "in full canonicals" and at Bury that of the Duke of Wellington in Field-Marshal's uniform. Seven thousand came to Framlingham to celebrate, at Woodbridge 1,700 people dined in the main street, at Chelmsford, in defiance of the Churchwardens, the Reformers occupied the church to hoist flags and ring the bells. Similar rejoicing was reported from smaller places, including Thaxted, Langham, Nayland, Great Glemham, Boxford and Polstead. Two Bildeston workers, arrested for firing a cannon, were given a week in prison by resentful Justices, only to be met on release by a large procession and a gift of money. Hopes were high. An Essex observer remembered how "men appeared to have imbibed the notion that reform . . . would bring down in a shower every earthly blessing and that a tide of milk and honey was to overflow the land".[31] The number of people whose expectations had thus been aroused can only be guessed, but certainly those who in Essex and Suffolk had demonstrated, petitioned and celebrated the Bill's passage, exceeded 100,000.

The Act enfranchised £10 householders in the boroughs, giving the urban middle class a majority in Harwich and Bury St. Edmunds, and increasing their influence at Ipswich, Sudbury, Colchester and Maldon, not only by giving them the vote but by disfranchising previous 'outvoters' living at a distance, among whom were many workingmen. At the same time the aristocratically controlled boroughs of Aldeburgh, Dunwich and Orford lost both their Members and Eye lost one of its Members. The middle-class victory was, however, a limited one. The addition of the larger tenant-farmers placed the county seats more firmly under the control of the landed interests; nor was this counterbalanced by any enfranchisement of the middle class outside the boroughs. The latter gained nothing; Samuel Courtauld of Braintree, Robert Garrett of Leiston, Daniel Gurteen of Haverhill, the Marriages of Chelmsford and other substantial industrialists outside the boroughs remained unenfranchised despite their wealth and importance. The absence of the Secret Ballot left businessmen, shopkeepers and master artisans so exposed to economic pressure from their rural customers that, even at the first election after Reform, the Tories captured six of the ten Essex seats and by 1841 they held them all. The same trend, though less pronounced, was to be observed in Suffolk. The whole rural area, and some of the towns as well, were soon back under the firm control of the landed interests, the Anglican church and the Tory party.

The Reformers' disappointment did not result in any serious revival of their movement. While the struggle had been in progress, the more radical of them in both counties had planned to develop the local Reform committees into the nucleus of a Liberal party, but such organisation as was created was used merely as electoral machinery for Whig candidates.[32] The old Reform movement had ceased to exist, nor before 1866 did it make any significant recovery. When the Chartists advanced their Reform policies in 1838, theirs was the only radical movement in contention.

Rural Workers' Movements

From 1750 to 1790 farm workers and their families usually had enough to eat, with weekly wages approaching 9s., wives and daughters earning 3s. each from spinning and a stone of flour costing 1s. 6d. An expanding agriculture gave full employment, and young men could and did move to London if dissatisified or if eager to improve their prospects. The Poor Law gave a basic social security, albeit at subsistence level. Social protests were confined to brief periods of high prices, such as that of 1772, and on these occasions protesters were apt to demonstrate their loyalty to the social order by avoiding the theft of food and confining themselves to enforcing its sale at customary prices.[33] In the scarcity of 1795 there was anxiety about the behaviour of the rural poor, but the Justices and Vestries then adopted, at least for periods of high prices, a scale of family allowances varying with the number of children and the cost of wheat, the 'Speenhamland System'. This prevented starvation and, as wages slowly rose, only rarely in 1796-1814 did labourers cause the authorities any concern. In 1815-16, however, the post-war depression set in, ex-servicemen returned to the villages, wages fell to between 8s. and 10s., while woollen spinning had completely ceased, with almost no alternative work taking its place; food prices, on the other hand, were about double those of 1750. Attempts were also made to lower the level of poor relief. As villages became places of distress and discontent, observers noted that other changes had been taking place which intensified social division. The labourers had by now become a distinct economic class. In Essex and Suffolk their numbers had grown to perhaps 65,000 in 1815 and were to reach 78,000 by 1841, so that with their families they constituted the great majority of the rural population.[34] They increasingly resided, not in cottages close to farmhouses, but in rented property in the village or one of the growing hamlets. Young labourers now rarely lived in farmhouses. "The farmers keep no labouring servants in their houses", wrote a Great Henny farmer, "it being cheaper to pay them weekly wages". By 1834 yearly hirings were few and men were employed by the week, even by the day, so that personal ties with the farmers were further weakened. A farmer reported that "labourers being in general employed by the day, their services are at an end every night, without any notice whatever. They are hired and discharged daily, according as their services are wanted". The labourers, given the chance, changed their employer readily, "owing to their not being brought up under the farmer's roof, which formerly made them attached to the particular farm, as well as in every respect more tractable and more respectable", as a Little Waltham farmer put it.[35] The estrangement was intensified by the New Poor Law of 1834, which withdrew the existing social security system at a stroke just when the fall in living standards had made its retention essential to all labouring families. While farmers welcomed the consequent fall in the poor rate, the labourers now felt completely abandoned by those who controlled their villages. From 1815 to 1850 they and their families were poverty-stricken, normally exhausted by adversity and cowed by a stern control, but often bitterly resentful and sometimes driven to open protest or secret revenge; their record of machine-breaking, strikes, animal-maiming and incendiarism was so continuous and so extensive as to leave no doubt of their general alienation. Considered in terms of the Reform movements of the period, here in the villages lived the discontented masses to whom radical leaders might look for the popular support which in industrial regions came from factory workers.

The first protests occurred in 1815, as soon as living standards began to fall.[36] At this stage labourers reacted openly, if illegally, their target often being the threshing machines which, though a rarity in 1805 when Arthur Young surveyed the region, by 1815 were being made in some numbers in local foundries. After harvest in 1815 there were attacks at Kenton and Monk's Soham in central Suffolk. At one trial, it was reported, "the prisoners were called upon for their defence, but except for stating the difficulty of obtaining employment which they attributed to the use of such machines, they had but little to urge". At Rattlesden and Hundon in Suffolk, and at Lawford, Mile End and Finchingfield in Essex, the destruction of machines was made the occasion for large demonstrations, sometimes by almost all the labourers of the village. At Clare the crowd carried a machine into the market place with full ceremony and burnt it. Layer Breton labourers, accompanied by their wives, asked a farmer not to use his machine and, on his refusal, carefully packed it up and led his horses back to the stable, but when they returned to find it in use again they destroyed it. North-west of Braintree 200 men for two successive days visited farmers known to possess threshing machines and mole ploughs, destroyed a number of these and dispersed only at the news of an armed party moving against them. At nearby Sible Hedingham a crowd destroyed some machines and, when four of its leaders were led off to Halstead House of Correction, rescued them, chased the constables into Halstead and besieged them in the houses where they had taken refuge. The ensuing demonstrations in the Halstead streets drew workers in from other neighbouring villages. The crowds occupied the town for three days, breaking the windows of the larger houses, repulsing the Yeomanry and dispersing only when Dragoons arrived from Colchester Barracks. At Brandon in north-east Suffolk there was an even larger protest by labouring families from the rural area. The first incident was a demonstration against high prices on a Thursday afternoon by 200 women and boys, which was dispersed by the reading of the Riot Act. Next day labourers marched into the town and, despite the presence of a dozen soldiers, won a promise of 2s. a day in wages and lower flour prices. On the Saturday, 1500-strong and bearing a banner inscribed "Bread or Blood", they badly damaged the house of a profiteering butcher; arrests followed. Despite the Combination Acts, there was at least one attempt at trade unionism. A Wattisham labourer was sentenced "for conspiring with several others with a view to inducing labourers to form themselves into a society for raising their wages".

The failure of these open actions and the punishment that followed persuaded some discontented labourers that the safest form of protest was the incendiary fire. This was not an entirely new method, but it had been used on any scale only when prices rose in 1800.[37] In 1816, while machines were attacked in some villages, fires occurred in others, at Henham, Dengie and Langham in Essex, at Gedding, Kettlebaston, Drinkstone, Hadleigh, Stanningfield and Wickhambrook in Suffolk. For a fire at Martlesham a discharged artilleryman was among those arrested. Machine-breaking continued, but arson now so predominated as to have become the normal mode of protest. A Suffolk observer wrote that "it has become something of a *fashion*, . . . such a mode is the most practised, without discovery. *Custom* has pointed this out to every aggrieved labourer".[38] He also thought the culprits to be mainly youths who, being the last to be given farm employment, had to earn a small dole in parish gravel-pits where "they brood and vow vengeance".

After a lull during the economic recovery of 1824-8, unemployment and protest returned in 1829, when it was reported from Essex that "a great number of labourers are out of employ . . . in almost every parish". Wages fell, poaching increased and Chelmsford Gaol was filled. There was a bout of fires near Witham, machine-breaking and incendiarism at Toppesfield and four attacks on threshing machines in central Suffolk.[39] Then in November 1830, the *Ipswich Journal* reported the start of 'the Swing riots':
"It is with the deepest feelings of regret that we are obliged . . . to record a series of tumults and acts of atrocity committed in the different counties of this once peaceable and happy island; and that, too, not as heretofore, by factious demagogues in large and populous towns, but by the peasantry".[40]

Not every area was affected, but in many villages where no incident was reported, there are records of special constables enrolled, staves handed out and other precautions taken. Justices in the Rochford area told the Home Secretary that "no man's property can be considered safe" either from machine-breakers or "the still more mischievous work of the incendiaries". They attributed the troubles in Essex to agitators from outside, and there is no doubt that the events in south-east England did provide the stimulus in Essex and Suffolk, as the following notice, allegedly issued by a labourer from Stapleford Tawney, near Romford, indicates:

Samuel Whitbread, Laborer
Stapleford Tawney, nr. Romford, Essex

To the hard working (but ill used) Laborers of Stapleford Tawney, Stanford Rivers and other Parishes.

Countrymen,

The time is now come when the poor laborer is determined to have more of those comforts that he produces, than he has at present. In the counties of Kent, Surrey, Sussex, Hampshire, Berkshire, Wilts, Lincolnshire and Norfolk, the laborers all have *struck* for *higher wages,* they say they won't starve upon 8 or 10s. a week any longer. They go to the farm houses after they have got together as many laborers as they can, perhaps 200 or 300 men from 5 or 6 different parishes and *make* the farmers promise to give them 14s. a week in Winter and 15s. in Summer, and now the men have 14s. instead of 10s. They don't mind the farmer bouncing and blustering. They said they would have it and now they have got it. The men in Kent and Sussex that first struck began to plan the thing on the Sunday and went about it on the Monday. If Essex rises, it will make 10 Counties, and I know this, that it is the fault of the laborers themselves if they have 10s. a week instead of 14s., which the brave men of Kent, Sussex and the other Counties are getting. This is good news, my boys, make good use of it.

I am,

A Poor Man's Friend,

They make every man leave off work and join them. No more 10s., a week, my lads.

Show this letter to your fellow Workmen, as I know what they will say and what they will do. Beware of Spies.[41]

The first incident in Essex was an incendiary fire at Rayleigh where allegedly "a fine young man of thirty-four", with arms folded, watched a barn burn, saying "this is just as it ought to be" and "he wanted it to be the same as in Kent". Convicted of being himself an arsonist, he was hanged. Fires followed at Little Baddow, Thaxted and Braintree, and threats of them at Writtle and Roxwell, but strikes rather than arson now predominated. At Mile End, just north of Colchester, nearly four hundred met from several parishes and requested "certain conditions of employment", that is a rise in wages. The Colchester authorities were alarmed enough to prepare a defence force, but a local Justice quelled the strikes and had their leaders punished. In three quite separate areas similar events occurred; at Sheering, near Harlow, where a strike led to a charge of compelling a fellow-labourer to leave his work; at Ridgewell, in the north-west, where workers were partially successful in their wage demand; and at Arkesden beyond Saffron Walden where labourers paraded the village bringing out their fellows, before besieging the Vestry to demand better rates from the farmers there. Other strikes took place at Henham, Clavering, Steeple Bumpstead, Finchingfield and probably Ridgewell. The movement was at its strongest in the Tendring Hundred of north-east Essex. Dovercourt labourers asked 2s. 3d. a day. Great Clacton labourers, when refused an increase, went on strike, as did those of Peldon and other villages across the Colne. It was when strikes failed that machines were attacked. Crowds paraded Great and Little Clacton, Great Holland and Walton, looking for them. "The villages of Kirby and Clacton are in a complete state of insurrection, some of the labourers declaring that they could help themselves and that they would do so". At Ramsey, where 200 labourers were parading, a fire occurred which brought the military from Harwich, together with the Mayor, a *posse* of richer citizens and the fire-brigade, but no sooner had they departed with their prisoners than "the mob" destroyed a threshing machine.

Retribution was swift. Justices, despite their own testimony that the labourers had been seeking higher wages by peaceful means, felt that they must "check this spirit of insubordination". The Lord Lieutenant chaired the Shire Hall meeting of magistrates and leading landowners, which decided to arm special *"posses"* against the "illegal assemblies". The response was quick. At Danbury, the Baddows and other villages around Chelmsford, for instance, 450 Special Constables, a hundred of them mounted, stood ready to answer any summons, and a similar force was mobilised from around Colchester. 576 Specials, 140 of them mounted, were enrolled in the twelve villages of the Halstead area. On Tendring Heath nearly a thousand assembled for a man-hunt, described by the Master of Essex Foxhounds as follows:

"Dec. 11th. Rode to Hundred Heath; a vast assemblage of horsemen went through Thorpe, down to Kirby and Walton, by Holland and the Clactons, took 12 or 13 men who had been instrumental in breaking six or seven threshing machines, came home by St. Osyth and then to Brightlingsea, where these fellows had taken water for Bradwell — they had left the

Clactons in the morning. Despatched eight or ten men after them from Brightlingsea".[42]

He returned the next day to his hunting. At the ensuing trials some fifty men were sentenced to prison or transportation.

In Suffolk the movement was stronger than in Essex, but similar in pattern, with the labourers attempting to gain wage increases by open pressure and generally not resorting to violence or arson until their claims were rejected. Almost all districts were involved. In some villages farmers actually supported the labourers in the hope that their demonstrations might win the reductions in rent and tithe which most of the farming community was by now urgently seeking, and the outcome was just what they had counted on. The pattern of events was as follows. A crowd of labourers would ask farmers to raise wages, only to be told that this was impossible with prices so low and tithe and rent so high. At Whepstead, having received such a reply, they marched to the rector to request respectfully that he should reduce the tithes, which he did on condition that the labourers received the full benefit, to which the farmers agreed. The same sort of process occurred at Whelnetham, Bradfield, Rushbrooke, Weston, North Cove, Ellough, Toft, Ringsfield and Willingham. Some clergymen forestalled such pressure by voluntary abatements and some farmers withheld tithe altogether — at Brome, Oakley and Elmswell for instance. At Mellis farmers signed the labourers' petition for tithe reductions and at Bradfield refused service as Special Constables, one of them explaining, "when my rent and tithe are reduced, I have no objection and also will advance my labourers' wages". Landowners now came under moral pressure and some voluntarily reduced rents, usually on condition that wages should then be raised. The unemployed tried to improve their position, persuading some parishes in the north-west to replace gravel-pit work by full employment on farms, at 9s. for single men and 11s. for married men. At Hadleigh the unemployed working on road-repair asked for 2s. a day and were instead given farm work at 1s. 10d. The method of relief used in these places was the Labour Rate by which the farmers between them employed all the labourers proportionately to their rateable value. The same reform was won in some Essex parishes and was seen by labourers as an important guaranteee. On the other hand, where concessions were refused, violence might follow, as around Walpole where a force of Special Constables was mustered to suppress protests. A thousand labourers marched in from surrounding parishes, shouting "we are starving" and "down with rents and tithes". When a Colonel Bence arrested a "ringleader", they rescued the prisoner, roughly handling both Bence and Lord Huntingfield. Generally the authorities kept firm control. When a joint meeting of farm labourers and Ipswich workers was called on Rushmere Heath outside the town, the Justices held regular soldiers, the coastguard, militiamen, gentlemen and farmers in readiness, their anxiety being all the greater because of the urban workers' involvement. The authorities easily dispersed labourers coming to this meeting and dismissed those who managed to reach the Heath with a mixture of warnings and promises. When 'Swing' subsided and some of its leaders appeared in the Suffolk Courts, they turned out to be fairly young, with an average age of twenty-eight, men whose youth had been spent amid the unemployment and poverty of 1815-30; those who were tried in Essex Courts were much of the same age. They could not fail to see that, in places where they had not been completely defeated, their gains had been small and precarious. Their own punishment for leading open protests was in contrast to the ease with which many of those who resorted to arson had escaped detection.

Though crushed, some labourers were not yet completely cowed, partly because their livelihood remained too miserable to permit apathy and partly because poor relief, which was now part of their incomes, was already being reduced in quantity even before the New Poor Law denied them outdoor assistance altogether. They may even have shared the general belief in 1831-2 that Reform would improve their lot, if reliance may be placed on the reports of their attendance in force at Reform meetings in villages and small towns, their barracking of the formidable Sir Thomas Gooch at the 1830 election, their presence at the Reform victory celebrations of 1832 and the temporary cessation of incendiary fires for the greater part of the period of the struggle. When, like urban workers, they became disillusioned with Reform, some turned to trade unionism for help. During 1833-4 there was combination in at least three villages against wage reductions.[43] At Stansted Mountfitchet, in west Essex, over a hundred struck, called at the farms asking for the cancellation of an intended 1s. reduction, released the horses from the ploughs and went peacefully home; their moderation and openness gained them no credit, for their leaders were tried on charges of intimidation. A reduction at Cressing, near Braintree, caused a strike which quickly collapsed because the labourers had insufficient food to see it through. Around Eye, in north Suffolk, "large assemblages" met in several villages "to oppose combination by combination" and to prevent a 15 per cent reduction. For three days they went around the farms bringing out so many others that the reduction was cancelled, this despite the action of the Justices of the borough of Eye and some county Justices in bringing in Suffolk and Norfolk Borderers to induce them "to return to their labour without being shot at". Finally in 1836 the first attempt to found a permanent trade union took place in north-east Essex, where the workers had not been completely dispirited by their failure in 1830 or subdued by the measures then taken against them. The contiguous villages of Great Bentley and Thorpe-le-Soken were the centre from which the union spread to other villages in the Tendring Hundred and also across the Colne to Peldon and Layer-de-la-Haye and to Wormingford, north-west of Colchester, until at its height it had enrolled 1,200 members. Subscriptions were 1s. a month and strike or lock-out pay 1s. a day. It apparently sought a minimum wage of 12s. a week, with beer, or 1s. 6d. in lieu of it, and a sliding scale which allowed the wage to vary with the price of flour; harvest pay was to be £6, with beer; and no union member was to work where a threshing machine was used. The farmers started the Tendring Agricultural Association to defeat the union and crushed it quite quickly, partly by dismissals and partly by the usual charge of intimidation, which was employed against unionists at Little Bromley, Ramsey and possibly elsewhere. The event, however, made an impression perhaps even deeper than the Swing events. It was called "a disaffection almost bordering on revolution" and the Judge at Essex Assizes thought that the "combination of labouring men, who had no property, to direct their masters in what way they are to employ their capital, is a subversion of the principles of civilised society".[44]

Labourers found additional reason for collective action in the introduction of the New Poor Law of 1834. This, besides condemning them to the possibility of spending their last years in the bleakest of surroundings, also put them at a serious disadvantage throughout their working lives. The rule that the unemployed and their families could receive relief only in the new workhouses caused labourers to accept almost any wage rather than risk dismissal. Precisely this was the intention of many supporters of the Act, as early official reports on its operation made clear and as a correspondent of *The Times* reported from Suffolk. It was also implicit in the following report in the *Colchester Gazette:*

"Several agricultural labourers from Writtle, with large families, have lately been driven by necessity to accept relief in the union workhouses. Four of these families, making a total of 30 persons, were detained in the Writtle and Chelmsford workhouses for several days, but their establishments were not broken up. They were all eventually assisted with small loans and have again rejoined their wives and children. The men appear to have received a useful lesson and with additional zeal have resumed their labours".[45]

Farm workers felt threatened by this weakening of their bargaining power and they also saw how the Act ended the work schemes being run for the unemployed in a number of parishes and how it made impossible the system of full employment maintained in some places through a Labour Rate. Conflict first occurred when able-bodied claimants were offered lower rates of relief, or assistance in the form of bread instead of money, as temporary economies in advance of the completion of workhouses of the new type or, as soon as such workhouse accommodation became available, were refused outdoor relief altogether. At Sible Hedingham, where unemployment was severe, 170 protesting labourers were quelled only by the reading of the Riot Act and the arrest of seven of their number. Thirty-four men from Dedham, when refused their normal allowance, marched to the Justices at Colchester Castle, but were sent about their business with a warning against trying to intimidate the Bench. At Halstead, Stebbing, Dunmow, Thaxted, Great Holland, Letheringham, Stradbroke and probably many other places, Relieving Officers were threatened or actually assaulted and in several places had to be given protection. At Thorndon, near Eye, a group of claimants invaded the office where the Relieving Officer was paying the new lower rate and stopped the proceedings in defiance of the Constable. When a Justice signed an order for arrests, 200 labourers demonstrated outside his home before escorting the arrested men in triumph to their homes. Seven men were arrested when a crowd at Ardleigh intercepted a waggon carrying bread to the local Relieving Officer.[46] The scope of protests widened. Near Stradbroke labourers stoned the carriage of the Rev. Henry Owen, a Justice who was resolutely implementing the new system, and then tried to wreck the conveyances of the local Guardians as they went home after a Board meeting. Next, as the new workhouses inexorably approached completion, labourers turned to direct action against them. Those at Stradbroke, Laxfield and Bulcamp in Suffolk were attacked on the same night, just at the time when two similar buildings were being damaged at Ipswich. The Cosford Union workhouse at Semer was severely damaged, too, by a crowd of labourers and artisans, twelve of whom were arrested. At Sible Hedingham workhouse, then in use as a temporary institution prior to the completion of the Union workhouse at Halstead, a fire was started and, when firemen arrived, they were pelted with fire-brands.[47]

At the same time protests of a legal kind were also being made, possibly with the help of artisans or some other sympathisers from outside the ranks of the farm workers. Petitions against the Act circulated in a number of areas. When labourers from around Eye announced a meeting to plan such a petition, the Magistrates declared it illegal and threatened anyone attending with fines or imprisonment, but 500 arrived and applauded a speech in which the main recommendation was that all unemployed men should be allowed a piece of land to cultivate instead of having to seek poor relief. In villages around Wickham Market, in east Suffolk, over a thousand signed a petition for the restoration of "the mild, humane, generous, benevolent and noble Old Poor Law".[48] Labourers at Terling, Boreham, the Walthams and the Leighs, besides trying to negotiate with local farmers for a minimum wage, also petitioned Parliament for an end to the New Poor Law which they saw as "a system of terrorism" and "the total frustration of their hopes, of which the obvious tendency is to sink them into a state of the most abject slavery and destitution". Their alternatives were a basic wage, allotments, lower indirect taxes and "a well regulated property tax". The petition concluded:

"Your petitioners beg also to state . . . that they do not wish to be relieved from the toil and duties connected with their humble station in society; and while they wish at all times to pay due regard to all the just laws and institutions of the country, they feel it a grievance that, while the interests of the higher classes are scrupulously guarded by your honourable house, the poor should be treated as if they have no right to live in the land of their birth".[49]

There was a well-run campaign against the Act at Wickford, Rayleigh and Rawreth which developed into a Chartist Association a year later; a march by 500 labourers and wives into Halstead to protest against having to pay poor rates on their cottages; and meetings in the Felstead-Great Leighs area at which a scheme was discussed to engage a lawyer to represent labourers in Poor Law business.[50] Despite the failure of all these protests, the Act remained so live an issue that, when the Chartists sought support in Essex and Suffolk villages in 1838-9, they promised its abolition as one of the first reforms to follow the Charter's enactment. When Chartism, too, failed to bring any relief from hardships and the labourers had relapsed into sullen resentment, many of the incendiary fires that followed had as their victims the farmers who were Poor Law Guardians.

While open movements had been taking place and even more so after they had been abandoned as useless, incendiarism remained the most frequent form of protest. Immediately after the suppression of 'Swing', it re-started with fires at Basildon, Writtle, Brentwood, West Bergholt and Tendring in Essex and at Bedfield, Earl Soham, Earl Stonham, Beccles and Polstead in Suffolk.[51] Then, after a period of relative peace during the Reform struggle, the sad series of fires was resumed amid growing rural unemployment. At Wortham there were two incidents in 1833, followed a year later by a further two; in three of these cases the same family was the victim, possibly because one of its members was a Justice.[52] Despite executions for arson at Bures and Toppesfield,[53] every winter now witnessed fires and these occurred in every part of Suffolk, except the north-west, and in every part of Essex including the south where such protest had previously been rare. It had become clear that the outrages were not attributable to "one wretch" or "a desperate few", as was suggested at a Halstead meeting called to check the prolonged series of fires in that district. The same meeting was told how a reward of £700, almost equal to a labourer's life-earnings, had not revealed "the demon". An offer of £575 at Spexhall, near Halesworth, led to the burning of a stack of a man who had subscribed to the reward and a threatening letter to another. Incendiaries were obviously being protected by their fellow-labourers, who often assembled at a fire to watch their employers' discomfiture, regardless of the fire's effect on their own future employment. In one incident in Suffolk "the agricultural labourers not only refused to assist in subduing the fire, but occupied the time in the most wanton and riotous manner. They entered the house, consumed and carried off all the eatables that they could gain possession of". Another report ran as follows:

> "There was not observable here (as at the Halesworth fire, or as at Lowestoft where the labourers who assisted were pelted with stones and wounded) any disposition to impede those who tried to check the fire; but there was observable, among the agricultural labourers in particular who were going to or returning from the fire, a vast deal of levity, so that it appeared as if a fair, and not a wilful fire, had attracted attention, roused people from their beds and spread consternation around the country".[54]

By their conduct at many such fires the labourers both declared their own moral complicity in them and also imparted to the incendiarism of the period the character of a broad social movement. They gained little, if anything, from this method of protest except a general revenge for their own impoverishment, but, if asked why they resorted to it, they would probably have pointed to the punishment awaiting those who attempted to lead their fellows in movements of an open kind, as well as to the social and economic victimisation which in any village could make the life of an outspoken dissident a very unpleasant one.

Urban Working-Class Movements

There is evidence of widespread working-class organization in the cloth industry in the early eighteeenth century. The 8,000 weavers, woolcombers and other apprenticed clothworkers worked and lived in circumstances that were not unfavourable to combination, sharing as they did common conditions of apprenticeship, employment and wages and, although not employed in factories, working next door to one another in particular streets or neighbourhoods. At Colchester they frequented the same inns, the Weavers' Arms, the Woolpack, the Bishop Blaze and the Beaters' and Roughers' Arms, where they maintained 'clubs', presumably Friendly Societies like the one of 1700 that offered sickness and unemployment benefit for 6d. a month.[55] Increasingly, too, they felt themselves a class distinct from their employers, as the latter's businesses grew in size; on average in the 1760s Colchester firms employed nearly fifty weavers each. At Sudbury and Colchester some of them possessed the Parliamentary franchise, so that their petitions received attention. Sufficient cases have come to light to suggest that combination of some kind existed in the larger textile centres at most times in the eighteenth century. Braintree, Bocking and Coggeshall weavers seem throughout to have maintained their right to elect 'wardens' or stewards to represent them. 'Companies' of weavers at Braintree, Bocking and Witham, and of fullers at Braintree, Bocking and Dunmow, were reported in 1700 to be petitioning Quarter Sessions against their employers' use of non-apprenticed labour. Other organisations were a Friendly Society at Coggeshall and a Co-operative at Braintree and Bocking which in 1758 was buying flour wholesale to sell to members at cost price.[56] While the industry remained strong, the weavers' organisation could be effective, as was shown in the successful strike at Colchester in 1715 against wage reductions and other economies recently introduced by the clothiers, but as the industry's decline became serious the workers' attempts to protect themselves, though spirited, were undermined by frequent unemployment. The weavers of Braintree and Bocking in 1758, to the number of five hundred, stayed out on strike for fourteen weeks to retain their ancient right to keep the 'thrums' from their looms, but they were beaten in the end.[57] A strike at Colchester in 1791 for a cost-of-living increase seems also to have failed.[58] The clothworkers' tradition of combination did not entirely come to an end with their industry's collapse, but certainly exercised some influence within the youthful silk industry in which some of the sons of former woollen weavers found employment. It may also have helped to inspire the trade unions and Friendly Societies that were started among certain non-textile trades in the cloth-producing towns towards 1800.

A main cause of combination in non-textile trades in 1750-95 was fear of competition from cheap non-apprenticed labour. In 1752 Bury St. Edmunds bricklayers united against "persons who have no right to the trade" and in 1785 shoemakers at Saffron Walden, Chelmsford and Colchester formed 'Friendly Societies' with the same object. Another cause was the steady increase in food prices which led Coggeshall and Maldon carpenters in 1765 and Braintree bricklayers in 1772 to seek wage increases. Such organisations as were formed at this time were local self-governing bodies which might, however, like the shoemakers' societies of 1785, maintain some communication with one another.[59] The only groups known to have belonged to a larger combination were the Ipswich and Yarmouth seamen who in 1792 had joined a union of East Coast seamen. The Ipswich men struck work and picketed the quay but were driven off by dragoons and a corps of local gentlemen; the Yarmouth seamen were similarly dealt with.[60] These events coincided with the French Revolution, when any organisation of the poor was suspect, and the ensuing Combination Acts caused workingmen not to publicise any trade union to which they belonged. Little can be known of the working-class movement of this period, though a few events have come to light. A group of Colchester tailors, for once in a strong position because of the lucrative orders for military uniforms placed by officers at the Camp, won an increase in wages, apparently with the goodwill of their employers who did not report them for combining.[61] Also 'Friendly Societies' of carpenters at Colchester and Chelmsford were refused registration, probably because, as happened elsewhere, they were really trade unions using a Friendly Society title.[62] When the Combination Acts were repealed in 1824, several organisations were seen emerging into the open. Ipswich, Woodbridge and Harwich shipwrights now had strong unions, linked to the Thames union, and Ipswich sawyers were also organised. Seamen on the Harwich Post Office ships sought and won an increase in wages, as did the Ipswich seamen. Undoubtedly other organisations existed but still feared to declare themselves. It is known that a national union of brushworkers had branches at Bury St. Edmunds, Ipswich, Braintree and Witham, but none of these received any mention in the Press. Meanwhile Friendly Societies had grown rapidly, reaching a membership of 21,000 in Essex by 1815 and constituting a largely artisan movement which was giving workingmen some experience of organising and some training in administration.[63]

The artisans of the region, who constituted the main body of trade unionists in this period, now faced a difficult struggle to protect their living standards, which in most trades had fallen in real terms since before the War. In 1780 a carpenter had been paid about 12s. weekly and his wife and a grown-up daughter might together have got 6s. by spinning, but in 1830, though his wage would have been 16s. to 18s., his family were fortunate if they had any employment at all, while food prices had almost doubled. Shoemakers and tailors would have fared no better than a carpenter. Silk weavers earnt even less, but their wives were often silk weavers too and their daughters might be working in a silk mill. Workers were put at a further disadvantage when the New Poor Law withdrew from them the slender relief previously available at times of unemployment, short time or illness. The threat of the new workhouses, at this time of unemployment and poverty, probably weakened the resolve and courage necessary for the construction of a sustained trade union movement. On the other hand, three new developments favoured working-class combination. Artisans were becoming more numerous, amounting to 1,600 at Colchester and 3,000 at Ipswich by the 1840s, with corresponding increases in other towns. Secondly, artisan workshops were increasing in size and a majority of urban shoemakers, tailors and building workers were now employed in units of five or more workers, so that the journeymen tended to see themselves as a class separate from the master artisans and as having separate interests. Finally, many artisans belonged to nonconformist chapels, were members of Friendly Societies and supported political Reform, so that they, and even more their leaders, did not lack conviction and experience.

The occupations known to have been affected by some form of combination between 1824 and 1850 included tailors, carpenters, bricklayers, shoemakers, shipwrights, sawyers, seamen, stone-dredgers, silk weavers, brushmakers, papermakers, engineering workers and printers. Other occupations may have been briefly organised in 1833-4 when the Grand National Consolidated Trades Union (G.N.C.T.U.) tried to unite all workers in one organisation but even then it was probably the skilled trades that were mainly, if not solely, affected. Support was strong enough for the G.N.C.T.U. in Colchester to frighten its opponents into an attempt to boycott any business employing a trade unionist. Support was even stronger at Ipswich where the funeral of a member of the tailors' section was accompanied by 130 of his fellow tradesmen walking two abreast.[64] The movement seems also to have had a following in Chelmsford, Braintree, Needham Market and Yarmouth. The transportation of the Dorchester labourers led to a protest meeting at Ipswich against this "unjustifiable attack upon the rights of humanity". Nor were the 'Tolpuddle Martyrs' forgotten in later years in that town. Another meeting was held on their behalf in 1835 and, when they were finally pardoned, they were celebrated yet again, this time under Chartist auspices.[65] The episode of the G.N.C.T.U. soon passed but it had one not unimportant result, the acquaintance gained by some local supporters with the views of Robert Owen and his Socialist contemporaries who had helped to inspire the Union. An Ipswich worker said that his aim was now "a new state of society, where every man will be expected to render his due portion of labour for his own and the public good" and where workers would receive "the full produce of their toil".[66] A hostile Colchester paper, dimly understanding the Syndicalist views of some G.N.C.T.U. leaders, denounced this attempt "to invert the natural order of things by making the master obedient to the servant and the Legislature and the Government the passive tools to register and enforce the enactments of the mob".[67] Owenites were subsequently found in the region, both inside and outside Chartism, but of more consequence were those men, mainly trade unionists, who, without embracing the full Socialist philosophy and strategy, had gained from Owen both a distaste for the moral defects of a competitive society and a longing for a life of co-operation, harmony and enlightenment.

Whereas Owen himself thought politics irrelevant to the creation of a new society, by 1837 some local working-class leaders, including several who shared Owenite ideals, had come to believe that, without political influence and political independence, they could not protect the living standards of their class, improve its lot or create a more moral society. They had been slow to reach this position. Until 1815 workingmen had not even constituted a distinct element within the democratic movement, their political action being confined mainly to supporting, along with their wives, the food riots which took place in both textile and non-textile towns in 1740, 1757, 1765, 1772, 1789 and 1795. Certain weavers and other artisans did possess the franchise in Ipswich, Sudbury, Colchester and Maldon, but they took no independent position of their own at election time, easily succumbing to the bribes from either side, which their poverty made it hard for them to resist. It is possible, but far from certain, that it was in the early years of the French Revolution that some of them first took a serious look at politics. The quite untrustworthy Press of the period referred to a "Disputing Society" at Ipswich, a "Revolutionary Society" at Woodbridge, "rebellious publications" circulating in rural Bures and a "Jacobin" organisation at Chelmsford. Suffolk publicans were warned against harbouring dangerous clubs. There was also a response when Hardy and Thelwall, leaders of the radical London Corresponding Society, made a speaking tour in the region. A Bradwell-on-Sea man was given six months in prison for "having d—d the King, d—d the Nation and d—d the Constitution". One charge was abuse "of our happy Constitution", others were the selling of Tom Paine's works at Colchester and Saffron Walden. Yet the known occupations of the accused were clothier, bookseller, lawyer's apprentice, yeoman and "a considerable tradesman", with only one sea-waller to represent the poorer class.[68] The earliest known political involvement of a group of artisans occurred around 1812 when tailors at a large Colchester workshop were listening in their mealbreaks to readings of radical journals, including Cobbett's, and soon after the Peace Joseph Bird, bricklayer, freeman and "the Robespierre of Ipswich", first made his appearance in radical politics.[69] At Colchester D.

W. Harvey's support lay in the public-house clubs, one of which, the Loyal and Independent club, included both electors and non-electors. These consisted of one attorney, three small industrialists, five men employed in shopkeeping or commerce, ten in miscellaneous occupations and 17 artisans of whom six were shoemakers and three worked in the almost extinct cloth industry.[70] Cobbett visited the region several times, acquiring an influence that proved a lasting one; when he spoke at the Ipswich Theatre, artisans and their wives crowded the gallery.[71] In 1830-2 the anti-Reform Press often mentioned the predominance of working people at the meetings and, though these reports were intended to alarm middle-class readers, other evidence confirms them. Most of the audience at a Chelmsford rally, held in support of the two Reform candidates for Essex in 1831, were artisans or 'operatives', while Rigby Wason had a particularly strong artisan following at Ipswich. Throughout 1830-2 thousands of urban workers actively participated in the movement for the Bill which they saw as an instalment of an approaching democratic victory. It was they who supplied the pressure whenever the Bill was held up, issuing "inflammatory handbills" and throwing the Tory candidate's coach into a pond at Colchester, uttering "intemperate language" at Ipswich meetings and engaging in "angry talk" at Harwich. At Bury St. Edmunds "the trades" had a prominent part in the victory procession, with printers, brushmakers, curriers, tailors, carpenters, bricklayers and shoemakers carrying "devices applicable to their employment", while at Braintree, where silk workers were strong Reformers, the local Reform organisation celebrated victory with a manifesto stating that the struggle for democracy had only just begun.[72]

Poorer Reformers had expected substantial benefits from the 1832 Act and by 1835 they had been disappointed on most counts. They had believed that the new Parliament would quickly extend the franchise and end the Open Ballot. The obvious indifference, if not hostility, of local Reform leaders to further democratic measures brought swift disillusionment. The Secret Ballot was vaguely discussed in the region's Liberal papers, but only as a possible measure at some future date. Electoral corruption, once seen as the product of the old electoral system, was still observable in every constituency and that too on a broader scale because larger electorates had now to be bribed. It was said of the Maldon constituency:

"From 1832 to 1847 every election in the town of Maldon has seen a contest. All have been in character the same — all corrupt from first to last. In '32 the contest was only comparatively pure. In '35 the cost was much increased. In '37 the place was quite corrupt. In '41 'twas very much so. In '47 nothing could be worse".[73]

A few years later Sudbury so distinguished itself for electoral corruption that it was disqualified as a Parliamentary constituency by a Parliament mainly composed of men also elected by dishonest and illegal means, and here it was the Whigs, the pro-Reform party of 1830-2, who were more blatantly at fault. A measure of Municipal Reform was conceded, though its ratepayer franchise caused it to be, in the words of an Ipswich carpenter, "but a transfer of power, under a property qualification, from one party to another".[74] Nor was municipal corruption ended; the record of the Liberal majority on the new Colchester Town Council elicited from a Liberal paper the question, "if this be Reform, what is corruption?".[75]

Civil liberty had always been one of the Reformers' demands but, though the formal right of public meeting was now upheld, local trade unionists learnt how little freedom could be theirs in economic matters when in 1834 the Dorchester Labourers were transported and their fellow-members at Colchester were threatened with dismissal for membership of a trade union. Another extension of liberty expected but not granted was religious equality, particularly the abolition of tithe and of the compulsory Church Rate which fell on all ratepayers whether Anglican or, as many Reformers were, nonconformist. Essex and Suffolk Whigs, themselves mostly Anglican, supported their Government's retention of the Church Rate, Rebow of Wivenhoe Park riding down to a Wivenhoe Vestry to defend it against the objections of "cobblers and other unwashed members of the fraternity of Radical Dissenters".[76]

There had been hopes that, after Reform, reduction in Government expenditure and in taxation would promote economic recovery but, despite some progress in this direction, Corn Law Repeal was not wrung from an unwilling Parliament till 1846. The Corn Laws had no stronger champions than Western and Lennard, leading Essex Whigs each of whom wrote a pamphlet in their defence, and the Ransome family at Ipswich, makers of agricultural machinery; these had all been supporters of the Reform Bill in 1830-2. Quite the strongest cause for resentment among working men against their former Whig and Liberal leaders over social or economic policy was the introduction of the New Poor Law. During the 1830-2 campaign 'Reform of the Poor Law' had been promised to ratepayers as the means of lowering poor rates and to the poor as the means of making the system more humane. To the poor at that time an increase in the rates of benefit had become an urgent matter, since many parishes had recently reduced them at a time of acute poverty. The New Poor Law of 1834, though it pleased ratepayers, dismayed not only existing claimants but the whole employed population. It denied assistance to the able-bodied and their families except in a new type of workhouse where their diet was to be worse than that of the worst-off worker outside, the work was to be such as to make them wish to leave, and husband, wife and children were to be separated in different wards. The unemployed, underemployed and those in precarious occupations like silk-weaving were almost in terror of the new regime, while working people in all occupations now acquired that abiding anxiety about the workhouse that remained part of their collective outlook throughout the century. It was not only that they might well die in it, but they were also put by it at a disadvantage in relations with their employer who, in refusing a wage increase or imposing a reduction, could threaten a reluctant employee with dismissal and thereby with a choice between the workhouse or starvation; court cases in the region showed that some younger ones almost preferred the latter. A Suffolk labourer in 1840 called the system "the slave-driver's whip and chains to starve the poor into submission and to work for whatever pittance it affords them".[77] Finally, though the Law's advocates had promised that widows, orphans, the disabled and other unfortunates would suffer no loss of comfort, it is questionable whether this promise was kept or was even meant to be. The economies achieved were such that Essex expenditure on poor relief fell from an average of £255,000 in 1825-9 to £152,000 in 1838 and in Suffolk from £266,000 in 1833 to £146,000 in 1839. "The new law", wrote a Suffolk observer, "did more to alienate the poor from the middle and upper classes than any half-dozen laws of the present century". Among the Guardians administering the new system were quite a number of leading ex-Reformers, such as Thomas Butler of Witham and Samuel Courtauld of Bocking. Nor did critics fail to contrast its oppression with the Reform leaders' promises. This was to be almost a commonplace of early Chartist speeches, but it was briefly summed up by a Braintree weaver imprisoned for refusing hard labour under the new regime: "he had been for Reform and this was what they had got by it".[78]

By 1838 disillusion was complete. An Ipswich worker said, "we hardly know which is the Whig and which the Tory. We pass from Session to Session without a practical measure being carried out that will do us any good". As for the Liberal Reformers of 1830-2, a Colchester cooper saw "old independent burgesses, who assisted with all their energy to bring the Reform Bill into operation, now oppressed by the very men whom they then supported".[79]

Disillusion with the Whig Government grew after 1834 but the rift with Liberalism was sharper in some places than in others. At Chelmsford the Operatives' Reform Association, founded in 1835, continued to press for the full implementation of Liberal policies and remained attached to C. F. Branfill, Whig candidate for South Essex. At Colchester, where the radical artisans most of all wanted the return of D. W. Harvey who had stood down as Liberal candidate in 1835, criticism of middle-class Reformers was muted and represented only by the formation in 1835 of an Independent Club for "the humbler class of voters", which 46 Parliamentary electors joined. Led by William Wire, a watchmaker and a pioneer of Colchester's Romano-British archaeology, the Club operated in the Liberal public houses, much as Reform clubs had done before 1832, and concentrated on securing a voice in the nomination of Liberal municipal candidates. It had some success and grew in numbers until it had to divide into separate clubs for each ward.[81] More militancy was evident in a violent protest by nonconformist workingmen against the levy of a Church Rate in a Colchester parish in 1836. At an auction of goods seized from an ironmonger who had refused to pay the rate, "the people, who had assembled in number about 400 or 500, made a sudden rush towards the auctioneer, knocked him down and uttering loud cries against the Church and its exactions, tramped upon and completely destroyed the goods that had been seized and sold; after which they quietly dispersed".[82] Such militancy, unexpected in such circles, was deprecated by better-off nonconformists, so that the action reflected in the denominational sphere the divisions discernible within Reform politics; in Chelmsford too some nonconformists were preparing for direct action against the Church Rate at a time when their more respectable fellow-members were allegedly consenting to its imposition.[83] At Braintree and Coggeshall the breach with Liberalism came when workingmen who paid the Poor Rate combined to secure the election of Guardians sympathetic to themselves.[84] The New Poor Law had also created great bitterness at Saffron Walden, where the workhouse was set on fire in late 1835 at the same time as similar buildings were under attack in Suffolk. The report of the fire concluded:

"The alarm was much increased in consequence of the lower classes refusing to render any assistance, but who, on the contrary, evidently enjoyed the scene, shouting most hideously,

'Let it burn, it cannot be at a better place', 'Put it out yourselves' ".[85]

In Yarmouth, which, though situated in Norfolk, was soon to be linked with Suffolk Chartism, the local National Union of the Working Classes had not disbanded itself after it had completed its campaign in support of the 1832 Reform Act, and it quickly reacted to the failures of the Whig Government by taking up the Reform cause afresh and this time with a specific commitment to Universal Suffrage. It was still in touch with the London working-class radicals, so that the toasts at one of its social gatherings in 1834 were to one of the London leaders, Henry Hetherington, as well as to Robert Owen, William Cobbett, Tom Paine, Annual Parliaments, the Secret Ballot and Universal Suffrage. It also supported the G.N.C.T.U., collecting money for trade unionists locked out at Derby, and was still active in late 1835 in connection with the General Election in that year.[86]

The working-class radicals of Ipswich had been as quick as those at Yarmouth to show disillusion with the results of Reform. Immediately after the Reform Act they began to question the motives and intentions of the Liberal leaders. In June 1832, they took over a meeting held by the latter to choose Parliamentary candidates and to form a committee for the election campaign. Some non-electors led by John Goslin, a shoemaker, prevented the endorsement of the campaign committee recommended by the platform, demanded precise pledges from the Parliamentary candidates and permitted their endorsement only after those pledges had been given.[87] By 1834 distrust had spread. Even the *Suffolk Chronicle* conceded that the Whig Government hardly differed from its Tory predecessors and one of its correspondents admitted that "the Whigs were not straight, undaunted and vigorous defenders of public rights, but a trimming, timid, faltering knot of shufflers, unsettled and vacillating in principle . . . and heartless in the execution of their vaunted 'Reform' ".[88] Though Ipswich working-class radicals now briefly neglected politics and gave their energies to the G.N.C.T.U., on its dissolution they again made their presence felt at public meetings, intervening at any opportunity. When some Liberals sought the disqualification of poorer freemen on the grounds that they often took bribes, Joseph Bird accused the accusers of similar corruption and went on to demand democratic municipal reform, honest administration of charities and the Secret Ballot, adding that he would never again vote Liberal. At another meeting he upheld the right of any poor relief claimants, who happened to be municipal electors, to retain their vote. With two other future Chartists, James White and Donald M'Pherson, he helped form an Anti-Church Rate Association to remedy by local action in the Vestries the Government's refusal to abolish the Rate itself.[89] The New Poor Law however had become the most pressing issue. 6,000 people dismantled a building then in the course of conversion into a workhouse of the new type, shouted down the magistrates as they read the Riot Act and held the streets in defiance of the Dragoons. Next day, when attacking another intended workhouse, they were beaten off by Dragoons using the broadside of their sabres. Those arrested, a coachmaker, a shoemaker, a bricklayer and a sailor, did not include the known working-class politicians, but the latter were now criticising the new Law at every opportunity and were probably responsible for the "inflammatory" handbills circulating in the town.[90] John Goslin interrupted a Charity meeting to denounce the uncharitable nature of that Law and to demand Universal Suffrage to protect the poor from it. At a meeting to start Provident Societies to enable the poor to fend for themselves under the New Poor Law, he turned to the platform and said that "if these men felt towards us as fellow countrymen, they would give us our political rights by which we should be able to retain in our hands the fruits of our industry and to live in independence in the land of our birth". A Liberal meeting, arranged to focus attention on clauses of the Law rather than on the Law itself, was easily taken over by Goslin, Joseph Bird, James White and John Cook, Goslin declaring that "nothing but repeal would satisfy him", and they carried almost all of the 2,000 present in support of a motion for a return to the Old Poor Law. Finally, at the 1837 General Election White and Bird interrogated a Whig candidate on the issue point by point and then demanded Universal Suffrage, the Secret Ballot and Shorter Parliaments as the only possible protection for the poor.[91] The working-class leaders of Ipswich were by now Chartists in everything but name.

2
Chartism, 1838-9

Foundations

In February 1837, the London Working Men's Association (L.W.M.A.) drew up a programme of democratic reforms, comprising universal male suffrage, annual Parliaments, vote by ballot, payment of M.P.s, abolition of the property qualification for candidates and equal electoral districts. Called the People's Charter, this programme was sent to working-class radicals in various towns with an invitation to them to start their own Working Men's Associations (W.M.A.s) and to work for an Act of Parliament embodying the Six Points. A petition was then launched, as a means of persuading Parliament to enact the Charter.

The movement began in Essex and Suffolk when workingmen here responded to the L.W.M.A.'s invitation. The first Association was established at Rawreth, a village in south-east Essex where a recent protest meeting against the New Poor Law had demanded Universal Suffrage as the means of repealing that measure.[1] By the end of 1837 other Associations had been founded at Ipswich, Colchester, Braintree, Halstead and Coggeshall, while at Chelmsford the existing Operatives' Reform Association joined the new movement. Enthusiasm rose as scores of artisans came forward to voice their views at the weekly or fortnightly meetings which remained the movement's central activity throughout its duration. "A glorious era is dawning upon the useful classes", wrote the Braintree W.M.A. in one of the 'Addresses to the Working Classes' which it issued at frequent intervals during this period. Grandiloquently phrased and burning with moral zeal, these manifestoes proclaimed the emancipation of workingmen from ignorance and vice and urged the achievement of democratic rights by overwhelming moral pressure upon Parliament.[2] In this and other respects the region's W.M.A.s followed their parent body in London, but, as they took root in the working-class communities of the different towns, they each developed their own local characteristics. Indeed, the variety of leadership and outlook was a striking feature of this stage of Chartism.

As the largest town and the oldest centre of working-class politics, Ipswich was always Chartism's stronghold in the region. The W.M.A., founded in December 1837 at the Admiral's Head, an old radical resort, at first modelled itself on the L.W.M.A., seeking the support of thoughtful workingmen and inviting individuals from other classes into honorary membership. Dues were a penny a week, meetings were weekly and a new committee of twelve was elected every three months.[3] Its leaders were able men of varying opinions and personality, who between them linked Chartism with all the earlier movements of protest and radicalism in the town. At least four came from Liberal and nonconformist circles. Robert Booley, who delivered the first lecture, was a spring-maker at a large coachworks. A lay preacher, he brought with him the oratory, vocabulary and mannerisms of that calling, as well as a fair knowledge of political philosophy. He was the most volatile of the leaders, coming nearest to condoning Physical Force tactics in the excitement of 1838-9 but supporting the Liberal candidate, Henry Vincent, at the 1842 by-election and the 1847 General Election. The tailor, William Rushbrooke, was another nonconformist who revealed his full capacity for leadership only when, from 1859 to 1884, he was left as the last of the town's Chartists still alive and politically active. Henry Lovewell, also a tailor and a Wesleyan, had belonged to the Liberal Mechanics' Institute as a lad and had not joined the working-class radicals until about 1837; he seems to have remained in the Liberal Reform Club in his own ward at least until 1839-40, despite his having joined the W.M.A. in 1838. A second group had led the resistance to the New Poor Law. It included James White, master shoemaker, who sought and won election to the Board of Guardians in order to impede the Law from within, and Nathaniel Whimper, a wine merchant who apparently joined the Chartists less out of enthusiam for Universal Suffrage than because they had helped him oppose the New Poor Law. Charles Bird, master painter and the W.M.A.'s first chairman, had been their close associate. A third group were the trade unionists, with Owenite sympathies derived from the G.N.C.T.U., such as the carpenter, Robert Orr, and the tailor, Charles Harvey. John Cook, journeyman shoemaker and Owenite, avoided public speaking whenever possible, mostly expressing his views in forceful letters to the Press. His friend, William Garrard, a carpenter, was another trade unionist. Studious but militant, an able speaker and writer, while Chartism survived he never wavered, however depressing the prospects. The shoemaker, John Goslin, had moved steadily from Wesleyan preaching, through a period of devotion to William Cobbett — "old Cobbett" as he called him with deep affection — on through Owenism to a final position as a socialist, economic determinist and unbending advocate of working-class independence in politics. Presiding over these diverse groups were Donald M'Pherson and Joseph Bird. M'Pherson, a native of Inverness, a tea-dealer and auctioneer, had been an active Liberal and opponent of Church Rates, as a result of which during the W.M.A.'s first two years of existence he was credited by his associates with continuing Liberal sympathies. From 1840, however, he identified himself with all Chartism's main policies and became its chief spokesman in Ipswich. His repeated interventions at public meetings held by other bodies made him so much Chartism's best-known local personality that, after his death, one radical letter-writer in the press used to style himself 'Ghost of M'Pherson'. An able orator, he was invited to address meetings in Suffolk towns, at Colchester and Norwich, to which he travelled in his gig, and he was able to link the Suffolk Chartist centres together as he travelled about on his tea-dealer's business. Joseph Bird, bricklayer and Free Burgess, had been associated with almost all radical causes in the town, including the pre-1832 Reform movement, the 1830 campaign of support for the Paris insurgents, the G.N.C.T.U., municipal reform, opposition to Church Rates and resistance to the New Poor Law. In all these activities his main concern had been to voice the separate interests and feelings of local workingmen, among whom he enjoyed high standing. At least two years before the foundation of Ipswich W.M.A. he had already reached a position which was Chartist in all but name and so was readily accepted by his colleagues as their guide in Chartism's early years.

These dozen men all retained some of the convictions derived from the various movements which had initiated them into politics, but in general they remained united as long as Chartism lasted. Two other able men, a foreman coachbuilder and a journeyman hatter, afterwards joined them and together these constituted the most consistent and successful leadership in the region. They were young — M'Pherson, one of the oldest, was only thirty-five in 1838 — but more experienced than most of their Essex and Suffolk counterparts. They were always 'Moral Force' supporters in that they renounced violence as a political method, but they were also militants, eager to mobilise massive working-class pressure upon Parliament, and from 1841 sturdy supporters of Feargus O'Connor, symbol to them of Chartist unity and working-class political independence.

For a very brief period only, Ipswich Chartists, like other W.M.A.s, gave the impression of still being under Liberal influence. The first members' meeting declared itself ready for any "reasonable extension of the franchise" and published an Address to the largely voteless working class, deploring electoral corruption. Some Liberals in their turn welcomed the W.M.A.; at a Liberal dinner the toasts included Church Rate abolition, Daniel O'Connell and "Prosperity to the Productive Classes, the only real source of a nation's greatness, and the Ipswich Working Men's Association". The Chartists' first public meeting was addressed by Rigby Wason, former Liberal M.P. for Ipswich who was trying to reinstate himself in the borough and thought that the W.M.A. had enough votes to be worth conciliating. However, what impressed the reporter on this occasion was the oratory of Booley, Whimper and M'Pherson — "this brat will soon become a giant", he wrote. With growing confidence the Association now began to speak more frankly, petitioning the Queen to replace the "treacherous" Whigs with a Government pledged to Universal Suffrage.[4]

At Colchester the L.W.M.A.'s call had been addressed to some old associates in the town and there had been an immediate response, chiefly from artisans, a number of whom owned their own businesses. William Wire, the sage of the Association in its early months, was a master watchmaker and antiques-dealer. Other prominent members included three shoemakers, a cooper, a baker, a mill-wright and a tailor, all with their own businesses. Some, while still lads, had learned their politics in the 1830-2 Reform movement, some had been closely associated with the Liberal Mechanics' Institute and almost all of them were nonconformists. At first they stopped short of demanding Universal Suffrage, favouring a gradual extension of the franchise to educated workingmen. They also endorsed the current Liberal campaign for the Secret Ballot to protect already enfranchised shopkeepers from economic victimisation. One of them expected support for democratic change from the Queen because she was an educated woman, another preferred reform of the Lords to abolition. Members gave lectures on favourite Liberal topics, the History of Commerce, the Corn Laws, Machinery, Education and Temperance. On one occasion, "the meeting having been informed that three members of the Association had left their work in an unfinished state, without the knowledge or consent of their employers, their names were ordered to be erased". Their only criticism of employers was that some of them forced their apprentices to attend places of worship contrary to their consciences.

Education was seen as the key to progress, but children, the Association decided, should be taught much more than a little reading, writing and arithmetic. Adult education would help parents to set their children a better example. "Let it be seen", said William Wire, "that the working classes . . . are no longer influenced by intoxication. There is a Mechanics' Institute in the town, open every night; the subscription is only 2s. a quarter. That would be a much better way of spending your time — in pursuit of knowledge. 'Knowledge is Power', and you can command it; you would also be instructing your children and doing everything to render you worthy of your franchise". Such views came easily to the lips of a Liberal like Wire, but one militant Chartist, the fruiterer Benjamin Parker, also advised young men "to leave the pot-house and study politics. He would advise such as were not married, to look out for *intelligent* wives and they would find *them* the best helpmates". Only the New Poor Law produced strong anti-Whig feeling. Younger members, who had joined in some numbers and showed no reluctance to voice their views, supported the current struggle against it and one of them, W. G. Blatch, made a speech attacking bitterly and in detail the conditions in the new Colchester Workhouse.[5] These proceedings elicited from the Conservative *Essex Standard* the comment, "We seriously advise these people to attend to their respective occupations; they will by this course serve themselves much better than by troubling themselves with imaginary grievances and interfering in questions about which they know rather worse than nothing". The two Liberal papers gave vague approval, though they rejected Universal Suffrage and defended the New Poor Law. Meanwhile within the W.M.A. enthusiasm mounted, as membership reached a hundred by the Spring and over two hundred by the Summer.[6]

At Braintree and Bocking Chartism might have taken a more radical direction from the start. Some of the silk weavers were sons and daughters of local woollen weavers and had inherited their fathers' traditions of class solidarity.[7] Others had come from Essex and Suffolk textile centres, attracted by the employment prospects in a place where both funeral-crape and soft silks were woven, and about fifty had previously worked in the East London silk industry. By 1830 they had become a compact force of 500 workers, 60 per cent male and 40 per cent female, a third of them being married couples; they all worked at home. Some lived on the outskirts of the town or in nearby villages, but most formed a distinct community in south-central Braintree. Their livelihood had recently become very insecure, as the prosperity of the 1820s had been followed by a depression in 1830-2, a revival in 1833-6 during which they organised quite a strong trade union,[8] and a renewed depression from 1837, which brought much unemployment, short-time working and a reduction of wages to about 5s. Courtaulds withdrew their handlooms, re-issuing them only in return for a guarantee of higher productivity. Before 1835 the distress would have been mitigated by outdoor relief, but when the Guardians sought leave to pay it to weavers as a temporary measure, the Poor Law Commission sternly told them to offer assistance only within the workhouse. When sent there, several weavers refused to continue the hard labour set them, unless the diet was improved, and were sent to prison, cheered by a large crowd which also barracked the Justices as they left the Court. All workers felt threatened and those of them who paid rates next united to win seats on the Board of Guardians, but their champions proved powerless even to modify the regulations, which were soon fully in force.[9] The weavers were now in a mood for strong action and would have taken up Chartism with even greater spirit, had they not found Braintree W.M.A. already controlled by men quite unwilling to organise militant action of any kind.

The founders of Chartism in Braintree and Bocking were a small group of artisans who since 1832 had slowly moved from Reform politics through adult education to a tentatively independent political position. They appear to have been responsible for a manifesto issued by the local Reform organisation in 1832, which warned that the Reform Act was important only in facilitating the struggle for further political and economic reforms.[10] This radicalism from "a knot of journeymen bakers and shoemakers", as one newspaper called them, had no immediate outcome because the local Whigs, having allowed the existing Reform organisation to dissolve, started a Reform Club with the main object of canvassing for the Whig candidates. The poorer Reformers held a mock election at which the victorious candidate stood on a programme of Universal Suffrage and Secret Ballot, but otherwise the only result was the formation of a workingmen's discussion society under the guidance of Lister Smith, the Quaker son of a Halstead clockmaker and himself a tailor.[11] He had not stayed in his trade, for after delivering a lecture on Gas in the hearing of Samuel Courtauld, he had been given a technical position in the latter's Bocking works, which, except for a brief period in which he set up Braintree Gas Works, he occupied until his death in 1871. He once explained to a Chartist audience why, though a Quaker, he was nevertheless so convinced a politician:

> "It had been a matter of grave consideration by some of the most excellent and pious men whether the humble-minded Christian ought to leave the quietude of his private circle . . . to take a part in a great political movement, and from the very few of those eminently pious persons who had hitherto taken a prominent part in the political arena, it would seem that most had arrived at a negative conclusion . . . Now, he had more than once tried to reconcile to himself this fireside patriotism and, enjoying as he did the pleasure of his family circle, to make up his mind 'to study to be quiet and mind his own business', but when he looked around him on the poverty, crime, destitution and ignorance that pervaded this highly favoured land, teeming as it did with wealth and plenty, yet steeped in poverty and wretchedness, it seemed to be part of his own business to unite with his fellow-citizens and try to eradicate those dreadful evils which he believed arose from a system of the greatest misgovernment".[12]

Though an ardent supporter of Reform in 1830-2 and the author of a poem in its support, he always saw adult education as the main road to a better society. So, as disillusion set in with Reform, he started a fortnightly discussion group in which, as he recalled, he and some radical artisans:

> "marched with fair Science's banners wide unfurled
> and strove to aid the progress of the world".

They soon took larger premises, held weekly meetings and opened a Workmen's Library.[13] They had links with the textile workers through two of their members, William Shead and George Bearman, both of them weavers who kept public houses frequented by their trade. Lister Smith also tried to unite the two groups by starting a Co-operative Society to provide the unemployed with small-holdings and thus keep them out of the workhouse, but his credit with the textile workers was weakened by his rejection of trade unionism and his failure to condemn the New Poor Law as a whole. He would have understood, but would not have endorsed, the bitter comment of one of the weavers involved in the workhouse strike already described, that "they were treated as slaves, although slavery had been done away with in foreign parts".[14] This division between Chartism's leadership and its main potential supporters prevented, in the one centre in this region where this was possible, the kind of Chartist upsurge that in 1838-9 took place in some of the industrial regions of the North and Wales.

Lister Smith had already become an honorary member of the L.M.W.A., as had one of his Braintree friends, a carpenter called Parmenter, and his own brother Barron Smith of Halstead, their sponsor being none other than Samuel Courtauld.[15] It was this connection with the L.W.M.A. that occasioned the foundation of the Braintree and Bocking W.M.A. in the New Year of 1838. Its early pronouncements clearly reflected Smith's earnest belief in adult education and pacifism. "The knowledge gained at their Mechanics' Institutes has discovered to them their true interests and taught them to think for themselves . . . War is a game which, were but subjects wise, Kings could not play at". The Queen's Coronation was deplored, not on Republican grounds, but because its pomp would beguile the multitude and stunt their intellectual awakening. A petition to Parliament asked for a public system of education and Smith, in a lecture, argued that such a system, so essential to the creation of a new moral society, depended upon the enactment of the Charter and the Disestablishment of the Church which had hitherto encouraged religious bigotry in the schools. The W.M.A. supported shop assistants' attempts to shorten their working day, assuring them that "one united and vigorous effort, guided by a respectful bearing towards their employers, would secure for them an early relaxation from business, which would enable them to cultivate their minds". This moral zeal caused some working-class recruits to withdraw because they were unable to maintain such standards, though it did attract some middle-class Liberals who attended the Association's first public meeting and by their presence overawed the few would-be interruptors.[16]

At Halstead the situation was similar to that at Braintree. The handloom weavers were anxious about the depression and the recent mechanisation of Courtaulds' weaving section, which, though it directly affected only those making funeral-crape, was an obtrusive reminder to all handloom weavers of their own economic vulnerability. However, the silk workers here, like the woollen workers before them, had never taken the same militant stance as their counterparts at Braintree and only one weaver was to be found among the Chartist leadership at this stage, the Reformer and trade unionist, James Hunt. Leadership came mainly from the same circles as at Braintree, from Barron Smith, Lister Smith's brother and a Courtauld manager; from David Scarfe, a harnessmaker and an admirer of William Lovett; and from a watchmaker and a tailor. They had connections with the town's vigorous nonconformity, made up of at least six chapels amid a population of only 5,500. The Chartists adopted the

L.W.M.A.'s constitution, with its emphasis on adult education and the need for patient research into workers' wages and conditions. They started a library, for which they received books from well-to-do sympathisers, including Martineau's *Political Economy*. They did not respond when the suppression of power looms was demanded by local handloom weavers, who found it hard to follow so solemn a leadership, and they made no attempt to go out among the nearby farm workers who for two decades past had been sporadically demonstrating against low wages, threshing machines and the New Poor Law.[17]

The other silk-producing centre in Essex was Coggeshall, where the weavers numbered several hundred in a total population of about 3,500. They were running their own Friendly Society in 1834[18] and were also involved in a movement of local workers against the New Poor Law which defeated the nominees of the Squire and the largest silk manufacturer at the 1837 Board of Guardians election and replaced them with its own candidates. The W.M.A. was founded shortly after this election, but remained small. Its first public activity was to support the current non-conformist resistance to the Church Rate at nearby Braintree.[19]

In the market and county town of Chelmsford, too, Chartism's origins were hardly those of militant working-class politics. Some workingmen had been active, without being prominent, in the Reform campaign, and the G.N.C.T.U. had also received support in the town. The W.M.A.'s immediate origins lay in the Operatives' Reform Association, founded in 1835 with tentative support from Branfill, Whig candidate for South Essex. When this body first came under Chartist influence, it took up, not Universal Suffrage, but the Liberal demand for an enquiry into the Pension List. Branfill addressed it on 'The Wealth of Nations', criticising the Corn Laws, protective duties, tithes and high taxes, but justifying the New Poor Law. Only in Summer 1838, did it rename itself the Chelmsford Working Men's Association, after which Chelmsford remained a loyal Chartist centre until 1850.[20]

By April 1838, Chartism had thus gained a footing in one Suffolk and five Essex towns, as well as in one Essex village, and in each its followers still bore some mark of earlier Liberal and nonconformist allegiances. Most were artisans, a few were shopkeepers and publicans, and their prudence and moral zeal were reflected in their proceedings. Progress was slow. Farm workers and urban labourers were little affected, many weavers remained on the edge of the movement and most towns still lacked any Chartist presence at all. The Associations at first seemed content to continue their discussion-meetings with little attempt to publicise their cause among the working population at large. There was hope in their hearts, however, that reason and social morality were gaining ground among thoughtful workingmen and that, as Braintree W.M.A. saw it, the once "ignorant masses" were now "forward in intelligence far beyond the bulk of those classes which had looked upon them with contempt".[21] Their confidence was reinforced by news of the mass support being received by Chartism in the industrial districts and they began gradually to feel themselves part of a national movement. There was therefore a willing response when in the Summer of 1838, they were called upon by their national leaders to spread Chartism more widely and to gain signatures for the National Petition.

Chartist influence widens

Ipswich W.M.A. was the first to address itself to wider circles, its readiness springing from the new militancy that had first been observable at a rally to welcome home the Dorchester Labourers. Garrard, in the chair, commended trade unions as the workers' only answer to exploitation by the employers. A currier maintained that the 'Tolpuddle Martyrs' had defended their only article of property, their labour; if to defend one's property was a crime, why not transport landowners and clergymen? Booley declared that "the great reason why the Dorchester Labourerers should now be addressed was that, by their standing up against the strong arm of oppression, they had been the means of raising a moral and energetic power among the masses". They had won liberty for all other workers, making it impossible for the Government to arrest the speakers at the present meeting, as they would like to do. "If the Government were now to take two or three out of this Association and transport them, it would light up a flame in Ipswich that would enkindle the whole country". Chartists should emulate the bravery of these men. "Nothing but the independence, energy and union of the masses would gain what the people wanted". A collection was taken for the Dorchester Labourers and an Address adopted, condemning the Whigs as the authors of their sufferings. It was in this mood that the Association put posters up all over the town advertising a rally for the Petition. Two thousand people from Ipswich and rural Suffolk filled the Town Hall, hundreds being turned away. It was an impressive demonstration of the new independence of the working-class radicals, for the chairman and almost all the speakers were workingmen and they maintained a high standard of political argument for four hours. The chairman declared Chartism's aims as the end of exploitation, repeal of the New Poor Law, equal opportunity and a decent livelihood for all who worked. M'Pherson said that workingmen, as creators of all wealth, were entitled to a reasonable wage; though a redistribution of property was unnecessary, exploitation must cease; a society based on 'Love thy neighbour' must be created, not by violence but by a mighty movement. Whimper condemned the Whigs as indistinguishable from Tories because they had imposed the New Poor Law, which a Chartist Government would repeal. Next John Goslin walked up from the audience and obtained permission to speak. He explained that he had stood aloof from the W.M.A., believing it to be yet another Liberal trick to retain control of working-class radicalism, but that night's militancy had won his support; "we want a fair distribution of the produce of our labour", which the Charter would ensure; a General Strike and the boycott of dutiable goods would achieve the Charter without bloodshed; the North would lead and the South should follow. Booley declared that the workers were now quite able to run the country. No hand was raised against the Petition, and some took copies away for signature in their villages.[22] An astonished Editorial in the Tory *Ipswich Journal* noted that the speakers had been mostly artisans, formerly supporters of Liberal candidates, and that they seemed to have learnt their oratory in Dissenting Chapels; the outcome of their proceedings, it warned, could only be a general pillage. The Liberal *Suffolk Chronicle,* despite the anti-Liberal tone of some of the speeches, declared that, as a result of the meeting, "the contest lies between wealth allied with bigotry and ignorance, against poverty aided by intelligence and honest integrity".[23]

Other public meetings followed. Ipswich Town Hall was again full when Cleave, from the L.W.M.A., lectured on Moral Force. Their rulers, he said, did not fear Universal Suffrage so much as the moral and intellectual independence it would foster among the workers; open, manly and temperate conduct by every Chartist was essential to success; they must be reasonable and patient, petitioning time after time until Reason had its way; women must help by forming their own Women's Associations to fight for the Charter, as well as making their homes havens of liberty, sobriety and enlightenment. Another crowded meeting heard James White, who as a Guardian had worked for every possible reform within the framework of the New Poor Law which he hated so heartily. He reported how, with other Chartists, he had persuaded the Guardians to permit the aged poor, forced into the workhouse by cuts in their allowances, to receive visits and parcels from friend and relatives; the Governor was now empowered to give the aged poor some tobacco or snuff every week. He urged the meeting to defeat reactionary Guardians at the next Board elections. Opinion in the town was now going Chartism's way, causing one of the two Tory M.P.s to raise the question of its legal suppression and particularly to denounce the despatch of delegates by the W.M.A. to meetings in London. In September delegates had gone to a rally in the Palace Yard at Westminster and this had created disproportionate alarm among anti-Chartists; a similar reaction was observable in other towns of the region and indeed, throughout Chartism's existence, much anxiety was aroused whenever local Chartists demonstrated their identity with the national movement.[24] This they were increasingly doing by their promotion of the National Petition. The initial number of signatures in Ipswich was 2,500 and more were to follow. This was no small achievement; workingmen, knowing how the Open Ballot exposed voters to economic victimisation, needed much resolution to run similar risks, as they saw it, by signing a document which was to be inspected by their exploiters in Parliament. The 2,500 signatories can be seen as almost the same number of convinced supporters. Figures of signatures from the whole region are not available but by Easter 1839, 6,914 had been sent in by Ipswich W.M.A. both from the town and from those places in Suffolk for which Ipswich acted as the centre, and other Suffolk Associations probably sent in their signatures directly to London. For the two counties 18,000 is a likely total.[25] Measured by these figures, Chartism in this region accounted for about 1.4 per cent of the movement's total strength, a percentage consistent with the scanty evidence available for its relative strength at other times.

Meanwhile, Colchester Chartists were spreading a more moderate message under the guidance of William Wire and of the L.W.M.A. to which they regularly wrote for advice. Wire and his friends still hankered after the return of D. W. Harvey, whom they had made an honorary member of their W.M.A. despite his coolness towards Chartism, and they were also ready to support the Liberal Free Traders whose dislike of Chartism was hardly concealed. However, once committed to a public campaign, the Association proceeded with vigour. Its rally, held in the New Market Place in the High Street because the Mayor refused it the Town Hall, was "the largest meeting remembered in Colchester for many years". By 6.30 p.m. 200 W.M.A. stewards were managing about 3,000 people around a platform flanked with anti-Corn-Law banners and occupied by 50 Chartists from Colchester and other local Associations. A normally moderate cooper opened with a speech containing sentiments rarely, if ever, heard before on a public occasion in Colchester:

"To remedy the present evil state of things the Birmingham Petition would be laid before them, which demanded that every man should be properly remunerated for his labour and that he should not be deprived of what the Almighty had created him to enjoy. That Almighty Being did not make one man rich and another man poor. The wickedness of man had effected this. Man had taken the power into his own hands; he had heaped together the riches of the world and had said, 'now I have the power, I will treat the poor as the off-scouring of the earth; they shall have just so much of good as I like to give them and no more'. Under such a system as this the people have been labouring, and it was this that brought the Working Men's Associations into being. The rich man lived on the produce of the poor man's labour".

A brush manufacturer followed with a largely Liberal speech and with references to the benefits of Universal Suffrage in America. W. G. Blatch, shoemaker, then attacked hereditary monarchy, the Reform Act, the New Poor Law and Malthusian economic policies, all of which the Charter would bring to an end. After greetings from Ipswich and Braintree W.M.A.s, a vote was taken in favour of Universal Suffrage with only twelve dissentients. A local shoemaker then defined Chartism's main aims as lower taxes, higher wages and Corn Law Repeal. There followed the most interesting speech of the evening, from John Goslin of Ipswich. The Established Church and the Corn Laws, he declared, were merely instruments of class-rule; in the continuing struggle between classes the landowners, who had ruled previously, were nowadays being challenged by the merchants and industrialists, who, having grown rich on the National Debt and war contracts, were destroying the relics of the old regime; when the latter finally overthrew the Church and the landed aristocracy, the workers could have their chance to intervene in this historical process to establish their own control; Whig and Tory were no different from one another, because they both tried to rob the worker of the greatest possible amount of the value created by his labour and their only quarrel was over the spoils; all wealth was produced by the worker but taken from him in rent and profit; armed force upheld this system, but a General Strike could win both the Charter and a society "to make us happy, free and social beings". Other speakers followed, including a veteran Reformer with a vision of a hundred Cobbetts in parliament, and the meeting ended four hours after its commencement with a virtually unanimous vote to adopt the Petition.[26]

The W.M.A. was elated, as additional signatures were added to the Petition, membership reached 250 and further crowded meetings were held. When, in October, Cleave addressed another rally, "the room and all the avenues to it were filled to suffocation". One report presented the occasion as entirely successful. Cleave attacked upper-class education as the cause of upper-class profligacy and urged moral teaching in schools and an adult-educational system suited to working-class needs. "But what are you doing in Colchester? You have had your party colours, you have had your price and pots . . . but have you anything like good principles at heart? Are you anxious to aid us in redeeming the working classes? All you who are willing to pledge yourself solemnly to aid the Working Men's Associations in working out their regeneration, hold up your right hands . . . Now let us see who is on the contrary. (Cries of 'not one' and tremendous applause.)". M'Pherson followed with a passionate plea against War. "Very shortly you will have the recruiting sergeants to enlist and send you to Canada to put down the Canadians; but let your reply be, 'No, we have to redress our own wrongs at home'. I entreat you not to lift a murderous arm against the Canadians; they only ask what we ask for . . . No, do not take the shilling; there is murder, there is slavery in the offer". However, another account, probably written by one of the militant minority in the W.M.A. gave a different picture. "Colchester. There was a great meeting at this place, a gathering of the working classes for the purpose of meeting a deputation for the Working Men's Association of London. It was hoped that the 'Great Lion of the North', Mr. Feargus O'Connor, would be present and long before the meeting was to commence, the Angel Inn was crowded to excess to hear him, but they were disappointed. The only deputation was Mr. Cleave from London . . . Mr. Cleave addressed the meeting in a very long, desultory and vague speech". The moderate Chartist leadership of Colchester would seem to have been at variance with the feelings of at least some of its own supporters.[27]

Chelmsford Chartists were also campaigning for public support, having changed the name of their Operatives' Reform Association to the Chelmsford Working Men's Association. It had been represented at the Colchester rally, had sent delegates to the Palace Yard meeting and, in December 1838, announced its own rally for the Petition. This was to be held in the Theatre and Branfill was to be chairman. The *Essex Standard* warned him that these were not "the times for well-meaning men to play the moth round the flame of revolution" and handbills were circulated urging all "who value their own respectability" to stay away. Two thousand people from Chelmsford and nearby villages did attend, however, and hundreds could not obtain admission. "Greasy smock frocks were lounging in aristocratic boxes and hob-nailed boots rested on the stools intended for satin slippers, while women and children filled up the crevices". Delegates came from four Essex Associations, and Cleave and Henry Vincent from the L.W.M.A. Branfill nervously argued that an improvement of the 1832 Reform Act, with a limited extension of the franchise, would be enough to end the Corn Laws, high taxes and War. The crowd, enthusiastic at first, fell silent as he proceeded and it obviously preferred the speech of Robert Hull, the local W.M.A. secretary, with its advocacy of a Labour Theory of Value, its refutation of Malthus and its plea for a system of higher education designed to inform the workers about public affairs. Cleave recalled the help Chelmsford had once given in the fight against the Newspaper Tax and urged a campaign in the villages, which the W.M.A. subsequently tried to carry out. Henry Vincent told his "fellow slaves" that it was the upper classes who, in wielding state power, monopolised Physical Force. Among the local speakers was John Thorogood, shoemaker, once a leader of the 1830-2 Reform struggle and soon to become 'the Church Rate martyr' when he preferred prison to payment of the Church Rate. The W.M.A. celebrated this success with a supper at their favourite inn. The event was marred only by the dismissal of some of the speakers at the insistence, it was alleged, of rich customers of the firm that employed them. Another result was that, when asked a few months later by Romford Chartists to chair their Petition rally, Branfill made his excuses; by that time the anti-Chartist pressure was too strong.[28]

The Braintree rally in November showed that the weavers were now ready enough to demonstrate for Chartism. Hundreds of them, coming from their looms after 6.00p.m., were shut out of the town's largest hall by 400 women and youths from the silk factories, who had occupied all the seats. Weavers were also shut out of a similar and larger rally at Halstead in December, but some of the speakers went outside to address them. This was a great day for the Halstead Chartists. Before the meeting an impressive march of their supporters had met the deputations from other Associations and escorted them into the town, and the total attendance was twelve hundred. Women were present in large numbers from the handlooms and the factories. The excitement probably sprang from the recent extension of Courtaulds' power-loom factory, but if the crowd expected support from the speakers for their bitter reaction to this event, they were disappointed. Lister Smith, who was in the Braintree delegation, told them, "I have heard a person say 'Down with the power-looms', and I do not wonder at it. However, I will say that I think power-looms have been beneficial to the manufacturing interests. If the manufacturers had them not, they would have to manufacture their goods at a dead loss. If the power-looms were shut, what indescribable distress would follow in Halstead".[29]

Into the countryside

Cleave had told Chelmsford W.M.A. at its rally that, to become an effective working-class movement in this region, it had to win over the farm workers and this the Chartists already understood. "It is the agricultural labourers we want to enlist", Garrard of Ipswich wrote. There were some grounds for expecting a favourable response. At the Chelmsford and the Ipswich rallies people had been present from villages and country towns, some of them coming from a considerable distance. Though it was still the only one of its kind, the Rawreth W.M.A. in south-east Essex was a genuinely rural organisation, the existence of which suggested that farm workers could become Chartists. Ipswich W.M.A. took the lead in Autumn 1838, when some rural workers asked it to help them organise associations in their villages. It issued a statement that:

"It is the intention of the Ipswich Working Men's Association to re-echo the sound through the county of Suffolk, until every village and town ring with Working Men's Associations. They will send missionaries into the country to preach the true and faithful doctrines of Radical Reform, and there is no doubt that success will attend their efforts".

The L.W.M.A. was asked to issue an Address to the Agricultural Labourers of England for use in this campaign. However, Ipswich Chartists faced formidable opponents in rural Suffolk, because few regions were more firmly under the control of landowners and farmers and all previous attempts by labourers to secure even limited concessions had been so easily crushed. Letters to the Press showed ruling circles in Suffolk quite ready now to deal with the "emissaries sent forth to the peaceful agricultural districts to operate upon the poor labourer in the midst of his privations and gain him over to the ranks of the anarchists".[30]

The Ipswich Chartists' plan was to move first into those country towns from which supporters had come to their rally and then, having formed W.M.A.s in them, to co-operate with these in spreading Chartism into nearby villages, a sensible approach because for villagers the nearest market centre was often the focus of social and political activity. In November came the first confrontation, when Ipswich delegates spoke at a meeting at Hadleigh, a former textile town of about 3,000 inhabitants, where Gould, a blacksmith with Owenite convictions, was already an active Chartist. A veteran working-class Reformer chaired the meeting, which was a large one. A strong W.M.A. was formed, which issued a statement of aims attacking the Corn Laws, the New Poor Law and child labour in factories. The significance of the event was illustrated by the warning to workingmen of Hadleigh from the *Ipswich Journal:* "If they array themselves in active hostility against property and order, is it not evident that an ignominious defeat, disgrace and punishment must be the inevitable consequence of their insane attempt? . . . The Government has its eye on their proceedings and we would therefore caution them to take warning from the examples of 1830 and 1831. Let them remember that hanging was then the reward of attacks on property and may be so again". When, early in 1839, Hadleigh W.M.A. planned a second meeting, it failed to find a meeting-place, the printer declined to print the posters and the bellman was forbidden to cry the meeting. The Chartists took the bell and cried the meeting themselves and, despite a steady snow-fall, over a hundred tramped out to a bleak field some distance from the town to hear the speakers.[31] From now on in this part of south Suffolk the Chartists found it increasingly difficult to proceed. When Ipswich W.M.A. arranged a meeting at Bildeston, a small town of 800 inhabitants near Hadleigh, farmers threatened to boycott all artisans attending and the local chairman, a tailor, was told that his business would suffer. Clergymen visited the cottages urging wives to keep their husbands at home. 600 labourers from a wide area did attend, but significantly no W.M.A. was formed. At nearby Boxford a meeting had to be cancelled when the local Chartists asked the Ipswich speakers not to come because of "threats and intimidation". Even in industrial Sudbury a meeting was postponed owing to threats of violence but the Sudbury Chartists continued with their plans and the meeting was soon held at which, with Ipswich and Colchester speakers in attendance, a strong W.M.A. was started.[32]

In other Suffolk country towns the Chartists were more successful. At Stowmarket in central Suffolk, despite attempts at intimidation, 3,000 people, including many farm workers, came to a meeting on a green near the town, while at Debenham, eight miles away, in the presence of police officers, 2,000 attended. Some workers from the borough of Eye, who had come the eight miles to the Debenham meeting, next held a rally in their own town at which, again in face of intimidation, "a huge crowd" heard two delegates from the Chartist National Convention denounce the New Poor Law and low farm wages. The Convention's programme to bring pressure on Parliament to grant the Charter was endorsed and a Chartist group founded, which was to enjoy greater stability than almost any of the other market-town branches. At Bury St. Edmunds, west Suffolk's largest town with a population of 12,500, belatedly in Spring 1839, an organisation was started that was to remain one of the sturdiest in the region. On the Suffolk-Norfolk border W.M.A.s were founded at Thetford, Diss and Harleston which drew support from the Suffolk as well as the Norfolk side. Finally at Woodbridge, long a Reform stronghold, M'Pherson chaired a packed meeting at the Shire Hall, and a Chartist group was started.[33] By Spring 1839, only Lowestoft and Haverhill among the larger Suffolk towns lacked a Chartist presence.

Partly parallel with these developments in the country towns and partly proceeding from them, a movement began among farm workers in central and east Suffolk. It was most vigorous near Saxmundham where the initiative came less from the Saxmundham Chartist group than from Ipswich W.M.A. and from the already existing W.M.A. at Friston, a central village with a population of about 450 where Hearn, a local shopkeeper, had been working for some time to create a "Suffolk metropolis of Chartism". The Chequers Inn here gave accommodation both for Friston W.M.A. meetings and for meetings of delegates from all the Associations in the area, as also did the Baptist Chapel. The Friston W.M.A. held the first large rally for farm workers in the area, which, despite alternative attractions hastily arranged by some of the farmers, a thousand people attended. They heard Booley speak on the text 'Go to now, ye rich men', Garrard attack the New Poor Law and M'Pherson ridicule the social pretensions of farmers' wives. This three-hour meeting in rural Suffolk, with lanterns hanging from trees, moved a reporter to write: "Never was there such a meeting in the rural districts", and the audacity of the labourers in attending it prompted letters to the Press recalling Swing and demanding the death penalty for arson and led a local landowner to threaten with dismissal any labourer on his estates who attended Chartist meetings.[34] However, the next meeting, held on Boxing Day, proved to be the largest ever to be held in the region in support of the Charter. A sympathetic journalist described the occasion:

> "At half-past nine in the forenoon, a large number of persons assembled at Bigsby's Corner, on the Ipswich Road, where they met the deputation from the W.M.A. of Ipswich, and escorted them in procession through Saxmundham to the meeting. The deputation took the lead, followed by the people walking five abreast, while several banners indicative of the principles of Chartism floated in the breeze. One banner represented the English loaf for 10½d., and the equivalent Russian and French loaf for 4½d. . . . 'Equal Rights, Equal Burdens' was another, and 'we will be slaves to nothing but our duty'. As the procession wended its way to Carlton Green, it acquired fresh strength, and when the place of meeting was reached, a waggon procured, and arrangements made for commencing business, there could not have been less than 4,000 persons present. At one time, it was said, there were full 5,000 . . . The day was delightfully fine; the sun shone forth in all his majesty and grandeur, and 'tipped the hills with gold', while all nature looked serene. The scene was indeed a most exhilarating one, though there was no music to enliven it, save the hum of thousands of human voices".[35]

For Hearn, who took the chair, it was a reward for his patient organising work. Booley opened with a prayer that the working people should be delivered out of the house of bondage. The speeches were rousing in tone and homely in language. Garrard based his pleas for Universal Suffrage, not on philosophical theory, but on the contention that "the workingman, who is able to conduct the affairs of his family circle, to plough, mow, reap and sow, who can make shoes and clothes, build a house and furnish it . . . is a practical man, a reasonable man, and ought to have the first right in political society".

Although 5,000 people had attended the rallies at Stowmarket and Debenham in central Suffolk, few W.M.A.s were formed in the villages there; at least, only one was reported in the Press, at Laxfield, a place with a number of artisans residing in it, a Liberal tradition and a record of farm labourers' protests, besides which there may have been one in a village near Stowmarket. In east Suffolk, however, the movement spread from Friston to other villages in the area and Associations were started at Sudbourne, Benhall, Middleton, Darsham, Wenhaston and also at Westleton, a large central village where support was particularly strong.[36] Hearn now found an effective ally in a country gentleman from Yoxford. John Goodwin Barmby was nineteen, self-educated and a prolific poet, described as "a young man of gentlemanly manners and soft persuasive voice, wearing his light brown hair parted in the middle . . . and a collar and neck-tie à la Byron". His letters reveal him as an already accomplished and witty dialectician, strongly influenced by Owen whom he knew personally, an internationalist, an utopian communist and a determinist. He denied charges of atheism, claiming to have evolved his own form of Pantheism from Spinoza and Shelley, the latter of whom he frequently quoted. His Chartist allegiance sprang from his sympathy for the dispirited farm worker and a belief that a Chartist society offered scope for "communities of united interest for the realisation of the fabled golden age upon earth". These visionary aims were tempered by some awareness of political reality, causing him to claim to be "more scientific than the Owenites". Without adhering to the so-called Physical Force party, he favoured vigorous tactics and sided with Garrard, Goslin and the more militant Ipswich Chartists. He in turn was welcomed by them as "one of the first political writers in the country on the side of the working millions".[37] Besides helping the village W.M.A.s to widen their activity, he also linked them with the Ipswich, Woodbridge and Saxmundham Associations in an East Suffolk Chartist Council, to which the recently formed Yarmouth W.M.A., though situated just inside Norfolk, also belonged. This move led to an attempt to found a similar Council in west Suffolk from W.M.A.s in the country towns there, one of which reported "a growing desire in the rural districts to join in the great national cause".[38]

No campaign was reported in west Suffolk villages, so that the east Suffolk movement remained the only success in rural Suffolk. Even so, it was no small achievement to have held the large public meetings of labourers in an area so completely dominated by its gentry and, more significantly, to have inspired the sustained activity of the village W.M.A.s, an achievement which was unprecedented and not to be repeated until the agricultural trade unionism of the 1870s. Although the only known local spokesmen were a country gentleman, a shopkeeper and half a dozen rural artisans, thousands of labourers openly appeared at rallies and hundreds joined the village Associations where some of them seem to have played a prominent part which they wisely concealed from the Press. However, Chartism's limited success would have been almost impossible without Hearn and Barmby and without the enterprise and courage of the Ipswich

Chartists; in Essex, where these factors were absent, rural Chartism was much weaker. If urban Chartists had been able to afford more time to organise support in rural districts, even in contemporary conditions a stronger movement might have ensued. Garrard thought that the labourers were so responsive that, if the National Convention would send an experienced delegate for only ten days, "by his assistance we could make Suffolk worthy of the cause and a county not the last, if need be, to raise the right hand of her sons in defence of liberty".

The villages where W.M.A.s existed shared a few special characteristics. Their populations were generally larger, and their artisans more numerous, than the Suffolk average. They mostly contained schools of some kind and also nonconformist chapels, which were an adavantage to Chartism in Friston and may have been so elsewhere. They suffered an observably lower level of incendiarism than the average Suffolk village, contrary to the routine anti-Chartist insinuations that Chartism and incendiarism went closely together. Otherwise there was nothing to distinguish them; they were no poorer than the rest of rural Suffolk.

Essex Chartists were less successful in rural campaigning, despite the attendance of many labourers at the Colchester and Chelmsford rallies and the early foundation of a W.M.A. at Rawreth, as already described. The reason for the latter success was undoubtedly the strength of the earlier Reform movement in this south-east Essex village and the presence there of Thomas Bedlow, a 52-year-old labourer who, during a life of sustained self-education, had left the Anglicans for the Peculiar People as well as teaching himself herbalism. He had been in early touch with the L.W.M.A. and, when in 1837 he organised a meeting against the New Poor Law, linked this protest with a demand for Universal Suffrage, so that it was a natural step to the formation at Rawreth in July 1837 of a W.M.A., the first in the region and, he claimed, the first in the land to consist largely of farm labourers. The list of its committee members shows an alliance of labourers and village artisans:

        Samuel Finch, basket-maker
        John Frost, coal carter
        Edman Layzell, farming labourer
        Samuel Creesey, farming labourer
        Henry Blackborn, farming labourer
        Richard Wade, farming labourer
        George Park, carpenter
        Timothy O'Rourk, tailor
        T. Bedlow, farming labourer, Treasurer
        W. Bedlow, farming labourer, Secretary.

Despite Moral Force professions, the Association's tone was militant. Thomas Bedlow's opening speech at the foundation meeting affirmed his belief in the centrality of class-struggle:

"Fellow working men, we are met here to form an association to be called the Working Men's Association or Democratic Association, and when so formed, to stand up by moral force for our rights . . . Let us tonight manifest by our proceedings that we will not cease agitation till we gain universal suffrage, which is the foundation of all our rights and will gain all the rest, whenever accomplished. There is a sworn hatred between the middle and poorer classes. My fellow working men, if you know not this, you know but little of the times. It is high time to awake out of sleep, for the enemy is in close quarters. And who are our nearest enemies is a question some of you can answer (My employer, exclaimed a farming labourer). Seeing things to be so, let us use moral force to disband them".

Bedlow concluded his speech with an attack on the New Poor Law in terms that revealed his own, and his hearers', awareness of its threat to wage levels. The Association looked for general support to Chelmsford, sending delegates to the rally there and obtaining the services of three Chelmsford W.M.A. members to speak alongside two local speakers at its own rally. Many labourers attended the latter meeting and voted to adopt the Petition, and Chartism now spread also to the adjacent villages of Wickford and Rayleigh.[40]

Otherwise, support for Chartism was limited in rural Essex. Chelmsford W.M.A. did call a meeting on Galleywood Common outside the town, at which, despite attempts by farmers to keep their employees away and despite the presence of the new County Police, 300 people heard speeches by "the Jack Cades, Robespierres and Marats of Chelmsford".[41] There was also much activity among rural workers in the Roothings, Hatfield Broad Oak, Harlow, Greensted and the Ongars, where workers gathered in public houses to hear the Chartist weeklies read aloud. "What spot", asked an observer, "can be supposed free from this foul infection, when it is seen to have pervaded even the quiet and secluded hamlets of Essex?". The Press was quick to attribute this to the presence of those of the Dorchester Labourers who had been settled on farms near High Ongar, but the likelier source, if source was needed, was one of the Chartist groups at Walthamstow, Epping, Waltham Abbey or Woodford, in the last of which W. J. Linton, the wood engraver, was then a very active propagandist.[42]

Meanwhile a few new urban groups had been formed, at Bungay in Suffolk and at Maldon, Romford and Witham in Essex. The Maldon group sent its contribution to the expenses of the National Convention with the following letter:

"Sir, The amount enclosed has been collected in this borough for the use of the National Convention. Although it may appear small, we as friends to the cause deem it our duty to acknowledge your body and to show that there is a germ of radicalism even in the Whig and Tory ridden town of Maldon, which may spread itself till it overshadows this dark and unintellectual part of the country".[43]

Chartism kept a presence at Maldon throughout the movement's duration, but never a strong one, perhaps because, as the letter implies, the borough's politics were so firmly controlled by Whigs and Tories, with the aid of lavish bribery. Romford W.M.A., however, received powerful support at its launching and went on to a full decade of effective activity.[44] By Summer 1839, as many as 27 W.M.A.s and 12 smaller groups had been started in Suffolk and non-Metropolitan Essex, and this list is certainly incomplete. The movement was now at its zenith. It enjoyed the confidence of most journeymen artisans and many unskilled urban workers in the region, while farm workers, when given the opportunity, had shown some readiness to respond. It therefore seemed for a brief time to be not out of the question for Chartism here to emerge as a widely-based popular force, if it could improve upon its rural position and begin to count its following among farm workers in tens of thousands. This was understood by the urban Chartists, on whose shoulders the work of expansion still rested, but, in the event, they were soon immersed in their own difficulties and quite unable to resume their rural campaign.

The wider conflict

In February 1839, the Chartist National Convention met to supervise the presentation of the Petition to Parliament, just as the Press began to report rebellious proceedings by Northern and Welsh Chartists. When Essex and Suffolk Chartists set out to collect money towards the Convention's expenses and to implement its programme of action, they were therefore joining a militant national movement and were no longer regarding themselves, or were being regarded, merely as the dissident wing of local Liberalism. Another result was that, by looking to the Convention for leadership, they were cutting their year-old connection with the L.W.M.A., to which they had hitherto reported progress and from which they had sought guidance. The process was hastened by delegates sent down by the Convention to arouse more support for the Petition in the region. These were men of a different spirit and outlook from Cleave and Lovett of the L.W.M.A. Gill from Sheffield, Deegan from Stalybridge and Duncan from Scotland brought something of the class-conflict of the North to Essex and Suffolk platforms, though they in their turn learnt of the difficulties faced by Chartists in rural areas. In Essex, they complained when they returned to the Convention, they had been greeted, not by cheering crowds as in the North, but by an implacable front of the powerful and wealthy, organised by the clergy and municipal authorities. They found Suffolk more responsive. The Mayor of Ipswich granted the use of the Town Hall which was again "densely crowded", though even here they met organised heckling which annoyed the majority of the audience by detracting from the effect of the meeting. In rural Suffolk they felt more at home because the audiences were large and enthusiastic.[45] These tours by Convention delegates widened the breach between the Chartists and the middle class. Tories reacted fiercely against the linking of the local W.M.A.s with what they saw as dangerous external influences, while Liberals were disappointed by the Convention delegates' attacks on "the monied tyrants", "the Shopocracy", the Anti-Corn Law League and the New Poor Law. Most Chartists applauded the delegates' militancy and went on to show, by collecting National Rent to finance the Convention, that they supported their national leaders and the direction they were taking. However, they now found their opponents uniting against them. When another Convention delegation visited Ipswich, the Liberal Mayor and the Liberal and Tory Justices impeded arrangements for the meeting, forcing the W.M.A. to resort to the bowling green of a beershop outside the town where the audience agreed to support a run on the Savings Banks to help win the Charter.[46] The Chartists feared that liberties would soon be curtailed by the new County Police, already set up in Essex and expected soon in Suffolk. M'Pherson told an Ipswich meeting that "very soon the inhabitants of Ipswich would be unable to go to Whitton with a shirt in a basket without being stopped . . . or go to Rushmere with two pennyworth of apples without being passed to the Station-house". At Colchester and Romford, when denied adequate facilities for holding their own meetings, Chartists retaliated by intervening at those run by Whigs and Liberals, further widening the breach, and the Liberal Press in its turn replaced news about local Chartist activity with lurid accounts of Chartist proceedings in Wales and the North and with anti-Chartist letters and hostile editorials.[47]

These developments subjected the Associations themselves to pressures that acutely divided them. Those under Liberal influence, Braintree and Halstead, hastened to condemn the so-called Physical Force leaders for their aggressive speeches, which, said the Halstead secretary, "if persisted in, would be our entire overthrow".[48] While these Associations urged unity with the new Anti-Corn Law League, Hadleigh and its very radical secretary regarded the League as the instrument of self-interested Liberal capitalists, and the new Sudbury W.M.A. denounced the Whigs as hypocrites for having once upheld Free Speech and now imprisoning Chartists for practising it. The strongest language was heard from east Suffolk, where, so far from disowning the Rev. J. R. Stephens for violent speeches, the Chartists remembered his work for factory children and vowed to seek his release "to the last drop of their blood".[49] The larger Associations, containing both pro-Liberals and militant Chartists, were divided in their reactions. Colchester W.M.A. did officially condemn the Physical Force leaders but also repudiated those of their own members who, in May 1839, joined the Liberals at a meeting to celebrate Peel's replacement as Prime Minister by Melbourne. At this meeting Cranfield, the master cooper, and other pro-Liberals offered the Whigs the W.M.A.'s support and agreed to accept a partial extension of the franchise instead of the Charter, whereupon the main body of Chartists present broke in with "we will have the whole", "It is our right" and "It is injustice to withhold a fraction of it". They then forced the chairman to allow M'Pherson of Ipswich to speak and loudly applauded his attacks on the Whig Government. "Three cheers for the Charter" were given at the end of the meeting.[50] At Ipswich too there was division. About sixty of the W.M.A. members were Parliamentary voters as £10 householders or free burgesses, while even more of them had the municipal franchise. This bargaining asset the W.M.A. tried to use to influence the Liberals, but at the municipal elections of November 1838 this policy caused an internal quarrel. In a move which it claimed was the first of its kind in Britain, the W.M.A. had decided to offer support to any candidate agreeing to consult his electors "in ward meeting assembled" on all controversial questions, but, in the absence of such a promise, to ask its members to abstain. One Liberal received Chartist endorsement on these terms, but another, by the name of Abbott, rebuffed the offer, causing the W.M.A. to distribute leaflets urging abstention in his case. Abbott, finding himself likely to lose without Chartist support, asked M'Pherson and Booley for help in return for a vague declaration of democratic intent. They agreed to this, but their failure to exact a specific pledge from Abbott was criticised by Goslin, who wished to boycott all elections until there was Universal Suffrage, and by the trade unionists, Garrard and Orr. When M'Pherson's explanation was accepted by a majority of W.M.A. members, Goslin resigned.[51] In June 1839, a similar issue arose when the Tory M.P. for Ipswich, Gibson, crossed to the Whigs and resigned his seat in order to fight it under his new colours. He arranged a meeting with the Chartists, who had apparently been receiving unofficial overtures also from the Tories, and assured them of his support for a limited extension of the suffrage, the Secret Ballot and Triennial Parliaments. He would gladly see W.M.A. members with the vote, he said, but not ignorant farm workers, and he admitted supporting the New Poor Law and the Rural Police Act. The Chartists contested every point with him, but cheered him as he departed and voted for him as the lesser of two evils. He lost by six votes because the Ransomes and other Whigs deserted him in view of his Chartist consultations and his Free Trade sentiments. When M'Pherson claimed credit for the W.M.A.'s steadfast support for Gibson, Garrard resigned and Joseph and Charles Bird seemed to have left with him. These dissidents, with Goslin, founded the Ipswich Chartist Association, which fully supported the National Convention and, while steadfastly refusing any dealings with Liberals, continued to co-operate with the W.M.A. in several undertakings, especially the campaign in rural Suffolk.[52]

These disagreements did not mean that active Chartists could be divided into Physical Force and Moral Force wings. The issue was now, as later, between those ready to allow Chartism to be an ally of Liberalism, albeit a critical one, on terms which would inevitably have involved acceptance of Liberal leadership and policy, and the great majority who had become determined to keep Chartism as an independent working class movement and never to accept any reform short of the whole Charter. The latter group supported the Convention and sought to implement its policies, but they were limited in what they could achieve. Colchester W.M.A. did consider the Convention's proposal for a General Strike to force Parliament to concede the charter, but felt it could take no action; its members were master artisans with their own businesses or journeymen employed in small workshops and would have found it difficult to lead a General Strike. The Association felt powerless even to persuade local workingmen to boycott exciseable goods, and the *Essex Standard* made merry at the picture of Lord Melbourne otherwise having to come, cap in hand, to beg Colchester's Chartists to light their pipes — "the town of Colchester and the Whig Ministry have each had a most fortunate escape", it wrote.[53] In rural areas some thought was given to a General Strike. The secretary of the Harleston W.M.A., on the Suffolk border, reported that his hundred members would have taken part but that wider support would not have been forthcoming because the villages between Harleston and Lowestoft had not even heard a Chartist speaker and so were not ready for such action. He thought however that a strike at next seed-harvest might be possible and that the labourers, with their potato-gardens to feed them, could stay out for a month; in the future strike action at harvest-time could be effective, "because the standing of corn, when it is fit to cut, is of more consequence than the standing still of a loom". He signed his letter "Yours till Death". In the Friston-Westleton area the labourers did not strike either, but they did plan a rally for late July, "as near to the commencement of harvest as possible, in order to strike terror into the hearts of those bigoted farmers and tyrant landlords in which that neighbourhood abounds", and they asked, unsuccessfully, for a visit by Feargus O'Connor because "he would make such an effect here that would long be felt and a blow could then be struck that our parson-Magistrates and tyrant-landlords would never get over".[54] There was talk of a strike in the Epping rural area, too, but to no effect.

In their helplessness some Associations fell back upon the routine of evening discussions which had been their main activity at the start, so that in the middle months of 1839, with their movement in crisis, they were discussing the Penny Post, the Corn Laws, Education and Astonomy.[55] Local politics also occupied some W.M.A.s. The Ipswich Association was planning to help approved Liberals win seats at the approaching municipal elections and Colchester Chartists took up an issue that achieved temporary notoriety in the town. On April 1st, 1839, the newly erected but not completely finished Hythe Bridge had fallen into the Colne. The Mayor, when told, had replied "It's April 1st — it won't do". But it was true and the W.M.A. resolved:

"As the possession of wealth has invariably been considered as a proof of the possession of wisdom by those in authority, and the Town Council has already expended £1,100 in the attempt to erect a Bridge at Hythe, and that attempt has entirely failed, this Association do volunteer to appoint a committee from its own body to draw up a plan for a substantial bridge, which the next 1st of April shall pass without finding it in the river".[56]

Other Associations were more spirited. Sudbury W.M.A. reported in October 1839 that "the glorious cause is waxing stronger at every meeting" and, when the National Convention dissolved, it urged the convening of a fresh one to lead a renewed struggle.[57] There were certainly other moves to continue the agitation for the Charter which went unrecorded because the local Press now declined to print such news. Ipswich Chartists were certainly preparing not only to repeat the previous season's rural campaign, now that the harvest was over, but also to organise a similar one in west Suffolk in co-operation with Bury and other Associations there. Fresh successes would have been won in rural Suffolk in 1839-40, had not the Chartists of the region, both moderate and militant, been stunned by the news of the so-called Newport Rising of November 4th, 1839, an armed but ill-prepared insurrection in which several thousand Monmouthshire workers marched on Newport in order, apparently, to initiate a more general uprising in favour of the Charter.

Most Chartist activities at once came to a halt, except that of petitioning for the pardon of the leaders of the Rising. All over the region people signed these petitions and even the *Essex and Suffolk Times,* now bitterly reproachful towards the Chartists, supported a policy of clemency as essential if British workers were not to be further alienated. Braintree W.M.A. collected for the relatives of "the Victims" and Ipswich sent them the money it had saved up to help finance a new Convention. This activity proved to be the occasion for re-activating the divided Chartists of Ipswich, who won a thousand signatures for a free pardon of the Welsh Chartists on the first day of their campaign. The preface to their petition showed that they inteneded to remain on the attack, declaring as it did that "the age does not require examples of blood and terror to render society secure; that can only be effected by an equal system of representation". Workers at Ransomes foundry had wanted to sign but the owners banned the collection of signatures within the plant, to the contempt of the Chartists who noted how "the clerks of the manufactory, disciples as they and their masters profess to be of the meek and lowly Jesus, members of the Peace Society and the Abolition of Capital Punishment Society, declined to allow the document to be carried among the men unless the prayer was altered from asking for a free pardon to entreating the Queen to transport the prisoners for life". The W.M.A. took the risk of booking the Town Hall for a public meeting and was delighted at an attendance of two thousand; it was "like a shot of electricity" and an answer to those who had rejoiced that "Chartism in this neighbourhood was defunct". Even where the response was less encouraging than at Ipswich, the defence of the Welsh leaders and their families occasioned some activity through 1840 when it might otherwise have subsided altogether, amongst other places at Chelmsford, Braintree, Halstead, Witham, Sudbury, Harleston, Eye, Stowmarket and Saxmundham. One way to proclaim undiminished support for Chartism was to display portraits of "the victims of Whig despotism" such as Frost and J. R. Stephens, orders for which came to Chartist headquarters from Rayleigh, Maldon, Bury and Braintree.[58] The release of the Welsh leaders remained a cause to which Chartists of this region kept returning through the next decade.

Chartists now found it increasingly difficult to present their case. So vehement was the concerted attempt to discredit them that they feared they would lose the rights of free speech and free association altogether. Even the Liberal *Suffolk Chronicle* called Chartists "insane" and "infatuated" and opposed any concession to their demands. At Harwich two Whigs devoted whole speeches to attacking them; Ipswich Mechanics' Institute and Chelmsford Philosophical Society, though professedly non-political, heard lectures against Chartism; the rector of Waldringfield was one of a number of clergymen preaching hostile sermons; and both Essex and East Suffolk Quarter Sessions hastened their completion of professional police forces. Chartists could be pardoned for fearing the suppression of their movement. "If the two factions should succeed in establishing their military despotism", one of them wrote, "I suppose that the mere whisper of Chartism will be punished as sedition and its advocates pointed out by a rabid Tory journalist or Whig demagogue as objects fit only to be hunted from the haunts of society". Another observer wrote, "Every species of crime and outrage is attributed to Chartism, and everyone who does not enlist under the banners of the Whig rampant or the Tory couchant, is set down as an abettor of High Treason".[59] It required courage to reaffirm Chartist loyalties, even in Ipswich where the movement remained strong enough to sustain its members' confidence, but more so in places where Chartist organisations were smaller and their members more easily identified. Some Associations were kept in being briefly to carry out petitioning and then fell into complete inactivity; this seems to have happened at Chelmsford, Colchester, Coggeshall and Romford. The Braintree W.M.A. condemned Physical Force methods, reiterated the justice of Universal Suffrage, urged unity with the Liberals against the Corn Laws, held two lectures on 'Moral Power' and 'Universal Peace' and, before dissolving, supported a public meeting at which the speaker was Sydney Smith, founder of the *Edinburgh Review* and no advocate of Universal Suffrage. Lister Smith's employer, Samuel Courtauld, had arranged this meeting and, in introducing Sydney Smith, referred to the "excellence of temper" of Braintree workers and the W.M.A.'s part in producing it. Nothing more was heard of the Braintree W.M.A. after this nor of the Halstead W.M.A., which had also passed a resolution against militant Chartism and for the Anti-Corn Law League.[60] A few individuals were still active in most Chartist centres, but only in Ipswich and, for a few months, in rural Suffolk did organisations continue to meet and carry out activity. However, the movement, though bewildered, was not utterly crushed and enough Chartists remained in sufficiently good heart to be capable of renewed activity when the situation became more favourable.

3

Years of maturity, 1841-4

Ipswich Chartists stood firm throughout 1840-1, refusing to disassociate themselves from the national Chartist movement and boldly counter-attacking its critics. The Newport Rising, in their view, did not impair the case for the Charter, which "remains and will remain uncontradicted till the end of time".[1] They were soon discussing strategy. Should they continue to organise pressure on Parliament to concede the Charter or become a mainly educational movement to elevate the masses and fit them for future enfranchisement? The issue was an immediate one, because they had to decide whether to support a new Convention called to meet at Newcastle. Barmby, already chosen as delegate by W.M.A.s at Eye, Stowmarket, Laxfield, Friston and Benhall, also wanted Ipswich's endorsement, but for Ipswich to adopt him was implicitly to re-enter the path of vigorous agitation. Gould, who had moved from Hadleigh to Ipswich, and Booley maintained that there was too much apathy for a militant policy to succeed and that, the last Convention having failed, a new one would do no better; the best policy would be to start more village Associations and collect money to start a Chartist daily newspaper. M'Pherson thought this attitude defeatist and persuaded the meeting to adopt Barmby, though it proved too late for him to attend. It was also decided not to support the Liberals at the next election, Garrard arguing that "the history of their past conduct, their silence on public affairs, their apathy now, is an impossibility of the two classes ever uniting again".[2] Instead of turning to the Liberals, the Chartists strengthened their links with the trade societies, five of which invited some of them to a dinner at which the toast was the People's Charter and the speakers on the trade society side turned out themselves to be Chartists, among them Orr, Harvey and Joseph Bird. Chartists and trade unionists also planned to build a Trades Hall for the use of all working-class bodies, but they could not raise enough money at this time of deepening slump. These and other cases of co-operation with the unions made it clear that the Chartists' policy in Ipswich was to build a broad independent working-class movement rather than to follow William Lovett and other L.W.M.A. leaders in their attempt to turn Chartism into an adult-educational association. They did not forget the farm workers as indispensable allies in the building of such a working-class party and prepared a "series of addresses to the agricultural labourers . . . with a view of instructing them in their rights, as men moulded by the same hand and governed by the same natural principles as the infamous aristocracy who now 'lord it over the working man's inheritance' ".[3]

It now also became clear that Ipswich Chartists still had the street crowds on their side. They dominated political life, allowing no public meeting to occur without a demonstration for the Charter. When an Anti-Corn Law League propagandist spoke on the Cornhill, two Chartists were there to speak for Universal Suffrage and at a Protectionist meeting in the same place M'Pherson virtually took over, addressing the audience on the iniquity of the Corn Laws, the hypocrisy of the Anti-Corn Law League and the justice of the Charter. "Henceforward", admitted the *Suffolk Chronicle*, "public meetings must be entirely composed of the select, or means be adopted to prevent the working classes opening their mouths at them".[4] This vigorous campaigning re-united the W.M.A. and the Ipswich Chartist Association, a process made all the easier now that the former had shed all pro-Liberal sympathies. Garrard co-operated with M'Pherson at an official County Meeting at Stowmarket, called to congratulate the Queen on the birth of a daughter. Stowmarket Chartists had distributed leaflets announcing that "representatives of the labouring classes" would attend and a force of police was brought in from several parts of Suffolk to control the situation. When the High Sheriff and six other gentlemen appeared on a balcony, they saw beneath them several hundred hostile Stowmarket workers. The High Sheriff moved a Loyal Address, whereupon M'Pherson and Garrard submitted a pro-Chartist addendum, M'Pherson observing that childbirth was somewhat more comfortable in a palace than in a workhouse. When the Sheriff declined the addendum, the crowd refused to vote on the Loyal Address, but when M'Pherson put the addendum as a motion they carried it with Three Cheers for the Charter.[5] Next, Goslin and M'Pherson turned an Anti-Slavery meeting at Ipswich into a demonstration against "the Bastilles", that is the new workhouses which they declared to be places of British slavery. The New Poor Law was fast becoming an even more acute issue as unemployment spread from the building trades to other occupations and the workless were refused all outdoor relief. When Chartist ratepayers in St. Margaret's persuaded the Overseers to call a public meeting on Poor Law administration, the large audience voted for total repeal of the Act itself and also launched a petition for this, which 3,000 people signed. "Feeling against the Act is intense", wrote the *Suffolk Chronicle*. "Public meetings on the subject are altogether out of the question hereabout. Neither Whigs nor Tories dare face 'the rabble' ".[6]

The situation was favourable to the foundation of a single Chartist body and in January 1841 the two wings disbanded their organisations and set up the Ipswich branch of the National Charter Association (N.C.A.), a new party of Labour established eight months previously. Its 'Address to the Unrepresented Classes of Suffolk' offered the Charter as the means of ending the New Poor Law, high taxes, low wages, long working hours and the other evils of industrial capitalism. Gould, who was now keeping a coffee-house and news-room, became chairman and Garrard secretary.[7] The old routine of weekly meetings with lectures was resumed, though the meeting-place was no longer a public house since most Ipswich members were now Temperance supporters. 200 people were now attending the more important discussions. An early lecture was by Goslin on Owenism, which he analysed sympathetically but critically. "The principles of the Socialists", he said, "may be good in themselves, but let us have the Charter which contains all that is necessary". This insistence on the primacy of the Charter and on the need for all social reformers to unite in its support was the answer which the movement always gave when offered alternatives to the Six Points, whether it was Temperance reform, adult education, Owenite socialism or Corn Law repeal.[8] The General Election of 1841 also found the branch united in rejecting any dealings with the Liberals; even Wason, once a favourite of working-class radicals, was rebuffed when he tried to re-instate himself, because he would not condemn the Whig "Black Government". M'Pherson condemned both "reptile factions", while Goslin urged support for the Tories because, by openly resisting all progress, they would cause the whole people to unite behind Chartism. However, Goslin reluctantly accepted the branch's policy of complete abstention. A plan to propose Barmby as a candidate was abandoned, apparently because he had left the region. Although during the campaign one of the Liberals proclaimed himself pro-Chartist and ready to support the Secret Ballot and the widest franchise Parliament would accept, the Chartists remained adamant and concentrated, with success, on interventions at public meetings.[9] The Ipswich crowds were with them and their influence continued to grow. However, their anti-Liberalism lost them whatever goodwill they still had with the *Suffolk Chronicle*, which now rarely mentioned them, so that at this, their period of greatest strength, the least can be discovered about their views and activities.

Chartism was meanwhile reviving in its other former centres. N.C.A. branches were formed at Sudbury, with weavers well represented among the membership, and at Bury St. Edmunds. It is not clear whether the groups at Saxmundham and Stowmarket became official N.C.A. branches but in the latter town they were strong enough, with M'Pherson's help, to dominate a meeting called to congratulate the Queen on the birth of another child. Activity was renewed also at Eye and Woodbridge, while at Framlingham the Temperance Society was reputed to be full of Chartists. Harleston again became an active centre. At Yarmouth, where an Owenite Institute was now in decline, the Chartists inherited some of its membership, the leading trade unionist of the town passing over to their side, and they soon built a sturdy N.C.A. branch.[10] In the villages there was no revival. The east Suffolk W.M.A.s had continued to meet well into 1840 and the Benhall Association had held a successful meeting against the New Poor Law, despite the presence of a contingent of the County Police. However, when Barmby left for London and later for Paris, the movement came to a halt. Nor was there a revival, except at Friston under Hearn's devoted leadership, though Ipswich N.C.A. wanted to repeat its earlier rural campaign. The Press referred to the survival of Chartist sympathies among the labourers, and individual villagers were kept in touch with the movement through the Ipswich and other N.C.A. branches, but, with the economic situation deteriorating and with the workhouse awaiting any labourer dismissed from employment, it was dangerous to be identified as a frequenter of Chartist meetings. A west Suffolk labourer complained at this time that "if anyone dare to advance the cause of Chartism, he is directly assailed as a general well-wisher to the destruction of property."[11] The urban Chartists, now that the elation and optimism of 1838-9 had passed, found it hard to spare the time and energy to undertake another rural campaign and yielded readily to the conclusion that, when town workers had created a powerful movement, farm workers would join it. The Harleston Chartist leader, commenting on the small attendance of farm workers at two open-air rallies in 1842, wrote:

"It is useless to attempt to organise them openly — the degrading serfism they are under will prevent them making any long-continued struggle. When the great mass of the operatives of the large towns, and all the really honest portions of the middle class are ready . . . , then will the men of the plough unite with their fellow-slaves in one grand final effort".[12]

In any case, legal political effort having proved fruitless in 1838-40, labourers were by 1842 turning to incendiarism as the safest form of revenge for their distress, so that Chartist approaches could have met little response even if Barmby had been there to help in the resumption of the rural campaign.

In Essex towns there was a strong revival. Colchester Chartists had re-assembled in August 1840 to celebrate the release from gaol of their friend, William Lovett, and had surprised themselves by the support they received. Several former W.M.A. members subscribed to Lovett's scheme for a Chartist initiative in progressive education, but when Lovett scorned any association with the N.C.A. and its leader, Feargus O'Connor, even Colchester Chartists preferred the N.C.A., which they formally joined in May 1841. The pro-Liberals had already withdrawn, leaving the leadership to more convinced Chartists, most of them veterans of 1838-9. The N.C.A. Council of seven members, elected in December 1841, contained at least five men who had been prominent earlier:-

James Clubb, flock manufacturer
Matthew Brown, cabinet-maker
Benjamin Parker, fruiterer
Thomas Rawlings, baker
William Flatt, tailor
Stephen Clubb, millwright, Treasurer
William Blatch, shoemaker, Secretary

The general membership remained predominantly composed of artisans, but it contained fewer masters and more journeymen. No Liberal paper was now published in Colchester so that the branch's activity went unreported locally, but the few reports for which the national Chartist Press could find space indicate a flourishing branch with a growing membership and greater public support than in 1838-9.[13] At Chelmsford several former W.M.A. members started an N.C.A. branch in December 1841, with a watchmaker as secretary. One very active member was the coachtrimmer R. G. Gammage, originally from Northampton, who later became a national leader and the author of a history of Chartism. He did not confine his campaigning to Chelmsford, but spoke also at Braintree, Colchester and Woodbridge. As in 1838, there were threats of victimisation against those joining, but the branch at once proceeded with the seeking of signatures for a new Petition.[14] It is unclear whether a branch was formally constituted at Braintree, but Chartism was at least as well supported there as before, especially by weavers and other silk workers, suffering as they were from a renewed depression in their trade. Furthermore, the leaders were more militant and readier to turn local Chartism into a working-class party with trade union connections, now that Lister Smith, though still ready to speak up for the Charter, had transferred his main energies into adult education. At Halstead, too, the Chartist group was firmly based among the handloom weavers. They had no N.C.A. branch, though they read the *Northern Star* and sometimes travelled the eight miles to Coggeshall where there was a branch, formed on the initiative of some silk-weavers who had moved there from

London.[15] Chartism now obtained a steadier presence in places where it had enjoyed only scattered support in 1838-9, such as Maldon and Witham, and made an appearance in other places where it had not existed at all, including Wivenhoe, Manningtree, Harwich, Sible Hedingham and Brightlingsea. At these places no formal N.C.A. branches were established, but, like similar groups in Suffolk, these Chartists looked only to the N.C.A. for leadership. The N.C.A. branches had fewer members than the W.M.A.s at their height. Voting figures for the National Executive of the party suggest that membership at one time reached eight hundred, but the evidence is far from certain; Bury St. Edmunds had about 80 members, Ipswich had about 100, with a further 150 close supporters.[16] However, N.C.A. membership imposed serious obligations, so that the really active strength of the N.C.A. in the region was probably at least as great as that of the W.M.A.s had been.

The N.C.A. was Britain's first national party to possess a popular membership and the first national working-class movement to command a faithful following in this region. It achieved greater cohesion than Chartism had done in 1838-9, both within its individual branches and also between these and its national leadership. This cohesion was founded in large part on a deep yearning for Chartist unity, bred amid the movement's quarrels of 1839 and reinforced by William Lovett's attempt to detach Chartists from the N.C.A. and by that of the Liberals to destroy Chartism itself by drawing them into the Anti-Corn Law League or the Complete Suffrage Union. When, in 1840, Ipswich W.M.A. discussed its political future, Booley "stressed the great importance of all the Chartists in the country being united". Chelmsford N.C.A. deplored the virulence of one particular internal dispute among the national leaders, warning that "denunciation only tends to create ill-feeling in our body, whereas every movement ought to be characterised by a spirit of kindness and brotherly love; and if differences exist, our sentiments ought to be expressed in a friendly manner; we therefore hope all bickering will cease".[17] As a result the Anti-Corn Law League seems not to have won the allegiance of a single active Chartist and the few who sided with the Complete Suffrage Union at Ipswich and Braintree did so very briefly indeed and without breaking their Chartist links. Not that wide differences of policy and outlook did not exist within the local groups. At Ipswich Garrard, Cook and Goslin saw Chartism as the political face of a comprehensive working-class movement, seeking to alleviate the immediate distress of working people and looking forward to their ultimate liberation from dependence on private capital, while for Booley and Lovewell the abolition of Church Rates still remained among the first reforms that should follow the enactment of the Charter. There were differences, too, between one locality and another, for instance between the pacifist and teetotal members of Colchester N.C.A. and the distressed Braintree weavers, meeting in their beerhouses to plan their economic struggle against their employers. Yet such diverse elements worked together to gain the Charter without which, they agreed, their particular programmes of social reform had no prospects of implementation. This desire for unity also reinforced the readiness of local branches and groups to forward the national campaigns launched by the N.C.A., including those against the Anti-Corn Law League and the Complete Suffrage Union which more Essex and Suffolk Chartists might otherwise have joined. In another campaign, the building of unity with the trade societies, the Chartists here achieved more than might have been expected in a predominantly agricultural region. They were, it is true, in no position to join in the 1842 General Strike, but they never condemned their fellow-Chartists in the North who were involved and at least nineteen branches and groups in this region sent regular donations for the dependants of those imprisoned. Indeed, Chartists here always generously supported "the Victims", perhaps because they felt so impotent themselves to join in the more militant activities of their northern comrades. One Sudbury Chartist, having given up all alcohol and tobacco and having sent the proceeds to the Victims' Fund, urged others to do likewise:

> "Brother Chartists, do not say you cannot go without spirits, beer, tea, coffee, sugar, tobacco and snuff, for a time. Think of the poor fellows in prison. They, I fear, will have to, and surely we can".[18]

The main channel by which N.C.A. policy became known in the localities was the Chartist Press, principally the *Northern Star*, which could be bought in Ipswich at Garrard's Radical Repository in Falcon Street or John Cook's Infidel Repository in Upper Orwell Street, where, as the name implies, Secularist and Owenite papers were also for sale. Other Suffolk centres received supplies through Garrard who was thereby enabled to communicate with Chartists all over the county and to help link them into an informal unity. Chartist papers could also be read at several beerhouses in Braintree, at Gould's Coffee Shop at Ipswich and at the Sudbury Coffee Shop and Reading Room kept by Joseph Goody. The Chartist Press did much to unify the movement here, drawing the local organisations into national efforts at times of high enthusiasm and keeping them in hopeful mood at less exciting times. In addition, with its informative articles on a wide variety of not directly political subjects, it furthered the process of self-education among individual Chartists and helped to inculcate a comprehensive outlook and philosophy among them.

Within the local groups fellowship was close. Women were welcomed as fellow-workers for the cause and are reported as politically active in Braintree, Coggeshall, Brightlingsea, Sudbury and Ipswich. In Ipswich they had a champion in Garrard, N.C.A. secretary, who, with his Owenite outlook, advocated their social as well as their political emancipation, and here women apparently became N.C.A. members. However, they seem not to have been elected to any branch office and even in Ipswich their main tasks turned out to be the collection of money for the Victims and the organisation of soirées, held in halls decorated with Chartist and Temperance banners, where for 6d. several hundred people would listen to readings, glees and songs for three hours and then dance for another three.[19] There were now whole families which tried to live their lives by Chartist values. At Sudbury, Ipswich, Colchester, Witham and Braintree children were named after famous Chartists. One notice in the *Northern Star* read, "More Young Patriots. At Braintree the wife of John Page was safely delivered of a daughter who has since been registered Eliza Feargus O'Connor Page".[20]

Among the wider public, Chartist influence was at least as widespread as in 1838-9 and far more lasting and, because of this and through better organisation, the Second Petition for the Charter in 1842 received perhaps double the number of signatures given to the first; this was certainly the case at Colchester, while in the market-town of Eye nearly 40 per cent of the adult male population signed.[21] Yarmouth members were so enthusiastic that they were represented with their banner at the head of the huge procession which accompanied the Petition to the House of Commons.[22] The branches held no large rallies in 1841-3 or, if they did, the Press ignored them, but they regularly used opponents' meetings to press their views, particularly at Ipswich where, for instance, six members appeared at a hand-picked gathering, called by the Mayor to start a coal fund in honour of a Royal Christening, and M'Pherson could not be stopped from giving an address against Charity and for the Charter.[23] At a by-election in May 1842, Ipswich Chartists were able to show that the street-crowds were on their side. Whigs and Tories had resolved to share the two seats, but Joseph Bird persuaded his fellow Free Burgesses to demand a proper contest. Two Tories therefore stood. Complete Suffrage Union candidates also presented themselves, but refused to adopt the Charter as their programme. Thereupon the N.C.A. decided not to vote and, with overwhelming popular backing, gave all candidates equally rough treatment. Disillusion with the Whigs gave the Tories victory, though the whole contest was once again annulled because of the bribery used.[24]

Though they took every opportunity to publicise their policies as widely as possible, Chartists now devoted most of their energies to a patient routine of educating and organising. In small country towns their task was to build firm organisations which would not melt away as the large crowds at the meetings of 1838-9 had done. Thus at Harleston, Walter Mason who, almost alone, had organised large open-air rallies of Norfolk and Suffolk labourers in 1839, in 1840-2 set out with some success to bring together into an N.C.A. group a smaller band of convinced Chartists whose task it then became to organise better-informed and more durable public support, though this did not prevent the group from conducting a further campaign for the Charter in the surrounding rural area and from gaining support not only from labourers but, to a much smaller extent, from Suffolk farmers.[25] The branches in the towns had the resources to attempt more important undertakings. One example was their arrangement of a tour for Dr. M'Douall when, on behalf of the N.C.A., he visited several towns to help the local branches make an alliance with the trade societies to which a number of Chartists belonged. M'Douall almost alone among the national leaders had perceived the movement's major weakness, the inadequacy of a mainly political programme in a situation where working people needed quick economic relief, and he had been remedying this weakness by a sustained effort to turn Chartism even more decisively into a party of Labour in close alliance with an enlarged trade union movement. His speech at Ipswich urged Chartists and trade unionists to prepare for a General Strike by which the Charter would be won and the way thereby opened for the reforms that the unions wanted; if Chartism were allowed to fail, he said, the Combination Acts could well be reimposed. His work at Ipswich and elsewhere was obviously successful. Colchester branch nominated him as the Eastern Counties' delegate to the new Convention and when the election came he easily topped the poll for that office. His advice to the Colchester Chartists in particular helped them to give leadership to the local trade societies during the next few years and at Ipswich he initiated a series of conferences at which Chartists and trade unionists discussed common problems.[26] However, trade unionism itself was too limited in this agricultural region to give support to the attempted General Strike of August 1842, which was in part industrial Britain's answer to Parliament's rejection of the Second Petition, designed once again to persuade Parliament to enact the Charter. On that occasion all that the Chartists here could effectively do was to continue telling unemployed and badly paid workers that the suffrage was their right and that, if they won it, they could themselves remedy their distress.

The rejection of the Second Petition and the failure of the General Strike disappointed the Chartists here but did not crush them. They were by now experienced politicians who accepted that their struggle would be long and hard, so that there was no collapse as in 1839-40. When Campbell, an N.C.A. leader, addressed a meeting of protest at Ipswich against Parliament's obduracy, he enrolled thirty new members in the branch. He and M'Douall spoke at a series of meetings at Bury, Colchester, Chelmsford and other towns. Suffolk Chartists also took up a scheme to join their comrades in Norfolk and Cambridgeshire in employing a full-time organiser to lead a missionary campaign in the rural districts, though this was abandoned when the man selected for the appointment was arrested during the Government's anti-Chartist drive of Autumn, 1842.[27] Meanwhile local branches and groups continued their weekly or fortnightly meetings as if there had been no General Strike and seem to have retained at least the passive backing of a working population still facing a deep economic depression and the distress which it entailed.

To Liberal invitations to renounce O'Connor's leadership and abandon their independent position, Colchester Chartists replied with "a whole-hog resolution in favour of the Charter and No Surrender". Other Branches passed votes of confidence in O'Connor, Chelmsford adding a resolution of support for "the talented, eloquent and patriotic Dr. M'Douall".[28] Ipswich N.C.A., which specifically attributed the attacks on O'Connor to the desire of Chartism's opponents to break its independence, had at once to face a trial of strength on this very issue when, in yet another election called because of corrupt practices at the previous one, it had to meet the challenge of the Complete Suffrage Union (the C.S.U.), recently formed by Liberals as an alternative to Chartism.[29] The usual attempt was made by the unofficial Whig-Tory coalition to take one seat each without resort to the polls, but a contest was ensured when firstly Thornbury, the contractor for Ipswich's new wet dock, and secondly Henry Vincent put themselves forward. Vincent had begun his political career in the L.W.M.A., had then been sent as Convention delegate to the West of England and South Wales and finally had been arrested for some fiery speaking in Monmouthshire, where the admiration of the militant miners had led him to say, "When the moment arrives, let your cry be, 'To your tents, O Israel'. And then with one voice . . . 'Perish the privileged orders! Death to the aristocracy! Up with the people and the government they have established' ".[30] In gaol he repented and issued a declaration recommending adult education and Temperance as the paths to progress. He naturally supported Lovett's new scheme but, finding it impossible to detach Chartists from the N.C.A., he abandoned relations with the mainstream of Chartism. Instead, he began to build his own career, lecturing not unprofitably to middle-class audiences and waiting for a by-election at which to further the Parliamentary ambitions he had long cherished. He polled well at Banbury, with some Chartist support, and, when the Ipswich election was called, immediately presented himself without first seeking Liberal endorsement. On arrival his first act had been to address a huge crowd which had gathered to acclaim this professed champion of Universal Suffrage and was delighted to hear him say that he had come "as the unpurchasable, the unflinching, the indomitable opponent of that aristocracy which has placed, kept, held the Government in the hands of the few". He next courted the Liberal-nonconformist vote with attacks on the Anglican church, the aristocracy and militant Chartism. As a C.S.U. supporter he received the endorsement of radical Liberals and, because of his acceptance of the justice of Universal Suffrage, that of the Chartists as well. The Whigs, however, led by the Ransomes, ignored him and, to win them, Vincent now omitted all reference to Universal Suffrage. This was to reckon without the mass-support enjoyed by the Chartists who attended the Nomination in "rather strong force" and with their own band. Before an immense crowd, which still believed Vincent a Chartist, M'Pherson methodically questioned him on each of the Six Points, obliging him to endorse them all. Thornbury too was forced by the crowd to profess strong democratic principles and the Tories also underwent close interrogation. Vincent's unwilling admission of support for Universal Suffrage lost him decisive Whig votes, the Tories winning both seats with 651 and 641 votes against 542 for Thornbury and 473 for Vincent, but for the Chartists the crowd's overwhelming backing for their policy made the occasion a triumphant one.

Though disappointed at Vincent's defeat, the Liberals were elated at his high vote; "henceforth the political battles in this Borough will be the People against the Tories", wrote the *Suffolk Chronicle*. The Chartists had mixed feelings. "The People against the Tories", they felt, was intended to mean a strong Liberal party, with Chartists in tow, a situation from which they had been trying to escape from the start. Yet, although Vincent was no longer a Chartist in either name or deed, the 10,000 people who had escorted him to his lodgings after the Declaration did so because they thought he was. So the dominant issue in 1842-3 remained one between Chartism and Liberalism, with the former striving to retain, and the latter to annex, the popular enthusiam for radical Reform. The Liberals formed a C.S.U. branch under the chairmanship of Fraser, a draper who had been captivated by Vincent's political charm. Their chief success was the adherence of five Chartists who sought to remain N.C.A. members while utilising Vincent's popularity to promote Universal Suffrage through the C.S.U. Two of these, Booley and Lovewell — and probably the other three — were strong nonconformists. About sixty Liberal electors joined, including several municipal candidates, and the *Suffolk Chrinicle* gave every possible publicity. The N.C.A. opposed it a scheme "to throw Chartism into the shade". M'Pherson said that "the present attempt originated in the middle classes and, knowing how deeply they had deceived the people, he could not feel confidence that the present move, which was essentially a middle class move, boded any good for the operative masses". Except for Booley who for a few months addressed meetings for the C.S.U., the waverers quickly re-committed themselves to the N.C.A.[31] In Autumn 1842, the Chartists smothered an attempt by the C.S.U. to move into the leadership of the Reform cause, when it called a meeting to choose four Ipswich representatives to a national conference at

Birmingham, having first taken precautions against any Chartist being chosen. However, workingmen attended in such force that Garrard and M'Pherson were elected, along with Fraser and Vincent. At the Conference the Chartists who had been chosen as delegates at similar meetings all over the country prevented the C.S.U. from replacing the Charter by another Reform programme, Garrard and M'Pherson voting with their comrades. On his return Fraser called a public meeting at which to denounce them, while Garrard declared himself so disgusted by the local C.S.U.'s conduct that he published a warning to Chartists everywhere, "I implore you to stand firm and elect your own men. Depend upon it, if you temporize, you are sold . . . The professions of such men are hollow and deceitful". He was also fully aware of Vincent's complicity in the C.S.U.'s attempt to edge the Chartists out.[32] The C.S.U. soon collapsed at Ipswich, as did its Colchester, Sudbury and Woodbridge branches, so that the Chartists were left as the unchallenged leaders of radical Reform.

There was one place where the C.S.U. made its appearance without involving any real danger to Chartism. At Braintree a meeting was called by Parmenter, a former W.M.A. leader, at the Six Bells, once the regular Chartist meeting-place, to consider the formation of "an association for the political enfranchisement of all classes". His aim was the "stirring up and informing the people on the various points of the Charter, as he believed that most of the dislike the public had to that document was more on account of its name and the unwise manner in which it had been advocated by some of its too ardent friends". Parmenter's sincerity was accepted by Lebeau, a weaver and a firm N.C.A. supporter, who seconded the proposal. Another W.M.A. veteran, George Walford, promised that "he would never disown the Charter or shrink from advocating its points, but he wished to do so in a manner most likely to obtain the support of the middle class, for it was through the exercise of their franchise that the working classes would obtain theirs". Even the man who proposed that the new body should be called the Braintree and Bocking C.S.U., "wished it to be understood that he was proposing nothing short of the Charter itself". The N.C.A. supporters, however, would not accept a C.S.U. connection, one of them arguing that "the meeting should not appear to compromise the principles of the Charter . . . by adopting a name that might be seen to announce to the world that they were ashamed of the Charter. He did not believe that the middle classes would be won over by so doing, and they would seem inconsistent to their principles". The advocates of C.S.U. affiliation won a majority but their new organisation seems to have dissolved almost at once.[33] However, its challenge may have been the cause of a lecture given soon afterwards by R. G. Gammage of Chelmsford, to "thunders of applause" from a large audience at Bocking. The chairman was Lister Smith whose speech showed that, even if he was no longer willing to act as the leader of local Chartism, he remained its supporter.[34]

If the aim of the C.S.U.'s promoters had been to win public support away from Chartism, from 1843 their mission became less urgent, as Chartism itself lost its vigour and initiative. The Chartists themselves and their artisan supporters, in this region as in others, were approaching political exhaustion, the former out of disappointment, the latter because of their long economic distress and Chartism's inability to mitigate it in any way. There was no diminution of discontent and, with even partial recovery two years ahead, most working people were struggling to avoid the workhouse. In 1844 numerous Suffolk able-bodied men applied for poor relief, almost all of whom, when offered the workhouse, preferred semi-starvation at home. About 1,300 Colchester families were receiving charitable help. Artisans tramped the countryside in search of work. To none of those could Chartism offer practical assistance, preoccupied as it was with the Six Points, though it did its best to help the trade unions in their work. Even its hitherto devoted membership dwindled. Its active Ipswich members fell to about twenty, their comrades at Colchester could be described simply as "the Chartist club" and in the rural areas of the two counties, it was stated, "the want of an efficient organisation is greatly felt".[35] The stronger branches did not abandon public work; those at Braintree, Bury St. Edmunds and Sudbury in particular seem to have struggled on with some success. Coggeshall Chartism, hitherto persistent but subdued, enjoyed a lively revival, partly because a leading London Chartist, T. M. Wheeler, took a special interest in the town. Supporters were attracted from a wide area to its weekly discussions and public meetings. The branch was also firmly in support of Feargus O'Connor, in spite of its strongly nonconformist affiliations.[36] Individual Chartists remained active in smaller centres like Lavenham, Stowmarket, Brightlingsea and Witham. Not until 1845 did Garrard write to the *Northern Star* to lament that in Suffolk the apathy of the workers and the economic victimisation of active Chartists had virtually ended N.C.A. activities in "this dark part of the country", so that he and his comrades had now become "silent observers of the progress the people's question is making".[37] However, he failed to do justice to his fellow Chartist, M'Pherson, who still intervened at so many public meetings, including some under the most august patronage, that the issue of the Charter could not be forgotten in the town for the briefest period. He was always patiently heard out and came to be known almost affectionately as "Mac." even to his opponents. He himself explained that "the question of the franchise was dear to his heart and that was why he brought it forward on every occasion".[38]

One result of their weakness was that Chartists failed to meet the Anti-Corn Law League's challenge with the same firmness as they had that of the C.S.U. The League was by 1844 entering the final stage of its brilliantly conducted campaign to persuade Parliament to repeal the Corn Laws. The Chartists were themselves strong opponents of the Corn Laws, but as soon as the League started in 1839 and invited Chartists to join it, they had at once reacted by proclaiming the prior necessity of the Charter. "As for the Corn Laws", said G. F. Dennis, "let us get Universal Suffrage, and *we* will repeal them". Romford W.M.A. tried to take over the earliest meeting held by the League in the town and put forward the Charter as the only solution. Barmby assured a Suffolk village meeting that "until we have equal political rights, the starvation act must exist".[39] As the League pressed ahead without regard to the Chartists, the latter began to harass it. "In the quiet little village of Walthamstow", they took over a League meeting and replaced Sydney Smith, the official speaker and a native of nearby Woodford, with their own spokesman. At Ipswich M'Pherson, Booley and other N.C.A. members waged a continuing war with the League, dominating its public meetings with accusations that the League's capitalist leaders wanted Repeal only in order to reduce wages to sub-subsistence. M'Pherson told a Liberal rally that "it was not the Corn Laws that had produced distress but class legislation" and that the League was the creation of the industrialists who were using it to advance their own interests. In 1844, when the League was advancing towards victory, Chartists were still moving amendments in favour of the Charter at League meetings. Even after Repeal M'Pherson gave the League no respite and was still claiming priority for the Charter at a meeting which the Free Traders held against the Malt Tax in Autumn 1846. Elsewhere in the region Chartists had abandoned the struggle against the League at an earlier date and at Colchester they seem to have been present to support Cobden when in 1843 he won a remarkable victory over the Protectionists at an open-air debate in the town before an immense audience of farmers and townsmen. After Repeal the Chartists of Essex and Suffolk generally defended Free Trade and actively opposed the re-introduction of Protection.[40]

These theoretical controversies over Free Trade took place in the midst of a working population urgently needing some relief from current insecurity and distress but no longer entertaining hope of a Chartist victory. Where Chartists were able to take up issues directly related to economic and social problems, they evoked a better response than when they offered what seemed a political solution. They had never abandoned their opposition to the New Poor Law which continuing unemployment had now made a threat to every workingman. Several allegations of inhumanity were made against the Poor Law authorities in 1844, one of which concerned the death of an old man at Nacton Workhouse in Suffolk. Though an enquiry acquitted the authorities of positive cruelty, they were widely felt to have been at fault and a very determined man, William King, who had been an inmate at the time of the incident, devoted himself to exposing them. With M'Pherson, Garrard and Whimper, he addressed large meetings at Ipswich and Woodbridge with such success that some Liberals and Tories joined his campaign. When another scandal arose in connection with Wickham Market Workhouse, the enquiry was held in such secrecy that the Press protested and withdrew. This campaign was strongly supported by artisans, who were now rarely seen at political meetings of the normal kind.[41]

In a similar field Chartists could claim minor successes in this period of political apathy. The *Northern Star,* widely read even at this time, was still encouraging readers to support the trade union movement, and the Chartist artisans of the region, mostly trade unionists themselves and followers of Dr M'Douall, responded where they could. When T. S. Duncombe, a pro-Chartist M.P., headed the opposition to a repressive Masters and Servants Bill, Garrard organised a petition against it at Ipswich, while at Braintree and Sudbury Chartists and trade unionists combined to oppose it.[42] A National Association for the Protection of Labour had been set up with N.C.A. backing and at its 1845 conference the Yarmouth unions were represented by J. Royall, once an Owenite and now a Chartist. Under the National Association's auspices a union for tailors had been started and a branch of this was formed at Colchester by the group which had for some years been upholding the Chartist cause within that trade. The leaders were William Barrett and Thomas Plummer, an advocate of Temperance and pacifism, and, although the male tailors feared and resented the competition from unapprenticed tailoresses living in the north Essex villages, these two men persuaded their new branch to invite the female "white slaves" to join. The stated aim was "to raise themselves from their fallen position by the support of the principle that fair wages for labour, and fair remuneration for capital, are not only beneficial to our class but to every class in society" and their methods were "unity, sobriety and perseverance". The members were even persuaded to transfer their meetings from a public house to the Mechanics' Institute, a change which the branch survived, at least for two years. Plummer also organised a Maldon branch and represented both towns at the union's 1847 conference.[43] Colchester Chartists had influence in the Shoemakers' Society, the secretary of which, Chapman, was a Chartist. G. F. Dennis, former W.M.A. secretary, seems to have been the Society's adviser; as a master, he may not have qualified for direct membership. In the brief boom of 1846 the Society had organised a Closed Shop among the town's 500 shoemakers and, by arrangement with other Shoemakers' Societies, was preventing any shoemaker from entering the town to work at below the Society's rate. To circumvent this 'blocking', one employer, a Mr. Mills, brought down three Londoners to work for him but, on being apprised of the situation by the Society's committee, they returned home. One of them, Duggin, was again sent down by the London agent of Mills, only to find on his arrival that Mills had given in to the Society and had paid a £1 fine for his previous attempt to circumvent the Closed Shop. Duggin stayed in the town and was drinking in a public house when he was threatened by a man called Wisbey, who, "though a tailor, appeared to have espoused the shoemakers' quarrel", as a surprised journalist wrote, presumably not knowing that Colchester tailors were also organised at this time. Wisbey was prosecuted, rebuked by the Mayor and fined 15s. Despite evidence in favour of the Society by G. F. Dennis, the Court warned that it was going to proceed more severely against its secretary, Chapman, but this threat was not carried out, possibly because the magistrates were subsequently told that trade unionism itself was no longer illegal, a fact of which they were not the only eminent persons in the region to be ignorant.[44] The very existence of the Shoemakers' Society and of its Chartist leadership would have gone unreported but for Wisbey's action, and it is almost certain that in other disputes and trade union activities of 1844-6 Chartists were involved. These included partially successful moves by Colchester and Ipswich shop assistants to obtain a reduction of their excessively long working day, a reform which the Chartists had long advocated. There were also two strikes by the 500 girls in the Colchester silk mill and one by Harwich stone-dredgers; others certainly went unreported.

Chartists thus showed readiness and ability to assist urban workers in their economic struggles; after all, they had themselves mostly belonged to the trades which they were trying to protect. Yet they failed to respond to the urgent complaints that arose in 1843-5 from the 80,000 farm workers of Essex and Suffolk. These took the form of a sustained wave of incendiarism, starting in Essex in 1843 and spreading next year to central and west Suffolk. Though the actual perpetrators tended to be young farm workers, some of whom had been badly affected by unemployment, these were so consistently protected by almost the whole working population that the several hundred fires of these years must be seen, not as terrorist actions by disgruntled individuals, but as a form of social protest supported by the mass of the rural poor. Few incendiarists were punished because few were caught; of those arrested a majority had to be acquitted for lack of evidence. The impoverished village population ignored rewards offered for information, although these might be equal to several years of their wages, in some cases to much more than this. Indeed, they sometimes flocked to a fire in a mood of hilarity, where they "openly exulted in the progress of the flames" or roasted turnips in the heat. Firemen were obstructed and their hoses cut. The countryside was heavy with sullen resentment among the labourers and deep anxiety among property-owners. Lord Western wrote of mid-Essex at this time, "Dreadfully changed are the tempers of the working-classes towards the higher. Where is the country, besides this, in which the farmers cannot go to bed without the fear that their blazing stacks may rouse them from their midnight slumbers?".[45] The *Suffolk Chronicle*, no friend of the rural establishment, condemned "this hell-born demoniacal system . . . a reign of terror".[46] The Press noted with surprise that good employers suffered along with the bad; at such a time of general class confrontation personal virtues counted for little.

If this was indeed a general social protest, it merited some response from Chartist groups now seeking to identify themselves with all current movements of working people. Chartists, of course, sympathised with the distress of the farm workers and at Colchester some of their more irresponsible supporters seem to have impeded firemen setting out from the top of North Hill to put out a fire in the adjacent parish of West Bergholt. Their leaders, however, had always deplored incendiarism, boldly speaking out against it at their Suffolk rural meetings and predicting that the advance of Chartism among the labourers would be paralleled by the decline of incendiarism. William Gould, the Hadleigh blacksmith, challenged an anonymous allegation that Chartist speeches incited arson. He maintained that Chartists were:

"the very men whose life and best exertions had been spent in teaching their agricultural brethren the folly of such-like crimes. Why, I have myself, hundred of times, when talking to my fellow-brethren of the plough, reasoned with them in some such fashion as the following: 'Every stack and barn destroyed by fire not only lessens the quantity of food in the nation, but cuts off the means of employment for several industrious men who would be able to pass away several of the winter months in thrashing and dressing the burnt corn'. Men may be fools enough to imagine that it is only 'serving a bad master right' to destroy his property, but in nine cases out of ten that property is insured . . . Let us view the subject in whatever light we may, it is the poor hard-working men who will be the greatest sufferers in these calamities. I have at all times freely stated my view of the matter, whenever I saw, or fancied I saw, an individual express anything like indifference at the dreadful news of such and such a stack or barn being wilfully set on fire, and I do not believe there is a farmer or landed proprietor in the kingdom who has done more to expose the folly of such proceedings than the members of the Working Men's Associations. Talk about political agitation as instrumental in midnight burnings — why, any man, not quite an idiot, would look for the real cause in the *absence* of political knowledge and political agitation among the great portion of the agricutural peasantry".[47]

When in 1844 arson was at its height, William Garrard published a statement firmly rejecting incendiarism as a method of achieving social progress and begging labourers instead to unite in support of the Charter, the winning of which would pave the way for a government ready to help them.[48] However, politics could offer no immediate relief to the labourers. They needed more food and, failing that, they wanted revenge, but Chartism could not provide the first and would not countenance the latter. N.C.A. branches and groups seem never to have explored ways of transforming the labourers' incoherent protests into a legal, purposeful movement for social betterment and, had they done so, in the 1840s they would have had poor prospects of even limited success. It was this failure, probably an inevitable one, to organise the rural workers who in this region constituted the majority of the working population, that condemned Essex and Suffolk Chartism to remain a minor force within the national movement.

4

Recovery and Final Decline, 1846-58

For Chartism to recover, some fresh initiative was needed, and this was provided in 1845 when its leaders founded the Chartist Land Society. Individuals were to buy shares in the Society by instalments and, if successful in a lottery, were to be awarded the lease of a smallholding on an estate purchased by share subscriptions and mortgage loans. Whatever the administrative failures and financial miscalculations, the scheme was a far more astute piece of opportunistic politics than O'Connor, its originator, has been given credit for. It offered subscribers a chance of swift translation from employee to smallholder, it had some of the attractions of a Friendly Society and the excitement of a lottery, and it promised fellowship within a like-minded community such as Owenites had dreamed of. This region's subscribers were close enough to village life to entertain no illusions about its amenities and few would have relished becoming an agricultural labourer, but the independence offered by a smallholding did appeal to them. To the Chartist groups the scheme gave an unexpected opportunity to build up support for a seemingly practical undertaking that would tie subscribers not only to the Company but to the Chartist cause itself. One by one, the stronger groups took the scheme up, though one feature of the range of response was its inclusion of at least three of Chartism's weaker centres as well, those at Maldon, Witham and Brightlingsea. There was also one place which formed its very first connection with Chartism when a Land Branch was formed in it, Exning in west Suffolk, probably the only agricultural village to have its own Chartist centre since the closure of the east Suffolk rural W.M.A.s in 1840.[1]

The first Land Branch was at Sudbury, where Joseph Goody, a baker, had maintained Chartism through the difficult years after 1842 from his Coffee Shop and News Room where supporters from the town and nearby villages could read the Chartist Press and discuss its articles. Before the end of 1845 he had sent in some £13 in subscriptions and had held a large publicity meeting at which a petition for the free pardon of John Frost and his colleagues had also been signed. This Land Branch met regularly and celebrated the purchase of the first estate with a tea party. More significantly, Goody proceeded to re-found the N.C.A. branch.[2] At Ipswich a Land Branch was at first slower to gain support, though ultimately it became the strongest in the area. In 1846 branches were founded at Halstead, Brightlingsea, Yarmouth and Chelmsford and in 1847 at Witham, Coggeshall, Braintree, Romford, Colchester, Maldon and Bury St. Edmunds. Support was by then sufficient for a federation to be formed of Essex, Suffolk and Norfolk Branches. The full amount of the contributions cannot be known, but the Essex and Suffolk branches sent in at least £800, probably more. Of the £800 about £300 came from Ipswich, a fair reflection of that town's importance in the region's Chartism. Interest was widespread, with publicity meetings attracting some of the largest audiences since 1838-9. At Witham hundreds attended a debate between supporters and opponents of the scheme, and a large Press correspondence reflected the widespread interest aroused in the region. By 1847 in a number of places, including Sudbury, Ipswich, Colchester, Halstead and Stowmarket the N.C.A. branches had been revived, mainly as a result of the activity generated by the Land movement. The so-called Chartist revival of 1848, sometimes attributed to the revolutionary events on the Continent, was thus under way by the Summer of 1847.

Confidence now began to return and it was reinforced by successful participation in the 1847 General Election, generally on the Whig side which, partly because of their own political isolation of recent years and partly in despair at the prolonged Tory electoral hegemony, local Chartists were mostly prepared to support. They welcomed the return for South Essex of Buxton, hardly a radical politician. In the North Essex election Halstead silk workers shouted for the Charter and against one of the Tory candidates when he tried to speak in the town. At Colchester the revived N.C.A. branch worked for Hardcastle, the single Whig candidate. A wealthy brewer and lawyer, he was equivocal on even the most tentative proposals for Reform but, in Chartist eyes, preferable to Sanderson, the Quaker Tory who had vowed "to defend the Constitution against the attacks of Whigs, Radicals, Repealers, Chartists and Socialists". With Hardcastle's wealth pitted against Sanderson's and a well-organised Reform Club creating a degree of anti-Tory fervour not witnessed since 1832, the Whigs secured the seat for Hardcastle and proceeded to win the municipal elections in November. The Chartists had been in the thick of the campaign, led by "the Dennises and the Wire-work" and at a monster tea-party G. F. Dennis, William Wire, H. S. Clubb and Thomas Plummer were singled out for special thanks. At Bury St. Edmunds the Chartists, who evidently included a number of Parliamentary electors, used this asset to exact from Bunbury, the Whig candidate, as the price of their support, a promise to vote for the free pardon of Frost and his colleagues. Several groups also collected for the national fund established to finance the various Chartist candidatures.[3] At Ipswich Vincent stood again, hoping to make a discreet alliance with Adair, the only Whig candidate. Though after years of lucrative lecturing to genteel audiences he had dropped almost all his Chartist connections, he still nominally supported Universal Suffrage and was therefore accorded Chartist endorsement. He was in a dilemma, however, since he needed both to avoid any radical utterances in order to secure the votes of Adair's Whig supporters and at the same time to assure his Chartist and Radical-Liberal voters that he had not abandoned Reform. In this he was thwarted by the Chartists who forced him publicly to acknowledge his commitment to Universal Suffrage and embarrassed him by baiting Adair over his pro-Tory preferences. However, Vincent still hoped to receive Whig votes in return for his delivery to Adair of the second vote of the Chartists and Radical-Liberals but, though most of the latter obediently voted for Adair, 53 electors took the Chartists' advice and 'plumped' for Vincent, to his own chagrin because they thereby gave over a hundred Whigs, including a number who had led the local Reform campaign in 1830-2, the excuse to give their second vote to the Tory, Cobbold, rather than to himself. The Chartists were thus responsible for

Vincent losing his last chance of entering Parliament. They had dominated the public part of the election, forcing Vincent to compromise himself in Whig eyes, turning every occasion into a demonstration for the Charter and presenting their own programme for social as well as political reform. The crowd had been with them; when at the declaration of the poll it had been asked to demonstrate support for Universal Suffrage, "a dense forest of hands, thousands in number, were held up, presenting a most singular appearance, as the people kept clapping them". One reputation to suffer was that of the Ransome family whose intrigues in favour of the Adair-Cobbold coalition were repeatedly exposed before their fellow-townsmen; Liberals though they once had been, five of them voted for the coalition. Another was that of Vincent himself, whom the Chartists had exposed as a very dubious champion of Universal Suffrage. "I'll never give him my vote again", said one of them. A Sudbury Chartist declared that "Mr Henry Vincent had deserted the Chartists and the workingmen".[4]

In 1847 a depression set in over most of the area, first in the silk towns where hundreds of weavers were thrown out of employment, wages were cut and the workhouses began to fill, and then in the country towns and ports, including Ipswich. By early 1848 the whole of Suffolk was affected. "Paupersim flourishes everywhere", wrote the *Suffolk Chronicle*. "Workmen are thrown out of employment. Shopkeepers are doing next to nothing. The wealthy are living as close as they can. The shipping interests are in a state of stagnation. The agriculturalists are prognosticating deficient crops . . . If Chartism had never been heard of, there is enough in the character of the times to appal the stoutest Conservative heart".[5] The presence of unemployed workers at Chartist meetings was now specially noted in the Press.

Ipswich Chartists refounded their organisation and quickly enrolled a hundred members. An attempt to have the word 'Charter' omitted from the title of the organisation was defeated after strong speeches by M'Pherson, who said he "would sooner live on potatoes and salt than give up the name of the Charter", and Goslin who argued that "we were determined to assist in making the Charter the law of the land . . . and we could not with propriety adopt any other name; neither would it be manly or honest to secrete under false colours great, just and glorious principles". Affiliation to the N.C.A. was approved. Two of the former leaders, Pearce and Booley, who had at first tried to found a rival body under the title of the Ipswich Working Men's Association, soon joined their comrades in the N.C.A., so that by the end of 1847 the veteran leaders were re-united, Garrard, Goslin, Bird, Cook, M'Pherson, Rushbrooke, Lovewell, Booley and Pearce, together with some promising younger men, notably S. G. Francies, a hat-maker, and an operative called Chapman, "whose eloquence", according the the *Suffolk Chronicle*, "would have done credit to a candidate for Parliamentary honours".[6] At Colchester the N.C.A. branch was already meeting regularly in its own premises with a number of its former leaders again prominent and hearing lectures on pacifism, the history of Chartism and the Land Scheme.[7] By late 1847 most former centres were again active and enjoying more positive working-class support than at any time since 1842. Silk workers, including women and girls from the factories, had never been so actively pro-Chartist and even farm workers were reported to have recovered confidence in the movement. There was more middle-class interest than at any time since 1838; some

Ipswich Liberals, the Colchester Reform Club, the son of the squire of East Donyland and the daughter of the squire of Hatfield Peverel were allegedly Chartist sympathisers.

The movement had thus revived some months before the Continental events of Spring 1848. Chartists, both nationally and locally, had been internationalists from the start and recently had been moving to a pacifist position against what they saw as warmongering by the British Government. At Colchester, where Thomas Plummer had for several years been a speaker for the Quaker-led Peace Society, all leading Chartists had joined the Bond of Brotherhood. At Brandon, Suffolk, "the Fraternity of Nations" had been toasted at a recent Chartist supper.[8] For Chartists, however, foreign policy was inseparable from domestic politics; a class-dominated state, they claimed, easily resorted to wars which unenfranchised workingmen then had to fight. At a crowded meeting in Ipswich Town Hall, Thomas Plummer stressed the need for Universal Suffrage as the only guarantee of peace and a resolution was passed in favour of the Charter. Another large meeting a fortnight later was equally successful but, when the N.C.A. began to arrange a third meeting, news of the events in France caused the Mayor to refuse them the use of the Town Hall.[9] They then advertised a meeting on the Cornhill with handbills headed 'Peace, Law and Order. A Republic for France: the Charter for England'. The Magistrates called the meeting illegal, enrolled Special Constables and sought military aid. The Chartists advanced the meeting-time to noon to avoid the use of torch-light, some of them themselves enrolled as Constables and the rally was held with perfect propriety. Goslin's speech was yet again the most thoughtful; he asked for the application of the political and social principles of the 1848 French Revolution to the special conditions prevailing in Britain where circumstances made possible the same fundamental objectives without recourse to violence, provided the rulers of this country were not obdurate. John Cook, rarely heard on the public platform, sent a message to Paris, "we can assure you that the British people will never sanction a fratricidal war against their brethren of France". M'Pherson referred to the loyal sentiments which, as a newly enrolled Special, he naturally entertained, but confessed to a feeling of shame that part of the £48,000 annually devoted to British Royalty might well be used to feed the exiled Louis Philippe at a time when the British unemployed faced the workhouse. Booley praised the abolition of capital punishment in France, the plans to give work to the unemployed in national workshops and Louis Blanc's promise that, as the middle class had triumphed in 1789, so 1848 would be the year of working-class emancipation; to match the social policies of French Reformers, England should provide all able-bodied workhouse inmates with a plot of land. The meeting endorsed an address from the Ipswich Working Classes to the People of Paris:

"All Men are Brethren. Equality, Liberty and Fraternity. Heroic citizens — The thunder-notes of your victory have sounded across the Channel, awakening the sympathies and hopes of every lover of liberty. We hasten to express to you our congratulations and to thank you for the glorious service you have rendered to the human race . . . Honour to those noble soldiers who refused to turn their arms against the people. All honour to the troops of the National Guard who so gloriously fraternised with the defenders of liberty. The fire that consumed the throne of the royal traitor will kindle the torch of liberty in every country in Europe . . . Should Kings and oppressive Governments, unmindful of the lesson of the past, dare again to league against France and make war upon your liberties, assure yourselves, citizens, that the nations will not, this time, follow the banners of the tyrants. No, they will march on your side, for your cause is theirs. You are the advanced guard of freedom's army . . . Accept our fraternal salutations and our earnest wishes that the French Republic may triumph over its enemies and become a model for the imitation of the world. *Vive la Republique*".[10]

Similar meetings occurred elsewhere, but one of the most noticed events was a sermon at Colchester by the Rev. T. W. Davids, Minister of Lion Walk Congregational Chapel, which included the words:

"It cannot be denied that the Horizon of the World is critical in the extreme. New movements are in progress to which history supplies not the appearance of a parallel. I admit that issues — for I cannot honestly say Means — are thus far illustrious with high encouragement and brilliant hope . . . ENGLAND WILL NOT, CANNOT, LAG BEHIND. Leader of the World for generations past, ENGLAND must be leader yet. Here, too, power is descending to the MASSES; and it is the MASSES the Church of our day particularly wants to reach. The little that has been done God has eminently blessed. THE NATION IS IN OUR HANDS".

Meanwhile, the movement was chiefly preoccupied with yet another Petition for the Charter and with the London demonstration which was to accompany the Petition's journey to Parliament on April 10th. The Colchester secretary, the youthful H. S. Clubb, yet another member of a family which had served the cause in the town from the start, had united the N.C.A. and the Land branches into an Essex and Suffolk Chartist Union, the Council of which met in Colchester to organise the collection of signatures for the Petition as well as to arrange meetings in new centres. It had only a few days in which to hold its Petition campaign, but hundreds of people signed at Sudbury and at least 1,200 at Braintree, far more than had done so in 1838-9.[12] Its plan to send delegates to the new Convention was thwarted by the Colchester magistrates' ban on Chartist meetings within the town and the inability of national speakers to reach the alternative meeting on Donyland Heath outside the town at which it was planned to appoint a delegate.[13] In the end, only S. G. Francies of Ipswich represented the region at the Convention, but the Union did organise contingents from Ipswich, Colchester, Witham and Chelmsford for the April 10th demonstration, and *The Times* described the crowds of demonstrators from the Eastern Counties emerging from Fenchurch Street station for the last stage of their journey to the assembly point on Kennington Common. When the authorities overwhelmed the demonstration and prevented it from proceeding to Westminster, there was much disappointment in Essex and Suffolk but no evident inclination to abandon the Charter. A Colchester member was quoted as saying, "What does it signify? The Charter must become law before long, for if Parliament does not grant it, the people will take it"; the movement in the North, he argued, was powerful enough to force the Government to give in. Scorn greeted claims that many signatures to the Petition were faked. When Francies returned from the Convention, a thousand Ipswich people were enthusiastic enough to defy the magisterial warning and to hear his report and the N.C.A. branch prepared to send a representative to the National Assembly which was taking over the leadership from the Convention.[14]

As in 1839 and 1842 the Chartists had now to contend with Liberal offers to endorse schemes of Reform that fell short of Universal Suffrage, though always on the condition, stated or implicit, that Chartists should abandon their leaders. At Ipswich, where the *Suffolk Chronicle* supported such a compromise, one Liberal called a meeting in his ward to petition for Suffrage "extension", at which he begged Chartists to be practical and unite with the Liberals behind a limited programme. Booley, moving an amendment for the Charter, enquired whether Liberals had ever thought of adopting that document; almost the whole meeting voted for his amendment.[15] At Braintree Samuel Courtauld himself, whose workers were showing more enthusiasm for the Charter than at any other time, now called a meeting in the Corn Exchange at his own expense "for a full, fair and free discussion of the People's Charter". The Chartists co-operated and succeeded in bringing together an audience of 1,500 from Witham, Chelmsford, Coggeshall and Halstead as well as from Braintree itself, but, after Courtauld from the chair had denounced the N.C.A. and questioned the whole validity of the Chartist case, the feeling changed to one of resentment. A series of speakers, including at least one of his most trusted employees, Lister Smith, contested Courtauld's every point, nor was the audience afraid to barrack this most important of the town's employers. Courtauld's friends then moved a prepared motion for a limited extension of the franchise, to which the Chartists moved an amendment for the full Charter; the audience clearly being on the Chartists' side, Courtauld refused the amendment and dissolved the meeting.[16] At Colchester a strong radical group within the Reform Club had previously been working with the N.C.A. for Universal Suffrage. One of them, W. R. Havens, attended the National Convention as an observer and another, the Rev. T. W. Davids, at a Reform Club meeting called to discuss unity with the Chartists, was reported to have spoken in terms which "astounded the most out-and-out Radicals present and disgusted the more moderate members". However, after April 10th the radical Liberals formed a branch of the People's League, a new body which offered a 'Little Charter', including not Universal Suffrage but Household Suffrage. They very apologetically asked Colchester Chartists to accept their programme as an instalment of the Universal Suffrage which they admitted to be the people's due, and they just succeeded in fending off the usual amendment for the full Charter.[17] Chartism was not yet finished, even though the Press urged its supporters to admit defeat and abandon their campaign. Its answer was to vote confidence in O'Connor, support the families of their imprisoned leaders — the Victims as they were termed — and continue public meetings. Two national leaders, Dixon and Donovan, after addressing a large rally at Chelmsford, moved on to Braintree where they found their projected meeting condemned by the Magistrates, and 250 Specials, including Samuel Courtauld, sworn in to supplement the 150 County policemen. The meeting went ahead, with strong support from Braintree workers, including many girls from the silk factories, and from

Chartists of the surrounding area. Braintree N.C.A. reported to the National Assembly that "Chartism has spread very extensively. The *Northern Star* is widely read. To all appearances Chartism will soon be the all-prevailing sentiment in this district". The *Essex Standard* also named Braintree as one of the strongest Essex Chartist centres. At Ipswich a thousand people heard Dixon and Donovan on the Cornhill, at Bury St. Edmunds a packed hall voted confidence in the National Assembly and at Yarmouth 1,500 people attended a rally in the market place. Further public meetings were held in Braintree and Halstead, with silk workers again prominent on the platform and in a majority among the audience, and as late as August some Sudbury Chartists held a meeting for agricultural workers on the Green in the north Essex village of Wickham St. Pauls. Meanwhile Witham Chartists had been organising a boycott of the more anti-Chartist shopkeepers.[18]

Only in Autumn 1848 did the movement lose heart. It had withstood the attacks of the Conservative and Liberal Press, the prominently featured reports of the trials and punishment of its national leaders, and the local threats to deny it freedom of speech. It had been denounced by G. C. Round, M.P., Samuel Courtauld, the Rural Dean of Tendring, the secretary of the Essex Anglican Board of Education and a representative of the Church Missionary Society. Such prejudice had been created that even its Essex and Suffolk leaders feared arrest. Yet it was not this sustained barrage that finally demoralised the active workers in the Essex and Suffolk groups, but their acceptance of the truth that the Government and the propertied classes, almost as a whole, were determined not to concede the smallest measure of Reform. Once again they had been obliged to accept that the massive support for Chartism in the industrial regions, in which they had placed their hopes of success, was in the end impotent to force the issue. There were now no national speakers to tour the region and revive their spirits, for few of these remained at large after the Courts had pronounced their sentences. It was a sign of the movement's approaching disintegration when Ipswich N.C.A. had to issue an anguished call to former stalwarts, asking for continued financial aid for the families of their imprisoned leaders — "Chartists, remember the Victims".[19]

From 1850 Chartism, as such, ceased to be a major political force in the region, but in two localities it survived as an organised body until the N.C.A.'s dissolution in 1858. At Ipswich the two veterans, Cook and Garrard, kept the N.C.A. branch in being at least until 1855. As agents for the Chartist and Secularist Press, they maintained quite a large readership for these papers among Ipswich workers and a smaller one in the rest of Suffolk and so were able to preserve some informal unity among surviving Chartists in the county. When Garrard left Ipswich, Cook took on the whole burden of leadership, despite the difficulty he had always found in appearing on a public platform. "The People's Charter and No Surrender" he had written after the disappointments of 1848 and, as long as the N.C.A. survived, he continued to support it with as many fellow-Chartists as he could keep together and, when obliged to, on his own. He organised his old trade, the shoemakers, in resistance to the employment of non-apprenticed labour, chaired a meeting of Rushmere farm workers seeking a wage increase, championed the dependants of Crimean War soldiers when they were refused outdoor relief, joined in the continuing resistance to Church Rates and, with his old comrade, Whimper, campaigned on municipal matters. When Ernest Jones, then Chartism's national leader, toured the Eastern Counties in 1853, Cook organised a rally for him in the Corn Exchange, where, through pouring rain, hundreds of working people assembled for this last demonstration of Chartist commitment in the town.[20] Meanwhile the Yarmouth branch, which had started later and had been far less influential, entered what was to be its period of greatest influence. Among its able leaders were J. Royall, former Owenite; Thomas Fisher, a veteran of the 1830-2 Reform struggle; and a grocer called Chapman who had come over to Chartism from the Liberals. The main source of popular support was the vigorous trade union movement, to which the N.C.A. gave skilled and experienced leadership. During the long, bitter but successful strike by 1,500 seamen in 1851 it was Royall and other Chartists who advised the strikers, gained them wide backing in the town, organised a committee of other unions to support them and appeared in Court for those of them who were arrested. They also took an active part in a trades council set up in 1853-4. They remained zealous N.C.A. supporters, paying their dues, collecting for various Chartist funds and, in a national debate on Chartist strategy, firmly taking the side of Ernest Jones and the militants. When Jones spoke in the Masonic Hall, hundreds were unable to find a place in the immense audience. Though the branch declined after 1855, it did not close and still remained fairly active until the N.C.A.'s formal dissolution, when it reconstituted itself the Yarmouth Working Men's Reform Association.[21]

Elsewhere Chartism as an organised movement did not long survive the disappointments of 1848, though for two years it was kept in some sort of life by its obligation to support the Victims' Fund, with almost every centre contributing something. Individual Chartists remained politically active in a number of places, including Sudbury, Eye, Maldon and Braintree. At Colchester the branch seems to have closed in about 1850 when it split into two groups, a pro-Liberal one led by Blatch and a more independently minded one headed by William Barrett, a tailor, and Thomas Rawlings, a baker and the town's most faithful Chartist. The second group was not a formally constituted branch of the N.C.A., but it followed that body's leadership, reading the *People's Paper* which it supported by a special levy, and meeting regularly for discussion. It was not strong enough to arrange a public meeting for Ernest Jones when he visited the region but it did intervene at meetings held by other bodies. Its strength, and the continuing working-class support for Universal Suffrage, were shown in 1859 when the prospects of a new Reform Bill occasioned the calling of a Liberal meeting. Hundreds of workers attended, cheered loudly when the Charter and O'Connor were mentioned and by a large majority passed an amendment in favour of Manhood Suffrage.[22] The group had recruited some younger supporters and in 1858 seems to have been on the brink of re-constituting the N.C.A. branch just when Chartism was formally brought to an end.

5

Assessment

Chartist aims and methods
Essex and Suffolk Chartism, developing as it did out of several earlier movements and representing several social groups, had no single doctrine at its start and throughout its existence it never ceased to discuss its aims and methods. It is therefore impossible to list precisely the reforms which its followers here expected from a Chartist Government. In general, they accepted the programmes of political and social measures current within national Chartism, but it is observable that certain points within each of these programmes received strong emphasis here. Information about such preferences is provided by many speeches and by three formal statements of aims. The earliest of the latter is contained, by implication, in the toasts at a dinner held by Colchester W.M.A. at Queen Victoria's accession in 1838.[1] These, in order, were as follows:—
  The People
  The Queen, and may she govern with equity
  The Points of the Charter
  National Education
  D.W. Harvey and the Radicals of the House of Commons
  Wakley and the Dorchester Labourers
  Civil and Religious Liberty All the World Over
  Villiers, Molesworth and the Repeal of the Corn Laws
  The Working Men's Associations of the United Kingdom.
The chairman giving out these toasts was William Wire, then the W.M.A.'s teacher, and they reflect the views of those radical Liberals who were then using the W.M.A.s as a vehicle for protest against the Whig Government's deficiencies. None of the toasts were such as the L.W.M.A. would have deplored. State-provided non-denominational education was given priority. The surviving Radical M.P.s were still seen as the W.M.A.'s Parliamentary spokesmen. Acclaim for the Tolpuddle Martyrs was possibly as much a plea for Civil Liberty as support for trade unionism. Civil and Religious Liberty was a heart-felt concern for men who remembered the repressive Governments before Reform and, as nonconformists, saw the retention of tithes and Church Rates as the Whig Government's chief failure. Corn Law Repeal, the current Liberal preoccupation, was to be won under Liberal leadership. Abolition of the New Poor Law found no place. The outlook implicit in these toasts was to be superseded as the Liberals withdrew and as Chartism evolved its own philosophy and programme. The reforms advocated after 1838 did not exclude National Education, Civil Liberty, Church Rate abolition and Corn Law Repeal, but Chartists here refused to make Corn Law Repeal an issue separate from the triumph of the Charter, vigorously denounced the New Poor Law and the support given it by Liberals, and endorsed demands for factory legislation and other forms of protection for labour, reforms which many Liberals opposed.

Another statement of aims was made by an Ipswich worker on behalf of his fellow-Chartists during the 1847 General Election to a crowd of thousands.² It can be summarised as follows:—

Opposition to all religious coercion
Scrutiny of the Criminal Code
Universal non-denominational education, supported from public funds but free from state control
Taxes on the wealthy
Public assistance to the old and sick in their own homes rather than in the workhouse
The Charter

Church rate abolition and educational reform were thus still prominent, along with the liberalisation of Criminal Law, an old Radical cause, but taxes on the wealthy and reform of the New Poor Law were the demands of militant Chartism. The Charter was demanded as essential for the winning of the other reforms and for their implementation under working-class rather than middle-class control.

The Essex and Suffolk Charter Union of 1848 adopted the following programme:—

The Charter
Protection of the workers' interests
Work for the unemployed
An increase in wages to stimulate consumer demand and end the depression
An all-round programme of social reform
Less expenditure on the Church, Royalty, the Armed Forces and the Pension List
Restoration of the land to the people³

This programme came nearest to the thinking of local Chartists after 1838 and corresponded closely with the policies which the 1851 National Chartist Convention adopted in an attempt to make the N.C.A. the leader of the whole trade union and co-operative movement. What, however, was missing in all three foregoing statements was a programme of factory protection, restriction of working hours, minimum wages and similar reforms favoured by Chartists of the industrial regions; some Chartists here did refer to northern factory conditions as evidence of the general social injustice, but none considered the issue to be of importance to their own largely rural communities.

Two cognate issues frequently raised by Chartists in 1838 were Church Disestablishment and Church Rate abolition, on which the Whigs were clearly unwilling to legislate. "Let it be known that a large body of Chartists are Dissenters", wrote a Suffolk member, and indeed most of those whose affiliations are known were Baptists, Congregationalists, Quakers or Wesleyans, with a small minority of Secularists. They therefore joined the campaign against the Church Rate with enthusiasm. When the question arose at the Coggeshall Vestry, it was reported, "the Dissenters had collected their forces, amongst whom were Radicals, Chartists, etc.". John Thorogood, the Chelmsford shoemaker, went to prison rather than pay the Rate and at Ipswich other Chartists appeared in Court for similar defiance. Increasingly, however, Chartists became suspicious of better-off nonconformists, noting their dislike of Universal Suffrage; M'Pherson told Suffolk farm workers that "the Dissenters of

Stowmarket, of Hadleigh and of Ipswich will allow you to go to Heaven with them, but they will not allow you to have a vote". They predicted that, without Universal Suffrage, there would never be a Parliament ready to abolish the Rate and warned the Dissenters that, "as long as they continued to be the great impediment to granting the people the right of voting, so long would the unhallowed union of Church and State exist". They also sensed a weakening in nonconformist resolve to continue resistance to the Rate and contrasted it with the courage of men like Thorogood, claiming that "the Chartists were the only legitimate, the only persevering, the only determined Church Rate Abolition Society". Here too they linked the issue with the antipathy of middle-class Dissenters to Universal Suffrage. "Is it because Thorogood is a Chartist that the Dissenters of Chelmsford are quiescent?", asked a letter to the Press. Consequently, on this as on most particular issues, they refused to be diverted from the pursuit of the Charter.[4]

Corn Law Repeal was another measure urgently pursued by the region's Chartists in 1838-9, but, as on the Church Rate question, they quickly became wary of allowing their support for it to divert them from their central objective of winning the Charter, an attitude in which they were confirmed by editorials in the Liberal Press suggesting that they abandon their own leaders for those of the Anti-Corn Law League and advocating Repeal as the shortest way to defeat Chartism. They noted too how the League's spokesmen would not speak up for Universal Suffrage. In November 1839, when the League was first seeking Chartist support, a moderate Braintree Chartist suggested that its middle-class promoters were in fact saying to working people, "we will not assist you to obtain an extension of your rights, but whenever our own interests are at stake, we expect you to make use of all the power you have in support of them".[5] So they rejected the League's leadership and stressed that the Charter must take precedence over Repeal. They promised that a Chartist Parliament would at once carry Repeal but warned that, if Repeal came first, the employers would use the situation to lower wages and would succeed in this because workingmen would still lack the political power to stop them. Meanwhile their hostility to the League certainly blunted the zeal with which they pursued this issue. Whereas in 1838, before the League's foundation, Chartist speakers kept returning to it, thereafter they relegated it to the background of their programme. In this conflict with the League, the Chartists were the losers and after 1846 they accepted Repeal and were found defending it against renewed attacks upon it by the Protectionists, especially at the General Election of 1852.

Where they did concern themselves with particular social reforms, Chartists here gave precedence to the abolition of the New Poor Law; at Braintree, Coggeshall, Rawreth and possibly elsewhere the W.M.A.s had partly originated in movements against the Law. Ipswich Chartists made its abolition a central issue when organising the Suffolk farm workers in 1838-9, knowing as they did how effective the law was proving as a means of reducing wages in the many villages where unemployment was ever-present. A Hadleigh speaker sarcastically applauded the law because its injustices would turn every labourer into a Chartist. In 1841-3 they returned to the matter as the economic depression deepened and, if after 1844 they concentrated their criticism on particular aspects of the law, it was not because they had ceased to advocate its total abolition but because the law had by then been successfully imposed and it seemed a better tactic to mobilise resistance to glaring injustices in its administration. As late as 1852 Ipswich Chartists were still pressing the issue at the General Election. The New Poor Law can be said to have done as much to divide the Chartists of this region from middle-class Liberalism as the question of factory reform did the Chartists of northern England. They would not yield in their opposition to the New Poor Law any more than Liberal employers and ratepayers would in their undeviating support for it. On the other hand, Chartists shunned the Tory campaign of criticism of the law and would not join the movement of Maberley which was campaigning in the region for abolition. Goslin told a farm workers' meeting "when you have got the Charter, we will repeal the Poor Law".[6]

Chartists of this region, with their Moral Force convictions, saw in education an important means to political power, social progress and personal fulfilment. Melodramatically Barmby traced the history of English elementary education:

"Old George the Third was afraid of the too great ignorance of the people. He said to himself 'I'll give these poor wretches a little knowledge, or for want of it they will break my Crown around my head' ... And what use do you think they make of their Sunday School writing? Why, they write reports of the National Convention to one another, learn when the Sacred Month is to be, and where to get arms; and now a Newcastle collier can tell you the constitutional right of all adult Englishmen to arms and Universal Suffrage, as well as Blackstone himself ... and now the men of Birmingham and Manchester are studying and practising military tactics from the records of the French Revolution".[7]

Chartists rejected existing denominational education, which even the cautious Colchester W.M.A. thought biased and inadequate. They envisaged instead a national system, financed from public funds and free from sectarian influences, in which the quality of the teaching and the range of subjects would be far superior to the miserable standards in the denominational schools. Hull, Chelmsford W.M.A. secretary, said:

"What is education? Not merely learning to read and write and cast accounts; these are but trifles towards education and, unless the thinking faculties of the mind are brought into operation, all the scholastic education in the world will be of little avail ... I wish to see the day when men shall not only be able to read and write, but to have a superior education".[8]

Chartists did not, however, seek for workingmen a share of higher education in its existing form. M'Pherson "was confident that many men entered college for the purpose of brightening up their sense and yet returned greater fools than when they paid these seats of learning their first visit". Booley saw the mechanic's technical knowledge as the starting point for his further intellectual progress and his entitlement to further education:

"People in high life do not possess all the wisdom and knowledge, for the mechanic who is continually at work and has always under his consideration certain mechanical operations, has a practical knowledge that other men are unacquainted with. He is necessarily led to think, and when he employs his mind on other subjects, as a practical man he is more fit for the consideration of important matters than those who denominate themselves great".[9]

Booley returned to this theme on a number of occasions and other Chartists shared his view. As with other desirable measures, so with educational reform, Chartists felt that the Charter must come first and that, once this was achieved, better education would be a priority. Hull believed that "under the present system we shall never obtain such an extensive education as is desirable, because the Aristocracy, who keep us in the low state we are in, know that, if we become intelligent, we will not continue in our present bondage". Lister Smith thought the enactment of the Charter to be an indispensable prerequisite of educational progress because this would end the Church Establishment and thereby liberate the schools from stultifying denominational control. Until a public system could be created by a Chartist Government, another Chartist wrote, W.M.A.s should provide "a commodious room or rooms for the education of their children during the day, and proper teachers to instruct them — and themselves devote their leisure to improve each other in all useful arts and sciences. Democracy will then commence a revolution in the world".[10] However, though much adult self-education did take place here, there is no record of Chartist day schools being started in this region as they were elsewhere.

On economic policy Chartists here were not precise. Their criterion was the right of individuals "to receive the full produce of their labour", words which were as likely to be on the lips of the most cautious of them as on those of the most militant. Cranfield, Liberal secretary of Colchester W.M.A. in 1838, thought that "the rich man lived on the produce of the poor man's labour" and Hull, the more radical secretary of Chelmsford, contended that workers "do not receive the full produce of their labour". The latter also thought that the worker had a claim to the greater share of the product of industry — "without labour nothing can exist; the land is useless without labour; the money of the capitalist is useless without labour being brought to operate upon it". Yet, when translating these ideas into positive policies, the Chartists made modest demands. In this region of small businesses and workshops they never advocated public ownership of industry and they repudiated the *Essex Standard*'s accusations that "their covert object is a general confiscation of property, to be effected under the pretext of equal political rights". The closest that any Chartist came in public to a socialist position was when a Braintree Chartist weaver warned middle-class opponents that "they were useful only as *purveyors* of the produce of others and not as the producers of wealth and the communities and co-operative societies, which were now on foot in various parts of the country, would enable the producers in great measure to dispense with their services". Generally, they envisaged a Chartist Parliament erecting "a fair and equitable barrier between poverty and wealth", as a Suffolk farm labourer put it, or, in the words of an Ipswich Chartist, ensuring that the worker "may no longer be obliged to live on Charity but that he may live on his labour". The Chartists, said M'Pherson, "wanted that which was in the power of Government, a comfortable home". Precisely how workers were to be given this protection was not stated; no speakers are quoted as favouring a legal minimum wage. The nearest any of them came to making positive proposals was when they advocated lower indirect taxation, made possible by the state spending less on unworthy objects. Benjamin Parker, a greengrocer and one of Colchester's veteran Chartists, pointed to "the present system of unequal taxation, to keep up an army, navy and State pension list, all at the expense of the men who produce all the wealth". The same caution was observable when Chartists discussed the ownership of land, which had for years been an issue among radical workingmen. Hull of Chelmsford thought that "the soil on which we tread is, in a certain sense, the common property of all". Yet M'Pherson, when addressing himself to the land question, asked only that waste land north-east of Ipswich should be divided into plots for unemployed farm labourers. Plummer, the Colchester pacifist, wanted less spent on armaments so that a plot could be bought for all workers wanting one". The Land Company was welcomed because it would enable "industrious poor men to obtain small estates and independence". A few hankered after Owenite communities or Barmby's version of this ideal, but nobody here advocated land nationalisation any more than they thought in modern socialist terms when considering the future of industry.

On questions of sexual equality Chartists differed widely and their record was less enlightened than that of the Yarmouth Owenites who within their own community promoted an atmosphere in which women could take any place, or engage in any activity, open to men. The L.W.M.A., in formulating the Charter, had regretfully not demanded votes for women for fear of prejudicing the case for universal male suffrage, and this caution was equally evident among Chartists here, one of whom frankly declined to advocate women's rights till the Charter was won. Another denied women's entitlement to the franchise at all, but his view was not representative. Both Dennis and M'Pherson in 1838-9 urged the formation of Female Democratic Associations like those in Wales and the North and in 1841 women were invited to join the new N.C.A. branches. Some did, mainly wives of active Chartists, and they gave out handbills, collected for the Victims and helped at social functions, but none are reported as speakers or chairmen. Women's rights were not an issue which many Chartists here chose to raise, but some were more resolute than others. Booley, when criticised by the Ipswich Bench for leaflets inviting women to meetings, warmly upheld their right to attend. M'Pherson said that, as women could be as hungry as men, they had an equal right to a political life. Barmby argued that the suffrage could never be called universal if women were excluded and William Garrard thought that women's suffrage was mainly important because it was a step to their real emancipation, which was emancipation from social bondage as much as it was from political deprivation. Most were confused on the issue. Thomas Plummer, for instance, was bold enough to favour the organisation of female outworkers in the same trade union as male tailors who had served their apprenticeship, yet he was also capable of saying:

> "In proportion as woman became elevated and refined, as she grew in all the excellencies which constituted her true character, so would her sons and daughters become useful and virtuous members of society".[12]

Chartists were convinced internationalists, inheriting a tradition stemming from the French Revolution. The French rising of 1830 against Charles X had also met a warm response from Ipswich workingmen, including some who were later to be Chartists. The L.W.M.A. gave regular and detailed attention to international affairs and inspired Essex and Suffolk W.M.A.s to do the same. In January 1838, Braintree W.M.A. supported the L.W.M.A.'s petition for a conciliatory policy in Canada and urged Englishmen not to allow their Government to "hire them to massacre their brethren". M'Pherson, once a solider and now a pacifist, feared that Britain would provoke a war in Canada to divert attention from the demands of Chartism. Foreign issues were often linked with domestic ones, as when Braintree W.M.A. urged that the abolition of Negro apprenticeship in the West Indies should be accompanied by an end to political slavery in Britain. Chartist internationalism was not uncritical. The Irish were addressed by Colchester W.M.A. as "brothers in political bondage" but urged to fight for real democracy within Ireland. Barmby told Suffolk farm workers that "his Socialism made him regard Irishmen as brothers", though he, Lovewell and Booley also warned that British tyranny could easily be exchanged for O'Connell's. Warm sympathy was shown to victims of oppression. Negro delegates were assured of a large Chartist attendance when they toured the region. M'Pherson was a strong opponent of anti-Semitism. In the aftermath of the 1848 revolutions John Cook acted as Ipswich organiser of the Shilling Subscription for European Freedom, set up to help the families of political prisoners. At Braintree and Colchester internationalism led on to pacifism; all active Colchester Chartists in 1847 joined the Bond of Brotherhood at the persuasion of Thomas Plummer, the tailors' leader and Peace Society speaker, and were described in 1848 as 'the Peace party'. Chartists generally were regarded as opponents of War. In 1859 a correspondent of the *Suffolk Chronicle*, who wrote under the pseudonym of The Ghost of M'Pherson, purported to give the latter's news from the Radical Elysium where he now lodged. Radical Elysium, he reported, was next door to Classical Elysium and had been exercising a most beneficial influence upon the older institution; now convinced that War was evil, Ajax and Achilles had become great friends; an English army officer had recently arrived from India, had made a bombastic speech and then paused for a burst of cheering, which failed to break out; at first he was classified as deranged, but was later sent to the University, run by Solon and Cato, to be turned into a decent member of society.[13] Yet some working-class radicals did not reject force unreservedly. John Goslin thought certain kinds of wars were justifiable, especially if, like the American War of Independence, they were rebellions against tyranny. He also thought that truly democratic states should resist aggression by tyrannical ones, but that, when democracy prevailed everywhere, courts of arbitration could settle all disputes. Garrard refused ever to be a soldier "except he should at some future time, enlist in the cause of Liberty and Equality". Booley also thought that force was permissible in defence of true democracy and in the 1850s the near-Marxist John Cook even supported the war against Russia because Russia was a tyranny.[14] However, for Chartists of all persuasions the Brotherhood of Man was a deeply felt conviction which, they thought, should govern the foreign policy of all countries.

Time after time Chartists made clear that the enactment of the Charter was the indispensable prerequisite for the winning of any important social and economic reforms, because only Universal Suffrage would "send working men to the House of Commons", as Colchester W.M.A. saw it, or "bring a different set of men into power, men who understood the wants of the working classes", according to Ipswich Chartists. As at present elected, it was generally thought, Parliament would always represent the employing and propertied class. Referring to the Masters and Servants Bill of 1844, one Chartist wrote, "A masters' bill it is and no mistake. A servants' bill there never will be but those of an oppressive kind, until the People's Charter has renovated the House of Commons and displaced those who now usurp the ruling power".[15]

How then was the Charter to be won? Chartists here were firm believers in a Moral Force strategy. Several influences contributed to this, including their nonconformity, their past involvement in Liberal politics, their early connection with the L.W.M.A. and the generally cautious outlook of the master and journeyman artisans who largely comprised their active membership. There could be no mass meetings of militant industrial workers in this region, similar to those reported from Wales and the North; the largest rallies of farm workers in rural Suffolk were quiet by comparison and not calculated to inspire Chartist speakers with the belief that they could transform their audiences into a revolutionary force. In any case, the invincibility of the local establishment had been amply demonstrated by the ease and assurance with which it crushed and punished protesting farm workers in the Swing year of 1830. In the excitement of 1838-9 a very few voices were raised here to urge militant pressure on Parliament to grant the Charter. Several of these recalled the threats of insurrection by Whig and Liberal supporters of the Reform Bill and by the Irish nationalists. Lovewell, of Ipswich, no militant, claimed that "it was a fact . . . that at the public meetings in 1830 and 1831 the Whigs displayed flags with mottoes and spoke in terms equally, if not far more, violent than any that the Chartists had used. They hesitated not at that time to call upon the people to arm". Gould, of Hadleigh, wrote:

"What Irishmen could do, can be done by Scotch and English . . . and, with God's blessing, before you see two more Septembers, we shall be able to knock at the doors of Parliament with such an array of moral force in our van as will enable some 'short-sighted jack' to perceive the physical force in the distance, with all the Blue Bonnets too over the border, and I have no doubt whatever that, though Universal Suffrage will be deemed 'very inexpedient', civil war will be deemed much more so".[16]

Booley, the lay preacher, was moved by the excitement of 1838-9 to say:
"It is not always that Physical Force is necessary to produce the effects we desire; but it is the fear of Physical Force. Were I to meet three or four footpads on the road, I should look at the power opposed to me and should say, 'it is no use resisting.' They might not threaten me; they might not say they would take away my life; but they would ask me for my money; and as the power was so great against me, and fearing lest I might get a blow on the head, I quietly put my hand in my pocket, give them what I have there, and am glad to get away safe. Though the people may not be disposed to use Physical Force, yet from an apprehension there is something behind that will affect their persons and property, the legislators would yield us our rights".[17]

Such talk was rare and those engaging in it looked northwards for this power that was to frighten their rulers into concessions. The Newport Rising banished such ideas for ever and it was Booley who in 1840 said, "I, as a Chartist, hate the bare idea of Physical Force . . . it is anti-natural and anti-scriptural". Though only a few Liberal-minded W.M.A. members signed the Moral Force manifesto issued by William Lovett and his associates in 1840, the main body of the region's Chartists remained strongly opposed to Physical Force and carried this view into the new N.C.A., where they consistently upheld it. Thus, in the movement's revival of 1847, Colchester N.C.A. re-emphasised their "determination to overcome evil with good rather than by meeting violence with violence". The Press generally, the Liberal papers especially and the Tory papers more reluctantly, acknowledged the local Chartists' distaste for insurrectionary methods. The *Essex Mercury* noted "the peaceful and constitutional principles upon which Chartism, excepting by a very few uninfluential and isolated individuals, has always sustained itself in Essex and Suffolk". The *Ipswich Express* made the same point and the *Essex Times* specifically contrasted the "soberer views" of Essex W.M.A.s, with the militancy of Northern Chartism.[18]

In this region the Chartists were as devoted to Feargus O'Connor's leadership as they were to a Moral Force strategy. This combination of attitudes, found in most regions of Chartism after 1839, would be a paradox only if their Moral Force outlook had been one of reliance on adult education, the avoidance of mass pressure and a readiness to compromise with the Liberals. After the Newport Rising some former W.M.A. members endorsed such a definition of Moral Force, but to Chartists here the term meant the renunciation of insurrection and the use of such non-violent mass pressure as they were in a position to apply. They wished to employ legal methods, but to do so with militancy. A "poor mechanic" of Colchester thought that, to avoid a policy of intimidating the rich by "bloodshed and incendiarism", they would have to "appal them by our numbers". Their rulers, they thought, could be persuaded only by sustained mass pressure from a well organised working-class movement. "Nothing but the independence, energy and union of the masses would gain what the people wanted". They knew that the struggle would involve patient, dogged organisation and sustained activity; one Chartist told a Colchester audience that "he and his friends did not come to tell them that the Petition would make an alteration next week".[19] However, in discounting hopes of a swift victory, they did not resign themselves to the promotion of education, as some ex-Chartists seemed to be doing. They thought adult education important, not because its promotion might prove to a middle and upper-class public that workingmen were becoming virtuous and knowledgeable enough to be permitted the vote, but because knowledge could help working people to stand up for themselves as individuals and pursue their collective interests more successfully. Goslin did not want "an education that teaches me to wear out the verge of my hat by bowing to gentlemen, but that which teaches me to stand erect and meet that man who would oppress me, as an intelligent being" and another Suffolk Chartist wrote, "Workingmen, I say unto you, unite, get knowledge and agitate, and you will have your Charter".[20]

Chartists here did not believe that Moral Force principles obliged them to work with Liberals in a slow evolutionary progress to a wider enfranchisement. They doubted the possibility of such an evolution, because they saw the British state as representing not the interests of the whole nation but those of a propertied class determined to use state power to crush all challenges to its privileges, a class "at war with all other classes"; Parliament, the Judiciary, the Church and all public institutions were instruments for perpetuating the domination of that class; the Reform Act, "the Charter of the middle classes", had not altered political reality, because it had enfranchised only a section of the propertied classes hitherto excluded. Whigs and Liberals would yield the franchise only under intense pressure and were certainly not to be trusted as allies, since they had already broken their implicit promise to use the Reform Act to promote further franchise extensions and had instead employed their new influence to favour the well-to-do at the workers' expense. M'Pherson thought that "the dastardly Whigs ... are worse than the Tories. The people of England, in supporting the Whigs, had been trusting thieves in their homes". There was therefore general agreement among Chartists, including those of pronounced Moral Force views, that their movement must be entirely self-reliant and very wary of a Liberal party in which wealthy industrialists wielded so much influence. The Colchester W.M.A. secretary said in 1838, "I look on wealth with a suspicious eye, because I cannot see that men of wealth can sympathise with the working millions" and he advised his audience, "No longer put confidence in either faction. They are neither of them friends of yours. Combine together, lead yourselves. You do not want leaders". A Yarmouth W.M.A. member said that "the working classes must in future depend on their own efforts solely, for painful experience had clearly proved that the other classes would not only not assist them but would oppose every obstacle to their enfranchisement". That was said in 1839 and fourteen years later John Cook voiced the same view:—

"More than twenty years ago the middle classes called upon the working classes to assist them to get the suffrage, which they did; and they promised them, in return, to secure for the workingman his fair share in the representation of his country; but how have they kept faith with them? The answer that history supplies is crushing and will for ever be a barrier to the working classes being made tools of again for the political purposes of the middle class".

It was this new independence of outlook and policy which led the main Chartist groups here to proclaim confidence in Feargus O'Connor, particularly at times when they were being pressed to abandon their independence and co-operate with the Liberals. O'Connor seemed to personify their own achievement in establishing a party which deliberately put working-class interests first, made its own decisions and resolutely pursued the policies it had decided on. To the Baptist shoemaker, Charles Fish of Witham, O'Connor was being reviled "for standing up as the unflinching advocate of the British slave and for unsparingly exposing the infamous proceedings of the Whig faction". Nor was his popularity confined to Chartist zealots. The farm workers of east Suffolk begged him to address their pre-harvest rally in 1839 and the mere rumour that he would be speaking filled the largest available hall in Colchester to capacity, with many having to be excluded. Equally unexpected in this Moral Force region was the high standing of Dr. M'Douall, a militant of another kind who was the chief advocate of a vigorous trade union confederation working in unity with Chartism. There were, of course, variations in the intensity with which different Chartist groups and different individuals upheld this independence of outlook, but in general, as long as Chartism seemed to offer a realistic alternative to the orthodox parties, self-reliance and solidarity remained strong.

A handful of Chartists believed that their strategy ought to be based upon an understanding of the basic historical changes which they saw at work in Britain in the current century. John Goslin told a Colchester meeting:—

"Until half a century ago the rich had a fellow-feeling for the poor; though they depressed them and though they depressed the human mind and shut it up from freedom of thought, yet they had such a fellow-feeling as not to allow the poor to suffer from want. But after what was termed the Protestant Revolution and the establishment of a funding system, a new order of people arose who competed with the landed aristocracy in the government of the country. The moneyed aristocracy then became a powerful competitor with the landed aristocracy and, as the wars of the country increased and the national debt consequently increased, it was a natural result that the aristocracy of money should become more powerful than the aristocracy of land, so that in course of time the ruling principle of the government became that of money. It is that which is now the ruling principle of the government and ultimately it will not only swallow up the poor but the landed aristocracy and the church itself ... Then will be the time for the people to step in and push the principles we are advocating tonight".

Goslin did not then elaborate the details of how the people would take advantage of the class-struggle between landlords and capitalists nor of how they could become powerful enough to win, but he and others were convinced that the people's new strength came from the factory workers and miners whose numbers were constantly being augmented by the development of industrialism. Goslin's speech was made as early as 1838.

The ideas, policies and strategies mostly originated in the radical thinking and sustained discussion that had been proceeding in working-class Britain through the previous half-century, but they were accepted locally only because they seemed to local Chartists to illuminate the nature and causes of the distress they saw around them in their own communities and to indicate the means by which that distress might be alleviated. After they had been weighed in the movement's discussion meetings, they were put forward on the platform and in Press correspondence with obvious conviction and with impressive skill. Different speakers and groups, according to their own experience and outlook, placed differing emphasis upon particular policies and they might also use markedly differing arguments in support of the same proposition, and this was significant of the intellectual independence that characterised the region's Chartists. They prided themselves on what they often called their "rational" attitude, by which they seemed to mean an attitude of open-mindedness, thoughtfulness and logical reasoning. They exasperated some of their self-appointed advisers and critics by the self-reliance with which they scrutinised all ideas and policies offered to them. William Garrard wrote:—

"Oh Sir, it is gall and wormwood to the hearts of these men to know that we too can talk, we too can write letters to newspapers; to know that we can reason with our fellows ... This is the sum and substance of our offending".

The limitations of Essex and Suffolk Chartism

Essex and Suffolk remained a minor centre of Chartism throughout the movement's duration, constituting little more than a hundredth part of its strength. Probably £1,000 of the £80,000 contributed to the Land Company came from the region, as did a similar proportion of the signatures to the first Petition. No local Chartist played any part in the movement's national leadership, the only man to make speeches outside the region being M'Pherson, who ventured no further than Norwich. On one occasion only, it seems, did a local Chartist go as delegate to a Convention, when Francies represented Ipswich in 1848. The Chartists were aware of their insignificance, "Suffolk is but a speck. The hardy sons of the North and Scotland are our hope", said one Ipswich member. Another described the region as "this dark part of the country". National leaders rarely visited it, except for a brief period in 1838-9 and in 1848. O'Connor never came and, when in 1853 Ernest Jones tried to arrange a tour here, there were only two centres still strong enough to respond. Yet the local Chartists did feel a strong responsibility precisely because any success gained by them in so unpromising a region would convey an impression of their movement's ubiquity. The Hadleigh secretary urged the election of a Suffolk delegate to a new Convention in 1840 on the grounds that "an election of delegates for towns like Birmingham, Manchester, Nottingham and Glasgow was looked upon as a matter of course by the Whigs and Tories, considering that Chartism was so prevalent in those districts, but it would fill them with surprise ... if a delegate were elected for the county of Suffolk".

Within the limitations of local society Chartism's record here was not inconsiderable. With no large mass of industrial workers to give support, with farm workers numerically predominant among the working population, with a hostile agricultural establishment influential in the market towns as well as dominant in the villages and with economic victimisation an ever-present fear, it was an achievement to have kept the movement in existence for two decades, with no organisational break except possibly during 1845. Chartist activity was reported in nearly fifty towns and villages at some time. Tens of thousands of men and women attended Chartist meetings, thousands belonged to a Chartist organisation, however briefly, and hundreds acted as officials, committee members or speakers. The pre-occupation of the local Press with Chartism reflected the impact which it made; however humble the standing of Essex and Suffolk within the national Chartist movement, within its own localities it could not be, and was not, ignored. Furthermore, the Chartist Press, including the *Charter*, the *Southern Star*, the *Northern Star*, the *Evening Star*, *Notes to the People* and the *People's Paper*, had assiduous readers here and so to a lesser extent did Owenite and Secularist journals. These papers for the first time led many working people here to see themselves as part of a British working class rather than as merely the poor part of their own community.

Chartism was never a mass movement in this region because it never received widespread and sustained support from farm workers, the largest occupational group. Briefly in 1838-40 it gained a presence in several villages where less than 10,000 of the region's 80,000 farm workers lived, and it retained this for a year and half at most. Subsequently it could count individual farm workers among its supporters, men whose attachment was close enough for them to pay from their slender incomes into the Land Company. Such men were evidently attached to the Chartist branch in their nearest market-town — thus labourers from Bulmer, Gestingthorpe, Assington, Cornard, Kersey, Long Melford, Newton and Flatford paid subscriptions through Sudbury Land Branch, while those from Silver End, Hatfield Peverel, Great Totham and Little Leighs did so through Witham — but they did not maintain branches in their own villages.[29] Except in Rawreth and Wickford no farm worker was ever recorded as a speaker or an official, not even in those villages in which Chartism gained some footing in 1838-9; in rural Suffolk the known leaders comprised two tailors, a saddler, a shoemaker, a glover, a blacksmith, a weaver, a shopkeeper and a country gentleman. Nor were the region's Chartists able to claim much industrial support such as the stronger regions enjoyed at times of political excitement; no workers here, for instance, participated in the General Strike of August 1842. This represented no failure on their part, because the industrial workers were so few. Outside the silk industry, the largest factory was that of Ransomes at Ipswich, but their building in Old Foundry Road seems not to have employed many more than 200 workers in 1838-9 and it was not until the mid-1840s that the much larger Orwell Works was fully opened. Neither this nor the other foundries at Leiston or Peasenhall prove to have been the workplace of any local Chartist leader. In 1840 some Ransomes workers were ready to sign a petition for the release of the Newport Rising leaders, in 1847 a number of them were reported to be pro-Chartist and individual 'engineers' took shares in the Land Company, but there was never any upsurge of support from this quarter comparable to that given at certain times by industrial workers in the North and Wales. There were a few shareholders also in foundries at Romford and Brandon and in the Witham brush works, but nobody from these or other factories emerged to take responsibility in local Chartist organisations. The only railwayman known to have been a Chartist was a porter on Braintree station. As for the ports, seamen and fishermen seem never to have played a regular part in public life and, except for a few Brightlingsea fishermen who joined the Land Company, only one is recorded as an active Chartist, until in 1851 the Yarmouth seamen accepted Chartist leadership in their strike. No Chartist activity was reported from Lowestoft nor, except for a brief period in 1842, from Harwich, while at Ipswich, Colchester and Maldon the maritime occupations were virtually unrepresented in their local Chartist organisations.

Support did come from the silk industry. At Braintree, Halstead, Coggeshall and Sudbury Chartism was a force throughout its existence, deriving its strength chiefly from the silk weavers who supplied some of its leaders and most of its general following. This was particularly so at Braintree where, of the 26 local leaders known by occupation, 14 were from the industry, 12 of them employed in handloom weaving and two elsewhere. Factory women, though often wives or daughters of weavers, were less active in organisational work, but in 1838-9 and 1847-8 they were well represented at public meetings. In 1847-8, when a depression was causing unemployment, underemployment and wage reductions, the *Essex Standard* recognised in Braintree a situation similar to that in the militant Chartist regions and expressed grave anxiety about the outcome. However, the capacity of silk weavers to give sustained support was limited. They were almost as poorly paid as farm labourers, working long hours for a net 9s.6d. or 10s.6d. weekly, but paying normal urban rent for their house. Fluctuations in trade could leave them in a distressed condition for two years at a time and at the mercy of employers who could select the workers they wished to re-employ when the depression ended and were often in a position to close down operations in any town where they found the weavers troublesome. Consequently, though deeply discontented and sometimes very radical in outlook, silk weavers were in no position to build for themselves a militant union or to take collective action in support of the Charter for any lengthy period.

Chartism had no significant following here among the commercial, professional and clerical middle class, except in 1838 when some Liberals saw it as a possible instrument for the further reforms which the 1832 Act had promised but never delivered. Such people probably comprised most of the sixty £10 householders stated to belong to Ipswich W.M.A. in Spring 1838, and similar support was reported at the time from Braintree and Halstead. After 1839 middle-class Chartists withdrew, leaving only those individuals who had become convinced supporters and stayed on as local leaders, men like Flood, the Romford newsagent; Parker, a Colchester fruiterer; M'Pherson, the itinerant tea-merchant; Hearn, a shopkeeper at Friston; and George Bearman who kept a beerhouse at Bocking. There is no indication that such individuals were representative of their class or that they were supported by even a handful of their fellow-tradesmen. In 1847 middle-class people comprised only 4 per cent of Land Company shareholders in Essex and Suffolk, though, because of their business experience and personal confidence, individual middle-class Chartists who did remain in the movement were well represented among the local leaders, constituting 9 per cent of those who have been identified. As for Chartist farmers, only four are known; two were from the Chelmsford area, another led the small Chartist group at Sible Hedingham and the fourth, from Fressingfield in north Suffolk, evidently admired the Chartists as firm opponents of the Anti-Corn Law League.

The absence of middle-class support for Chartism here is in contrast to the situation in other regions in which, for instance, Chartist success at municipal elections was due in part to votes given by middle-class ratepayers. In this regard the main factor was the dominance of the powerful agricultural establishment over the Essex and Suffolk market towns, an influence which also weakened Liberalism after 1832. Being themselves so dependent upon agricultural prosperity, shopkeepers, millers, lawyers and others with market-town businesses supported the Corn Laws and other policies favoured by farmers and landowners and saw no reason for any radical political Reform that might upset the supremacy of the agricultural establishment. That Liberal minority among them who might have been glad to see further extensions of the franchise were reluctant to admit to such opinions, knowing as they did how economically dangerous and socially disreputable it might be for them to do so. The middle class in the boroughs, having now secured the Parliamentary and municipal franchise, rarely sought to use it to promote independent middle-class policies and tended to look upon it as a social privilege which was not to be shared with working-class people, especially when so many of the latter held such radical views. So far from being mildly sympathetic to Chartism, the majority of the region's middle class were at one with the landowners and farmers in stern opposition to it. The Complete Suffrage Union here was not inviting Chartism into an alliance, it was trying to oust it from the leadership of the working class, as the Press makes clear; when Chartism lost its influence and no longer remained an independent working-class force, the C.S.U. and similar organisations quickly subsided. This absence of middle-class support weakened Essex and Suffolk Chartism in two ways. Because commerce and all those dependent upon it constituted so large a part of market-town society, the Chartists were severely restricted as regards the circles in which they could hope to extend their following, so that even in the towns they could at best be only a minority movement. Secondly, those individual middle-class people who were ready to serve the movement were all the fewer. Such as they were, the latter were of some value to the Chartist groups, without impairing that working-class independence which gave Chartism its contemporary importance and its historical significance. Had there been even a few more such people, willing to serve Chartism on Chartism's terms, there might have emerged here some of those middle-class regional leaders who were to be found, for instance, in south and central Wales but were absent from Essex and Suffolk, where there was nobody with time and competence to unify the separate branches and bind them into an influential regional force. In Essex such initiative was entirely absent, while in Suffolk M'Pherson, who as a tea-dealer travelled the rural areas, alone tried to provide it in 1838-42, though he had to devote most of his time to Ipswich. As a person of high ideals and much self-assurance, J.G. Barmby during his brief sojourn at Yoxford unified the rural W.M.A.s and gave them some standing in east Suffolk; his casual service to Chartism indicates what might have been achieved by even a tiny group of more consistent regional leaders. In the event, the most useful contributor to regional unity was an artisan, William Garrard, who, as a journeyman carpenter with slender means and limited leisure, had to perform his unifying function mainly by post.

Three men only from the middle class stood out as good friends to Chartism, all of them Quakers. At Halstead, Barron Smith, a Courtauld factory manager, was the W.M.A.'s secretary during its first two formative years. His brother, Lister Smith, a Courtauld technician, performed the same service at Braintree, worked hard to gain Samuel Courtauld's support for the movement, did not desert it in 1840-2 and, much against his employer's wishes, spoke up for it in the public debate of 1848. He was still working for Universal Suffrage at the Election of 1852. At Ipswich, Chartism found a staunch, if austere, friend in W.D. Sims, a partner in Ransomes and a Quaker of the old school.[30] In his old age he was described as follows:

> "He was a Chartist in the days of Chartism. He used to take the chair at Ballot meetings before any well-seasoned Whig in Ipswich could be found to give countenance to the agitation. He believed in manhood suffrage and equal electoral districts. It was

curious to see him in those meetings. He seemed alone. His ways were not the ways of those around him. His words were not like unto their words. He was unmoved by their turbulence; his presence was a check upon the ebullition of their common notions and sentiments and modes of address. He gave no countenance to the abuse of classes. He used no strong language and he deprecated the vehemence of some of the disciples; but he was unflinching in his adherence to the principles. He has lived to see more than half his programme realized, and the men who have carried off the honours are the men who used to hold aloof and let Mr. Sims take the chair unsupported at meetings where Rushbrook, Bugg and Cook were the speakers".

Local leadership came chiefly from artisans. Of the 260 Chartists known by name as speakers, committee members, collectors of subscriptions or particularly active members, 146 are also known by their occupations, which were as follows:

		Per cent	Per cent
Artisans:	building workers	14	
	tailors	13	
	silk weavers	12	
	shoemakers	10	
	others	30	
	Total		79
In trade, commerce, innkeeping			9
Farm labourers			4
Miscellaneous			8

This predominance of artisans is consistent with contemporary comment. The audience at Ipswich W.M.A.'s inaugural meeting was reported to consist mainly of artisans who had been prominent in earlier Reform movements. Essex Chartists were contemptuously described as shoemakers and tailors. This was an exaggeration but of the 26 known leaders at Colchester seven were tailors and four shoemakers, while at Chelmsford, out of nineteen, five were tailors and three shoemakers. Hostile comments dismissed Sudbury Chartists as "a dozen tailors, shoemakers and weavers", Framlingham Chartists as "a few clod-pated tailors" and those at Debenham as "the lowest grade of mechanics". The Chartists saw themselves as mainly artisans; the W.M.A. secretary at Sudbury started his account of the Association's inaugural meeting, "The industrious artisans have by a bold effort ... ". In the early years master artisans, men with their own workshops, constituted an important minority of the leadership but, though a number of these men remained active like Rushbrooke, the Ipswich tailor, or Newman, the Saxmundham shoemaker, their relative importance declined somewhat as Chartism added social reforms to its political programme, so that by 1842 journeymen artisans became more prominent. It was to be expected that artisans, both masters and journeymen, should be prominent in the movement; with their experience in trade unionism, Friendly Societies, radical movements and nonconformity, they possessed some of the necessary qualities of leadership.[31]

If artisans provided the leadership, who constituted Chartism's wider following? Everything points to its rank-and-file also being largely drawn from the skilled trades. However, the mass-meetings of 1838-9 were so large that, even if most of the local artisans had attended them together with their wives, there must still have been people present from other occupation groups. Unskilled urban labourers and factory workers, comparatively few though the latter were, certainly came in some numbers. Light is thrown on Chartism's wider following by the list that has survived of the early Land Company shareholders in about a dozen of the region's towns. These men and women included some of the local leaders already referred to, but most belonged to the outer circles of the movement, having sufficient confidence in Chartism to invest in its scheme but not, as far as can be seen, taking responsibility in its political work. The shareholders who are known numbered 272 and of these 138 were artisans, just over 50 per cent of the total. The other occupations included 81 labourers, of whom the great majority worked on farms but a small minority were unskilled urban workers. There were also 'engineers' from Ipswich, Brandon and Romford foundries, workers from the paper-mill at Greensted Green near Halstead, brush-workers from factories at Witham and Braintree and a few Brightlingsea fishermen. There was also a wide range of miscellaneous occupations, including three gardeners, three shopkeepers, two farmers, two waiters, two navvies, and an innkeeper, a waiter, a brewer, a platelayer, a carter, a hawker, a milkman, a warehouseman, a clerk, an accountant, a schoolmaster and a hairdresser. The eight female shareholders who had an occupation other than that of housewife or housekeeper comprised three semstresses, two shoebinders, a dressmaker, a grocer and a baker. If these shareholders were representative of the Chartist rank-and-file, the movement would seem to have enjoyed some support from most sections of the urban working population. It also evidently retained a following among farm workers, which may have been larger than the Land Company figures show because many would-be shareholders from that class would have found the instalments beyond their capacity; certainly the labourers in the Witham area who took shares tended to be young, unmarried and therefore better able to pay.

In the minor Chartist centre of Witham the shareholders were fairly representative of the main occupations of the town and surrounding rural area. By 1847, 35 men had been enrolled, 23 of whom lived in the town and 12 in nearby villages which used Witham as their centre. Seven were artisans, comprising two shoemakers, two carpenters, a bricklayer, a painter and a tailor; among these was Charles Fish, the local Chartist leader. There were five brush-workers and one patten-maker from Witham's only industrial concern, a steam-driven factory making brushes, clogs and pattens; the workers there had a tradition of trade unionism. A single draper represented the town's busy commercial life. 21 were labourers, nine from the immediate vicinity of the town and twelve from nearby villages; most of these were farm workers, but one was a groom, one a gardener and two were probably non-agricultural. Only two men out of a total of 35 seem not to have been employees. The shareholders living in Witham were young, with an average age of about 23; a majority seem to have been unmarried and therefore better placed to pay for shares. Those with children of school-going age sent them to school and tended to keep them there after the usual age of leaving. The fact that some shareholders, particularly the farm workers amongst them, were related to one another confirms the impression received from elsewhere that Chartism was sometimes the creed of whole families. Most of the shareholders living in

Witham had been born in that town and continued to live there for years to come.[32]

Since Chartism's strength in this region lay with the artisans, the movement flourished in places where members of that class were most densely concentrated, the textile and market towns. Generally, the larger a town's population, the greater the number of artisans within it and the better the prospects for Chartism to gain a footing. Thus Colchester, with 500 building craftsmen, 400 shoemakers, 200 tailors and 500 other artisans, had a more numerous and more persistent Chartist presence than did Stowmarket with a total of about 200 artisans. The towns with over 2,000 inhabitants in 1831 were the following:

Yarmouth	21,115	Coggeshall	3,227
Ipswich	20,454	Brentwood	2,825
Colchester	16,167	Stowmarket	2,759
Bury St. Edmunds	11,436	Witham	2,735
Braintree and Bocking	6,550	Long Melford	2,514
Chelmsford	5,435	Halesworth	2,473
Woodbridge	4,769	Great Dunmow	2,462
Saffron Walden	4,762	Framlingham	2,445
Sudbury	4,677	Epping	2,313
Halstead	4,637	Eye	2,313
Harwich & Dovercourt	4,297	Thaxted	2,293
Romford	4,294	Prittlewell	2,266
Lowestoft	4,238	Hornchurch	2,186
Waltham Abbey	4,104	Newmarket	2,134
Beccles	3,862	Manningtree & Mistley	2,113
Maldon	3,831	Harlow	2,101
Bungay	3,734	Lavenham	2,101
Hadleigh	3,425	Brandon	2,065
Hedingham, Castle & Sible	3,414	Haverhill	2,025
Mildenhall	3,267		

Of these 39 towns, 28 are known to have had some Chartist presence, the exceptions being Saffron Walden, Lowestoft, Mildenhall, Brentwood, Halesworth, Great Dunmow, Thaxted, Prittlewell, Hornchurch, Newmarket and Haverhill, that is mostly smaller towns. Generally, Chartism's strength in the towns in which it was represented, corresponded more or less with the size of the population. Ipswich was the strongest, followed by Yarmouth and Colchester, Bury St. Edmunds, Braintree and Bocking, Chelmsford, Sudbury, Halstead and Coggeshall. There were exceptions. The movement proved less persistent in Woodbridge, Harwich and Waltham Abbey than might have been expected in places of their size, while it maintained an unspectacular but sturdy presence in the small towns of Eye and Witham. Brightlingsea, Debenham and Saxmundham were towns where, although the population was under 2,000, the Chartist groups were quite flourishing at different times. This relation of Chartist strength to urban population partly explains why the movement was stronger in east Suffolk and east Essex than in the western parts of those counties where towns were fewer and smaller.

The Response of the Establishment

Chartism presented to the region's middle and upper classes a challenge so radical that no concession whatsoever was made to its demands. Its opponents here were all the more unyielding because, with commerce and industry so dependent upon agriculture, the middle class was less at variance with the agricultural interests than was sometimes the case in the industrial areas. Each side felt more threatened by Chartism and other working-class movements than they were moved by social and political rivalry with one another. A Colchester Liberal, accusing the Chartists of endangering the security of property, had forecast that "the determination to preserve that security will unite Whig, Radical and Tory, who, merging their political distinctions, will unite in mutual defence".[33] The form which their political unity took was the strengthening of the Tory party, since many middle-class voters deserted the Liberals as the original instigators of mass politics, and supported the Tories who had always proclaimed themselves the bulwark against radical Reform and social upheaval. This process, starting after the 1832 Act, had been hastened by Chartism and it soon gave the Tories electoral supremacy in Essex and a strong position in Suffolk; significantly perhaps, the only time when Liberals recovered some electoral ground was 1847 after three years of Chartist decline. Radical Liberals dared not risk antagonising middle-class supporters by flouting this mood and supporting Chartism. J.B. Harvey did so briefly and saw his two Colchester newspapers forced to close down, as he himself recorded:

> "The middle portions of the electoral community opposed a movement which sought to confer the franchise upon the labour classes. They were swayed too much by selfish considerations, whilst the class above them in social rank treated them both alike with the insolence of pride. During the Chartist agitation ... the speeches of the humblest members of the working classes were reported without curtailment, a course of proceedings which played havoc with our list of subscribers and drove advertisers from our columns. Many who boasted loudly of their Liberalism spoke contemptuously of our giving currency to the 'revolutionary design of tailors and shoemakers'".[34]

In Ipswich 'the Coalition', by which Whigs and Tories divided the two seats, was reinforced by the accession of not a few Liberals, frightened by the candidature of Vincent whom, though he had become anti-Chartist, they took at face-value as an advocate of Complete Suffrage. The remaining Liberals in the two counties at times came near to abandoning their challenge, knowing as they did that the middle-class public, from which they had always drawn their main support, was virtually united against further Reform, and they had to be content at Parliamentary Elections with Whig candidates like Adair, Hardcastle, Rebow, Lennard and Western whose policies on crucial issues differed little from those of their opponents.

By uniting the main parties in opposition to its social and economic policies, Chartism ensured that its impact upon orthodox politics remained small. It was, however, not without influence on local institutions and policy through its indirect encouragement to well-to-do people to increase charitable and religious provision as a defence against its challenge. Such provision had been increasing since the French

Revolution and there had been no attempt to deny that one purpose of this was the containment of social protest and political revolt. The following report from Maldon is representative of scores of comments avowing such political purposes:

"Maldon. The Poor. A subscription has been entered into to supply the poor of this borough with fuel and other necessaries during the winter ... The whole arrangements have been undertaken by the benevolent ladies who superintend other charitable institutions of the town; and it is to be hoped that their efforts thus made to temper the winds of adversity to the poor of the town will awaken in them lively sentiments of gratitude and respect towards their benefactors. Nothing is more calculated ... to make the poor man bear his lot without repining; and we believe that nothing is more efficacious in closing his ear to the insidious suggestions of disaffected demagogues than the kind exertions of his more favoured neighbours to help him in his difficulties and administer to the necessities of himself and those who are dear to him. The poor freemen of Maldon have long ago seen through the delusive visions of *Reform* prosperity; and all the glowing promises of 'the Bill, the whole Bill' will not realise to them half the comfort that may be found in a bushel of good coals and half the consolation that is bestowed by the sympathetic attentions of the benevolent".[35]

Chartism, because it gave substance to the deep social anxieties that had been inspiring the well-to-do in their charitable and religious provision for half a century, reinforced these efforts and caused them to take a more purposeful and systematic form in order to meet the urgency of the new challenge. A characteristic of the new charity system that now evolved was the encouragement to donors to make regular contributions to well-run societies, each with its own category of recipient; an 1850 survey of Ipswich shows the success of this policy.[36] Haphazard and indiscriminate distributions were replaced by a carefully devised structure of charitable care. Much thought was given to ways of ensuring that every penny donated was used to the greatest effect and that the system operated in such a way as to help build the orderly society which its donors desired. The latter were urged themselves to participate in the distributions. John Glyde in his survey of Ipswich recommended personal visiting of the poor by donors to "teach men the value of their relative duties as members of society". Subscribers to the Colchester Lying-In Charity received tickets in return for their contributions and were asked to award these to deserving women, thereby creating a personal link that would reinforce the general dependence of the one class upon the other. The rural gentry and their families were encouraged not merely to give donations but personally to attend Ploughing Matches and Labourers' Fetes. G.C. Round, M.P., told patrons of Dunmow Labourers' Friendly Society that they had done well to be present when prizes were given to deserving labourers, "showing to the poor that, if they shall be distinguished by good conduct and prudent and provident habits, they shall receive such substantial marks of approbation of those above them as shall urge them to persevere in the paths of virtue". Another speaker added, "Who did not mark the deep gratitude depicted in every countenance clustered around the waggons today — showing the propriety that the lower classes should receive some proof of the approbation of those above them", while a clergyman asked how the poor could "bear the ills which Providence had placed upon them, unless they had the smiles of those above them". On such occasions some speakers felt free to attempt the crudest indoctrination. In 1848, at a labourers' gathering at Aldham, near Colchester, the same G.C. Round told his audience that "whilst they were engaged in the discharge of rural duties, there was a spirit abroad that was exciting the alarm and indignation of his Majesty's subjects ... but he knew of no man in that part of the country who would not spurn with indignation the very thought of being a Chartist".[37]

After the involvement of the patrons in charitable administration the next step was the enrolment of the poor themselves as humble subscribers. Their weekly pennies not only added to the size of the benefits but also, it was thought and intended, gave the recipients a direct interest in the economic stability on which their small insurance policies depended. The latter point was made over and over again. Members of Great Baddow Provident Society were told that "they now had a great stake in the country, and he would not have them forget that the welfare of the Society depended upon the peace of the nation, and they were bound to do all they could to maintain it, not by physical force ... but by quietly minding their own business and leaving the patching of the state to abler hands". The Mayor of Maldon also warned Provident Society members against imitating the militant Chartists and so creating a situation "in which Provident Societies, and whatever else is dear to us, would be in danger".[38] There was, however, always a possibility that the poor would seek the benefits of insurance through organisations under their own control, such as the numerous public-house benefit clubs, and the semi-official Essex Provident Society was therefore systematically promoted. Every publicity was given to cases of inefficiency and corruption in the more plebeian societies; Glyde conducted an able campaign in the Press against these at Ipswich. Meanwhile most farm workers could not afford Friendly Society subscriptions, so that for them allotment schemes were advocated. As Ipswich Chartists began their rural campaign a strong plea was made in the Press for every labourer to be provided with an allotment to raise him to "a humble sufficiency" and so secure his loyalty. Horticultural and Cottage Garden Societies were also promoted and during the 'Rebecca Riots' of 1843 a patron of the Sudbury Horticultural Society asked "how many of the sons and daughters of 'Rebecca' belong to Horticultural Societies? The quiet of the garden is no place for them".[39]

Religious observance was seen as another way of promoting political and social conformity. The *Essex Standard* wrote during the Chartist upsurge of 1842 that "building new churches will be much cheaper than raising new regiments" and on another occasion that "by sending the Bible to every poor man's cottage the further dissemination of the pernicious and infidel doctrines of those deluded persons called Chartists would be prevented". Referring to the 1842 General Strike for the Charter, the Archdeacon of Essex said:

> "The whole history of the late disturbances suggested a remedy ... There was the largest amount of obedience where the Church of England had the greatest authority. Though living in the focus of insurrection, persons in the districts in which new chapels had been erected and religious instruction provided by

the Church, abstained from violence, so that the word 'Churchman' was used to designate those who took no part in the disturbances".[40]

The richer laity expected the clergy to use their influence to combat radicalism among the poor. A Suffolk landowner, during the Chartists' rural campaign of 1838-9, asked them "from their pulpits, by pastoral visits and in private conferences, to impart information on subjects on which the lower orders at this time are extremely ignorant or grossly misled".[41] Chartists were often denounced from the pulpits. The Rector of Great Waldringfield preached two sermons recalling the gruesome punishments suffered by rebels in past centuries. An Ipswich Curate celebrated his arrival in the parish with an onslaught on Chartism as licentious and revolutionary. A Great Baddow congregation was urged to resist Chartism by every means short of force. The Bishop of Norwich, preaching in Suffolk, expressed outrage at the Christian Chartists who claimed God's authority for supporting the poor against the rich.[42] The list of such outright condemnations of Chartism is a very long one, but sermons preaching general obedience to authority, respect for the rich and noble and the preservation of class distinction were so frequent as to be commonplace in this region.

The influence of religion was made stronger and more extensive by the drawing of the laity into such parish work as the founding of chapels in new centres of population, the increase of seating in existing buildings and the promotion of a wider church life. All this was carried out with impressive resolve and success. At Colchester between 1820 and 1850 at least twenty major schemes of church and chapel building were completed and at the Ecclesiastical Census of 1851 the town was shown to have achieved a level of religious attendance well above the urban average. Perhaps the most effective joint undertaking of the clergy and laity was the sustained effort to ensure that all poor children were educated in a strictly religious atmosphere. The Bishop of London, at the height of the Chartist revival of 1841, told a Witham audience that "they who were now crying out for more liberty were not generally uneducated in secular knowledge, but were uneducated in religion. That was not the fault of the Church ... but of the nation and the Government in suffering the congregating of large masses, particularly in manufacturing towns, without having provided schools or sufficient means of religious instruction, the melancholy consequence of which had been the spreading of treason and infidelity". His colleague, the Bishop of Norwich, who was equally trenchant in his onslaughts on working-class movements, said at Ipswich that education without religion would lead to Chartism, Owenism and rebellion.[43] Advocates of denominational schools, particularly Anglicans, returned to this argument time and again.

The education of the poor had long been advocated as a means of habituating working-class children to acceptance of their place in the economy and in society. In 1812 the Tendring Hundred clergy had recommended parish schools for labourers' children as "the only means of rendering that most numerous and useful part of the community faithful and honest in their services to others and contented in themselves". The vicar of Coggeshall praised the Monitorial system, as used in Church schools, because:

"The order and subjection which are enforced in these schools and form the most striking feature in what may be called the machinery of the System not only correct the natural rudeness of the children and make them respectful in their demeanour ... but also has a manifest tendency to give them due notions of submission to lawful authority".[44]

Such claims were normal at all times but after 1832 education was promoted also for its direct political value. An Essex poet wrote:

"So shall licentiousness and black resolve
Be rooted out, and virtuous habits
Take their place ... "

Chartist militancy in 1839 led a Liberal editor to write that "Popular Education is the great *Panacea* for the national complaint" and a Conservative editor to support the plea that "Education would quieten the Chartist meetings and restore peace ... It would save the expenses of armies and police forces". An Ipswich M.P. told guests at the Mayor's dinner, "Depend upon it, that it is on an ignorant population that the Chartist demagogues ... produce their greatest effect" and went on to argue that Education was the remedy for Chartism. The other two periods of Chartist militancy elicited similar advice. In 1842 the *Essex Standard* attributed the General Strike of that year to the absence of the right kind of education and in 1848 a Colchester Conservative Councillor said that "there are two things that will save the country, emigration and education".[46]

Children's education could only be a long-run solution, but Chartism remained an immediate challenge. Its adult supporters sometimes seemed to have thrown aside all deference towards political and spiritual authority and respect for the values and attitudes which they had once accepted. It was the Chartists' intellectual self-reliance and fresh thinking on central political principles which were seen by some to be their most alarming characteristic. They and their supporters therefore seemed in need of immediate re-education, and it was the Liberals in particular who took the lead in starting Mechanics' Institutes and other societies designed to inculcate approved ideas and habits. In the process of study, it was hoped, workers would see the advantage of co-operating with the new economic order and, almost without realising it, would become reflective, sober and non-Chartist. Discussing the Newport Rising, a speaker at Chelmsford Philosophical Society said:

"When men are determined to seek for knowledge, when they see how those are honoured who possess it, they soon learn to love it for its own sake. They soon find they have lost all relish for riot and intemperance ... and while you find persons engaged in intellectual pursuits, always ready to assist all measures which afford a reasonable hope to benefit mankind, you find them the last to lend themselves to revolutionary measures".[47]

J. G. Rebow, of Wivenhoe Park, at the dinner of Colchester Mechanics' Institute, described the process of regeneration:

"Look at the man ... who has had the prudence, the foresight and the intelligence to seek his recreation in institutions like the present, who has passed his evenings in our library, where he may perchance in the first instance have lighted upon some work relating to his own profession and probably tending to his advancement in life. That may lead him to consult works upon the general trade and commerce of the country; in time he will admire the wonderful advancement and stupendous extent of our commerce; he will see how wealth is to be acquired by enterprise and honest industry, and will find by recorded examples that, however humble his present situation, he need not despair of one day placing himself upon a par with the highest in the land. Such is the privilege of living in an enlightened country like ours ... From works connected with his own temporal advancement he may proceed to consult the history of his country; he will there see how early the seeds of civil and religious liberty were planted in this realm, and how gradually the tree has grown to its present vigorous existence. He will see how, bit by bit and piece by piece, our constitution has been reared ... until it has become both the pride and ornament of our own country, and the envy of all the other nations of the world. He will also be able to derive from his studies these advantages — he will find that the constitution has gradually enlarged itself to meet the increasing wants and intelligence of each succeeding age, and he may be sure that, in the same manner, it will continue to enlarge so as to be commensurate with our wants ... With such feelings he will return to his home contented, happy, rich in mind and in the way of being equally so in purse; he will be satisfied with, and attached to, his native country and will look upon those who abuse England, only as her enemies and as ignorant of her high privileges".[48]

Essex and Suffolk Mechanics' Institutes were never part of the working-class movement, but rather the creation of people from the upper and middle classes. Liberal employers often controlled them and consequently much of their teaching was based on Liberal economic doctrine. Free discussion was rare; one Mutual Instruction Society was dubbed Chartist merely for permitting it. There was usually a rule precluding political discussion, but, in criticising working-class movements, officials and lecturers did not hesitate to break it. In November 1839, the Ipswich Institute heard a lecture which condemned Chartism, pronounced workingmen to be ignorant, expounded correct economic theory and urged the audience to attend Institute lectures to avoid falling victim to Chartist delusions. A speaker at Colchester Institute called Chartists "cut-throats and rebels". At Manningtree a lecturer on France took the occasion to denounce all radical philosophies. This discrimination against Chartist and similar viewpoints was regarded by the promoters of the Institutes as a major point in their favour.[49] The *Essex Times* argued that they had saved Britain from working-class revolution. The chairman of Stowmarket Institute said:

"I have heard it objected to Mechanics' Institutes ... that they have a tendency to engender principles of republicanism — radicalism — Chartism — and all the other -isms held to be inimical to the social order. Gentlemen, I must confess myself to the opposite opinion, or I should have declined the honour of acting as your Chairman".[50]

For the same reasons most Chartists shunned the Institutes. Some of them had previously been members and a few of these retained their membership, but most became suspicious of societies which banned free discussion and never put the *Northern Star* in their reading-room. The thoughtful workingmen, whom the Institutes sought to enrol, were exactly those who joined Chartist or Owenite organisations and after 1838 more such people were likely to be attending discussions under the latter's auspices than under the former's. An Ipswich Chartist wrote as follows:

"The Ipswich Mechanics' Institute has been declining in numbers for two years. The number of persons belonging to it who can strictly be called Mechanics is comparatively small; and this too, when the library is confessedly the best in town. The cause of this is well worth investigating. I think it may in a great measure be traced to the sectarianism of many of the rulers of the Institution and their not giving sufficient aid or stimulus to the working classes to endeavour to obtain and impart information. The working classes will not join the Institution, raised for their especial benefit, in consequence of the restrictions imposed by those influential in its management with respect to the kind and degree of knowledge to be imparted to them. The exclusion of all subjects of vital interest, and the prohibition of the study of moral, political and theological topics, save insofar as these square with the interests of the clergy and the wealthier classes, have gradually diminished the real value of the knowledge doled out to them by the privileged obstructors of progression, and they have betaken themselves to other sources for the supply of information more valuable and bearing more directly upon their position and interests. Mechanics' Institutes should be temples of free enquiry and I can see no reason why subjects intimately connected with our social and political condition should be excluded from the Institution".[51]

Those who promoted charitable, religious and educational institutions in this critical period, partly in an attempt to contain and roll back popular discontent and pressure for democratic change, mostly remained unaware of any self-interest on their own part. Indeed, they included hundreds of people who spent years of their lives in often thankless endeavours to promote social welfare as they saw it. Deep religious conviction and genuine humanitarianism underlay their activities and, as for the subordination of the poor which resulted from these, they were fully persuaded that this was in the poor's best interests as well as in accordance with God's command. Yet it is difficult to read contemporary speeches, sermons and press correspondence without perceiving how strong was the motive to defend the supremacy and interests of the class from which the promoters came. It was not accidental that at precisely this period of social crisis so much more effort than at any time previously should be devoted to this system of charitable, religious and educational care by which the poor were effectively supervised and then gradually fashioned into the deferential and conforming lower classes of Victorian Britain. It was all very effective and altogether beyond Chartism's power to counteract.

6

The Legacy of Essex and Suffolk Chartism

Contribution to later Reform Movements

Essex and Suffolk Chartism contributed directly and indirectly to the campaign for the 1867 Reform Act and to a much smaller extent to that for the 1884 Act. First, it had planted among urban workers deep democratic convictions, the apparent weakening of which in the 1850s was due, not to any doubt on their part about their right to the vote, but to a loss of confidence in their ability to obtain it. If farm workers seemed less convinced of their right, that was due to their more limited acquaintance with Chartism and their own complete lack of political assurance, though their democratic sentiments remained strong enough to come to the surface in and after 1872 in the National Agricultural Labourers' Union, which in its turn contributed not a little to the passage of the 1884 Reform Act in this region. Secondly, individual Chartists, while unable to maintain their own N.C.A. branches, still used every opportunity in the 1850s and 1860s to demand Universal Suffrage, finally joining in the successful campaign for the 1867 Reform Act.

Evidence that democratic sentiments persisted among workingmen was provided in 1852 by events in two places where Chartism had been an organised force in the previous decade. At Braintree during the General Election the two Tory candidates for North Essex had shown themselves strongly opposed to Universal Suffrage and one of them had shouted at an audience of workers, "I despise you from my heart as the vilest rabble I ever saw". As a result, with hundreds of handloom weavers at their head, a huge crowd prevented these candidates from being heard at the Nomination, stoned their carriages and caused them to absent themselves from the declaration of the poll. As they went under heavy police escort to the White Hart to celebrate their victory, they were again assailed and, even when they reached the inn, they and their party were stoned whenever they approached its windows. The M.P.s had to escape from this siege by leaving the building at the rear and racing for the safety of the railway station, pursued by the crowd.[1] Also in 1852 some wealthy Witham farmers proposed to the Vestry to make rates on small houses payable through the landlord and thereby to disfranchise the occupants, as being non-ratepayers. The purpose was evidently to put an end to the practice by which poorer ratepayers were combining to elect Poor Law Guardians sympathetic to themselves. There was a dramatic clash between the farmers and the working-class leaders, three mechanics and a labourer, who insisted on bringing into the open the point which had not been explicitly stated, that 541 small householders would lose their Poor Law Union franchise if they no longer paid rates. Farm workers on 8s. or 9s. a week welcomed not having to pay rates directly, but it was suggested to them by one of the mechanics that "the farmers could best remedy the matter by giving the labourers more wages so as to enable them to pay their rates and retain their votes". Many labourers had been brought along to the meeting by their employers so that, with open voting, the farmers' motion was carried and, after a poll had been demanded, this too at first showed a majority for the motion, but the poorer ratepayers quickly organised their forces and defeated it by 183 to 126. One of the Witham leaders seems to have come from a Chartist family, but no other Chartist involvement was apparent in either of these two events.[2] What was clear, however, was that urban workers still held the democratic sentiments aroused in the previous two decades by Chartism, despite the recent dissolution of the Chartist organisations.

Meanwhile, individual Chartists remained alert to any occasion for launching a fresh movement for Universal Suffrage. Few such occasions offered themselves in the decade after 1848, as the official parties, no longer harassed by Chartist pressure, resumed their partisan politics, within which Universal Suffrage found no place; most of the C.S.U. supporters of 1842-3 were now silent. In 1859-60, however, John Bright's unsuccessful proposal for limited Reform at once evoked a response at Ipswich, where the lead was taken by G. W. Rushbrooke, who, after temporarily moving to the Liberals, had now rejoined the working-class movement. When he and King, former editor of the *Suffolk Chronicle*, called a meeting in support of Bright's proposal, 2,000 workingmen voted almost unanimously for Manhood Suffrage, the Secret Ballot, Equal Electoral Districts and Shorter Parliaments. Rushbrooke's speech was more radical than any he had made in Chartist times. "Whence comes the wealth of this country? From the working men. It is they who have made England great. And what do they get in return? A third of their produce, the remainder being divided between the Government and the capitalist. Workingmen, I tell you, the power is with yourselves". With two former Chartists, Thomas Coe, a seamen's leader, and F. J. Bugg, leather merchant and Co-operative pioneer, he founded the Ipswich Reform Association, enrolling seventy electors and many non-electors. At the 1859 election King stood on its programme of Manhood Suffrage and Secret Ballot and easily won the show of hands at the Nomination, though the Whig-Tory coalition shared the two seats.[3] However, the Liberals were not allowed to forget the Charter, as F. J. Bugg's biography relates:

"The Liberal member for Ipswich knew when he came down ... he would have to encounter Mr. Bugg, that Mr. Bugg would put some ugly questions and demand plain answers. Mr. Bugg ... was the mouthpiece of the non-electors. He was an elector himself, but he had thrown in his political lot with those to whom an aristocratic Parliament denied a vote".[4]

Rushbrooke intervened at so many public meetings that, like M'Pherson before him, he came to be the acknowledged voice of working-class radicalism and, as such, had to undergo the *Ipswich Journal*'s description of him as unwashed, voluble, diminutive in stature and ungrammatical.[5] Meanwhile at Colchester, too, a large meeting of workingmen had supported Reform. Though here the radical Liberals had taken the lead, the still active group of former Chartists carried an amendment for Manhood Suffrage, winning loud cheers for each reference to O'Connor and Chartism. In 1860, when the radical Liberals called another meeting to discuss Reform, it was workingmen who filled the hall and a former Chartist who persuaded them to vote for the enfranchisement of all lodgers, as well as householders, as an essential part of any real Reform Bill. At a similar meeting in 1861 another former Chartist, Thomas Barrett, carried the proposition that any Reform worthy of the name must "enfranchise the great body of the working-class" in both town and village.[6] At Yarmouth, too, the Chartist group, now reconstituted as the Working Men's Reform Association under the leadership of the veteran J. Royall, held a Reform rally in the Corn Exchange which "was crowded to excess, chiefly by the working classes".[7]

When the Russell Government issued its 1866 Reform Bill, local Liberals had to decide whether to campaign for the proposed enfranchisement of poorer workingmen in the boroughs, a class which since 1832 they had been willing to see excluded. Their response varied from frigid detachment to a gingerly acceptance of their leaders' new policy, but the working-class public showed its enthusiasm by signing the petitions for the Bill which flooded in from every town and many villages in the two counties. An organised movement took shape when the Reform League sent speakers round the region.[8] The audience at Chelmsford comprised mainly workingmen, though among the speakers were several of the town's largest employers. Two working-class spokesmen conceded that, though the Bill would enfranchise few of their kind in this nonborough town, it did represent a step forward and should be supported. Halstead Town Hall was filled with workingmen who cheered when a Unitarian Minister mentioned the Charter. A Reform League branch was formed, with the Unitarian Minister and the group of former Chartists at its head. "This is a working-man's question", read the branch's first declaration, "and the committee of the Halstead branch of the Reform League recommend it to the serious attention of Halstead workingmen". When it held a large demonstration, it yielded the platform to the Courtaulds and their associates and acquiesced in the passing of a tepid resolution on Reform but, after the meeting, it at once resumed control and held it till the Bill's final passage. At Braintree, normally a far more radical town than Halstead, George Courtauld and other leading employers supported the Bill so strongly that, though at the main rally three original W.M.A. members sat on the platform and one of them made a speech, the campaign remained in Liberal hands. It was the same at Colchester where the former Chartists had already joined the more radical Liberals, who were supporting the Bill with moderate enthusiasm. Liberals were also in control at Saffron Walden where 800 workingmen attended the main meeting, at Harwich where the chairman was a former Whig candidate for the borough, and at Kelvedon where the leading figure was the Whig squire, Sir Thomas Western. At Brentwood, however, the Liberals stood aloof, apparently because the foundrymen who called the meeting were led by "the extreme section of reformers who advocate Manhood Suffrage", and when a Reform League branch was started, it enjoyed mainly working-class support. At Bury St. Edmunds and Yarmouth, both of them boroughs and therefore places where poorer householders could now expect the franchise, workingmen thronged to the meetings and at Bury seem to have been in control. At Ipswich Rushbrooke's group tactfully allowed the radical Liberals to take the lead, which at first they did in some numbers. They soon withdrew, however, allowing the Conservative paper to claim that "Mr. Gladstone's Reform Bill finds no great favour in Ipswich, even among the Liberal Party". The working-class leaders then took over and started a Reform League branch; "the matter now rested with the working classes", said F. J. Bugg. Open-air meetings on the Cornhill were followed by a large rally in the Corn Exchange, at which there was much sarcasm about Liberal timidity. John Cook was there and, when reference was made to the franchise being extended to householders, he interrupted with, "He was a supporter of Universal Suffrage. He would have none of their brick and mortar suffrage but claimed it as the right of every Englishman". Though always uneasy as a public speaker, he was persuaded to join the platform and put the case for Universal Suffrage.

After the passage of the 1867 Reform Act which enfranchised a number of workingmen living in Parliamentary boroughs, Chartism as such ceased to exert within the boroughs the influence that the denial of Manhood Suffrage had hitherto permitted it. Outside the boroughs, however, the still unenfranchised urban and rural workers remained interested in further Reform. At Halstead the former Chartists, reinforced by some younger men, started a Working Men's Association, a Co-operative Society and a Working Men's Club, in which they held regular discussions, including a series on the published lectures of Ernest Jones.[9] When the 1884 Reform Bill was proposed, they joined the Liberals in a campaign of support for it.[10] At Colchester, with a majority of workingmen already enfranchised by the 1867 Act, the ex-Chartists had joined the Liberal party, forming a series of organisations within its ranks, including a Liberal Working Men's Association, to campaign for a radical programme. They vigorously supported the 1884 Reform Bill, John Howe, a leading trade unionist, declaring that "he was an old Chartist, and manhood suffrage was one of the points when he was a boy, and they had been fighting for it up to the present time. He thought every man should have a vote". The Ipswich workers' leaders had formed a branch of the Labour Representation League and secured the adoption as Liberal candidate of William Newton, former Chartist leader and now national secretary of the Amalgamated Society of Engineers.[11] In 1884, they resolved "to assist fellow working-men outside the borough in obtaining the franchise" and demanded "full and complete manhood suffrage, for which they had been waiting a very long time", together with Equal Electoral Districts, Payment of Members and Triennial Parliaments. They also decided that, to overcome the opposition of the House of Lords, they should demand its abolition instead of its mere reform. Together with the trade unions they formed a large contingent in a pro-Reform demonstration through the Ipswich streets.[12] One outcome of this campaign was a decision to start an Ipswich Trades Council, the final link in the chain between Chartism and the modern working-class movement.[13] Rushbrooke, an old man now, remained an active member of the Ipswich Radical Association which organised much of this activity.

The gains of 1867 and 1884 had been available only at a price. Not only did former Chartists have to accept Liberal leadership, they would not even have been offered these two Reform Bills if they had persisted in old aims and attitudes. Comments by veteran Liberals showed that they had never forgotten the political self-reliance shown by workingmen in 1838-48 nor how once Chartists had scorned the patronage of either party.

E. H. Bentall, whose agricultural machinery factory had transformed the once rural village of Heybridge, recalled that, though a Liberal, he had formerly opposed even Whig Governments for fear that they might make concessions to Chartism and its radical economic policies, a fear which, he thought, other wealthy Maldon Liberals had shared. Such anxieties persisted into the 1860s. A Colchester Liberal cited current strikes as indicative of how workers would dominate politics if conceded the vote:

"May we not all learn a lesson from the builders' strike — the work of a confederacy against capital? The men, too, engaged in these combinations ... are soon to be invested with electoral power. The inevitable tendency of public opinion is in the direction of strengthening democracy. What sort of democracy is it to be? That country whose *proletaire* order — the class that has no property but is solely dependent upon masters and wages — outnumbers all the rest, cannot fail to be in constant danger of disorder if the issues of government are placed in their hands".[14]

Opponents of Reform sought to deepen this anxiety. In 1866 Colchester Conservatives were reminded by a visiting speaker of John Bright's words to workingmen, "Establish your new House of Commons upon Manhood Suffrage and the Ballot. The land is now divided among three hundred men, then it shall be divided amongst you". The *Essex Standard* wrote of a proposal to enfranchise £6 householders:

"In some constituencies the £6 voters will overwhelm in point of numbers the whole present electoral body. The important question to be decided is how far the poorer industrial classes may more largely participate in the elective power without acquiring that predominance in numbers which would enable them on all questions in which their own interests might be or might seem to be antagonistic to those of the other sections of society, to overwhelm every other class".[15]

The same doubts delayed the enfranchisement of farm labourers, especially after the success of their union in 1872-4. An Essex M.P., Col. S. B. Ruggles-Brise, said in 1874:

"The time had not arrived for Household Suffrage in the counties. I do not want to be liberal at the expense of other people. It seems to me that, by enfranchising the working classes as they now are, you are simply disfranchising the whole of the electoral body. I have great faith in the working men, but they have been deceived by agitators".[16]

When the Reform Bill was proposed in 1866, the *Ipswich Journal* sought to discredit it by reporting the presence of former Chartists at a meeting held in its support at Ipswich:

"It was in a great measure a masked meeting. Most of the speakers did not utter more than half their political belief. They had ulterior objects which they did not care to avow fully. The men who got upon waggons on the Cornhill in 1848, emulous of the revolutionists who then held possession of Paris, and raved about the People's Charter, were there and they did not tell the meeting that they had been converted to a belief in moderate measures. No; they have studied this Bill and they think they see in it the means of achieving the object which they sought to accomplish by another method in 1848. The more artless of them, however, confessed the truth. The Bill did not go far enough for them; they wanted Universal Suffrage".[17]

To carry Reform, the Liberals supporting it emphasised the greater danger of refusing some franchise extension. An editorial in the Liberal *Essex Telegraph* warned:

"The obstructor of all Reform creates discontent in the body politic and provokes a dangerous spirit of resistance. Physical Force Chartism was the offspring of Tory stubbornness".

The paper's editor, J. B. Harvey, tried to re-assure middle-class opinion by emphasising how workingmen had abandoned political independence:

"In those boroughs where the working classes already were in a majority, they were not found combining together to elect men of their own class, but rather to send those men who were best qualified to represent them in the House of Commons; and with an extended franchise, he believed they would find the working classes working in harmony with men of intelligence and right principles".[18]

Another Colchester Liberal, the miller Wilson Marriage, protested that modern workers "did not desire revolution, nor bloodshed, nor physical force", the last phrase clearly recalling Chartism and dismissing any connection with it. An Ipswich Liberal also pointed to the recent absence of protest by working people even when economic distress was at its worst. George Courtauld went further, calling the Bill "a fair and just concession to the intelligence, culture and consequent political importance of the great working classes of the country". Much was made of the orderly atmosphere at the Reform meetings in 1866-7. The *Halstead Times* wrote of a Chelmsford meeting that "as minors and females were not admitted, the audience, amongst whom was a large body of respectable men, presented a uniform, manly and intelligent appearance".[19] Some speeches by workingmen were also designed to allay middle-class anxieties, including one from William Potter, once a Braintree Chartist and still a weavers' leader:

"Mr. W. Potter, a working man, supported the resolution, expressing his opinion that the extension of the franchise to the working men would strengthen the Government and more firmly establish the throne ... From his experience of 40 or 50 years in that and neighbouring towns he observed that the working men had always conducted themselves with manly fortitude and paid proper respect to property and persons possessing it. They knew their esteemed neighbour, Mr Savill Onley, had opened his grounds to the working classes year after year and they had conducted themselves so well that he had never repented of it. Mr. Samuel Courtauld, of Gosfield Hall, had also thrown open his grounds to them and he did not think he had lost anything by it, but had gained a renowned name which would go down to posterity".[20]

Other working-class representatives were less obsequious, but equally ready to advance arguments which they thought would be acceptable to middle-class opinion. One recalled that "non-electors were members of benefit societies, which were self-supporting and entirely under the control of the members and would bear comparison with any societies, no matter to what class they belonged". Another claimed the franchise for workingmen because "they paid the greatest amount of taxation, they supplied the sinews of war, they rallied round the throne and supported the Queen". The patriotism of the working-class at this moment of supposed imminent French invasion was in 1866 cited also by an Ipswich speaker — "there were 22,000 Volunteers at Brighton ready to defend their country . . . they were mostly artisans". If in the 1860s such opinions were still voiced for tactical reasons, within a decade most working-class leaders had broadly accepted Liberal assumptions, policies and leadership. W. J. Bugg of Ipswich, at one meeting, "enforced the obligation which workingmen were under to the Liberal Party". John Howe, of Colchester, also confessed deep admiration for Mr. Gladstone. Even Thomas Rawlings, Colchester's most faithful Chartist, appeared on Liberal platforms in the 1880s along with other Chartist veterans. W. G. Blatch, Colchester's once militant Chartist, in "a stirring speech" to Women Liberals, attributed fifty years of progress to the Liberal party:

"Let them look at our country during the past fifty years and see how various institutions and laws have been improved until the English nation was the greatest on earth. The population of the earth was something like twelve hundred millions, and . . . one-third of all the people were under the control of this country and all enjoying the liberty and beauty of self-government and freedom. And all this was due to the policy of Mr. Gladstone".[22]

Five years after this speech F. J. Bugg was contributing generously to the local Fund for Queen Victoria's Jubilee.

Such attitudes may have prevailed all the more strongly because even some former Chartists had themselves become beneficiaries of the economy's revival. W. G. Blatch, a shoemaker, was by 1851 already an employer of three workers and subsequently also became a small-scale estate agent. At Ipswich, Bugg expanded his leather and shoemaking business until it had grown into one of the town's major concerns. Charles Richards, a Land Company shareholder of 1847, was by 1861 employing three men in his Witham carpenter's business. There had been no more stalwart Chartist than Thomas Newman who, from the foundation of the W.M.A. at Saxmundham in 1838 to the disappearance of Chartism from that town in 1850, had never wavered; in 1859 he was employing a number of men in his shoemaking works and found himself on the losing side when they went on strike. Nor was prosperity limited to master-craftsmen. John Howe, a journeyman carpenter, having founded the Colchester branch of the Amalgamated Society of Carpenters and Joiners, saw the real value of wages in his trade doubled between 1862 and 1892. Other skilled trades also fared well in the region, except for the disappearing handloom weavers. Mere economic betterment was not, however, the main cause of Chartist decline; after all, workers were even better-off after 1905 when independent Labour politics vigorously reasserted themselves through the region. Chartism lost its hold over the region's workers for a number of reasons. These included the determination of almost all landowners, farmers, industrialists and shopkeepers not to concede the smallest amount of political Reform to workingmen who might use it as the Chartists advised; the proven ability of those who dominated local society to maintain their control against all challenges from the working-class; Chartism's complete failure to unite all working-class sections in a campaign powerful enough to secure even minor concessions; the crippling disillusion and exhaustion felt by active Chartists as a result of the defeats of 1839, 1842 and 1848; and, only in the aftermath of these crushing disappointments, the prospects of limited economic and political gains for working people in return for their co-operation with the now well-established order.

Influence on later Working-class Movements

A few Chartist stalwarts died before their movement ended, some moved away from the region and others lost heart after one or another of its three defeats, but most were young and possessed an outlook that predisposed them to continue serving some radical cause. John Cook was 24 when he first sat on Ipswich N.C.A. committee and 39 when he finally stood down from Chartism. The four Colchester Chartist secretaries, whose ages are known, were 18, 22, 23 and 25 when holding office and three of them subsequently enjoyed long public careers, one living until 1921. Such men were valuable recruits to any cause, both because of their knowledge and skill and because they had already survived political disappointment and braved the danger of economic victimisation. Referring to victimisation, Garrard wrote "I have had my share of this" and there is reason to believe him. "It is not at all pleasant", he wrote, "for a man in this part of the country to take a prominent part in the agitation for the people's welfare and he is sure to incur the hatred of the master class by so doing, the end being loss of work and consequent privation as a reward". It was even harder to maintain a Chartist position in a small country town, as one Chartist leader observed during a tour of Suffolk: "To dare to be a Chartist in an agricultural town where the finger of scorn is pointed at one, is not the most enviable position in the world". As M'Pherson said, "Chartists were marked men".[23] They consoled themselves with the irrefutable justice of the Charter and the intellectual self-reliance which they had achieved in its pursuit. Goslin could say, after years of disappointment, that "he had suffered deeply ... Perhaps it was for the best. What was there that could equal the possession and exercise of a free mind?".[24]

This independence of outlook was all the stronger for having been reinforced by instruction and discussion in Chartist and kindred societies, where adult education was always a central activity. A Colchester member thought that "the acquirement of useful knowledge should be the chief object of Working Men's Associations" and, if few gave it such priority, the weekly discussion remained the invariable practice of W.M.A.s in 1838-9, of N.C.A. branches in 1841-3, of Land Branches in 1846-7, of revived N.C.A. branches in 1848-9 and, even after 1850, of informal groups like that which met at the Essex Arms in Colchester to discuss articles in the *People's Paper*. As late as 1851 Ipswich N.C.A. wanted to build a People's Free Hall for "the promotion of secular knowledge and the furthering of democratic principles among the people, wherein the working class can freely meet and freely discuss".[25] For nearly twenty years there was an almost unbroken process of adult education in which thousands participated and from which hundreds derived convictions that were to prove life-long. They also regularly bought the radical journals in which they found educational articles as well as political reports. An Ipswich newsagent found that "in these journals the articles are the productions of men and women possessed of much zeal and enthusiasm, joined with both tact and talent. Calmness in discussion, strict moral principle, particular exactness in the statement of fact, firmness, dignity and charity, are conspicuous in their pages".[26] Numerous Chartists were well-read and well-informed. Goslin was familiar with a range of historical literature, Cook could quote Shelley and Byron, Garrard had studied British and Roman history and M'Pherson was a poet. At Colchester, Blatch was to be the founder of the Ben Jonson club, Dennis wrote humorous ballads and Stephen Clubb was an inventor. Men of this stamp could prove a valuable asset to the mid-Victorian working-class movement.

There were other adult-educational channels which, though not officially Chartist, contributed much to the enlightenment of working-class radicals. At Ipswich, where a section of the Chartists were quite ready to work with the Owenites, for several years John Cook conducted a discussion group in which the main subject-matter was drawn from Chartist and Owenite journals. Its largely youthful members became familiar with the works of Burns, Godwin, Paine, Byron, Shelley, Bentham, Owen and Cobbett. In 1842 they discussed the Formation of Character, the Evidence for Christianity, Miracles, Determinism in Human Behaviour, and problems of Education and Economics. A member lectured on Paine at the anniversary of the latter's birthday, there was a series of discussions on the Chartist poet, Thomas Cooper, and a debate on Byron. The group kept a library of Humanist literature, held tea-parties and soirées and collected 700 signatures for the Sunday opening of the Crystal Palace. In one form or another this group seems to have met for a decade or more.[27] A number of future Chartists belonged to the Yarmouth Owenite Institute, which started in 1838 to meet every Sunday for the discussion of articles in Owen's journal, the *New Moral World*, and by 1839 had two hundred men and women at its readings, lectures and 'Social Festivals'. As attendance grew even larger, Anglican and Nonconformist clergymen held meetings to combat this Owenite 'infidelity', but the work continued to expand. A large hall was acquired to serve as a reading-room and lending library. There were tea-parties, concerts by the Institute choir, 'Festivals' at which babies were "named", and a Sunday School which taught "nothing but what was good and useful" by methods based upon "the best portions of the Pestalozzian system". An even larger hall was acquired, with superior facilities. Whole families joined and women were encouraged to play an equal part in the work. Next 'missionaries' from the Institute walked into the countryside, stopping to ask labourers "how they would like to sow the wheat for themselves", or travelled to Norfolk and Suffolk villages to address meetings of farm workers which often numbered 200 or more. Socialist Lectures were also given to holiday-makers on the Yarmouth Denes which were "literally dotted with knots of people discussing the merits and demerits of the system". Not until 1843 did the Institute decline, after which the initiative and some of the membership passed to the Chartists.[28] There was Owenite educational activity in other places in Suffolk, including Bury St. Edmunds, Lowestoft, Beccles, Bungay, Yoxford, Halesworth, Saxmundham, Yaxley and Wetheringsett.[29] Not all Chartists had groups of this kind in their vicinity to which they could resort, though Goody's coffee-shop at Sudbury and Shead's beerhouse at Braintree offered some facilities for fellowship, discussion and the reading of the radical Press.

This self-education equipped scores of Chartists with knowledge, intellectual skills and an outlook which would not permit them to retire from democratic or working-class causes even when Chartism had disintegrated. However, they came to the reluctant belief during the apathetic 1850s that they could most fruitfully use their experience within movements which seemed to offer better prospects of advance, however limited. Trade unionism was finding its operations somewhat easier in the economic recovery of the mid-Victorian years. The region's farmers were now prospering, as railways reached the rural areas, the best technical practice spread, prices kept up, and poor rates and wages remained low. Urban artisans indirectly benefited from this and their bargaining power was further strengthened by the availability of better-paid employment in London. The consequent growth of trade unionism was unobtrusive but wide enough to affect both skilled trades and occupations not hitherto involved. There was also a tentative movement away from the local autonomous organisations towards the new nation-wide Amalgamated Societies which offered some external backing and a training in business-like trade union techniques. Whatever the form taken, trade unionism certainly grew during 1850-70. Local organisations of shoemakers now existed at Colchester, Ipswich, Saxmundham, and even Bildeston where there cannot have been more than a score in the trade; at Colchester, where shoemaking was already a minor industry, a strike secured a wage increase in 1853.[30] Shorter hours were the first aim of the Ipswich tailors. They and their fellows at Bury St. Edmunds and Colchester subsequently abandoned their local organisations for the new Amalgamated Society of Tailors.[3] Meanwhile, the third pro-Chartist trade, the carpenters, were benefiting from the rise in population, the recovery of business and the consequent demand for new houses and commercial and agricultural buildings. At Colchester and Ipswich they struck with partial success for higher wages in 1853 and at Ipswich also for shorter hours in 1856. In both towns their organisations later gave place to branches of the Amalgamated Society of Carpenters and Joiners.[32] Other building trades were also partly organised. Though Ransomes at Ipswich had grown into the region's second largest industrial firm, under the owners' paternalist rule trade unionism had hitherto been slow to come. Its smiths were unsuccessful when they struck in 1847 but in 1852, when the Amalgamated Society of Engineers had been formed, they were successful in starting a branch.[33] East Coast seamen were engaged in several disputes, starting in the successful Yarmouth strike in 1851 and including a seven-year campaign of strikes and negotiations at Ipswich, where the seamen formed a branch of a new national union centred on the north-east ports. Manningtree and Mistley seamen had at first joined this Ipswich branch but subsequently set up their own.[34] Harwich and Brightlingsea stone-dredgers also went on strike, although their action was in response to worsening conditions in the declining Roman Cement trade.[35] Women workers were affected by the movement. Silk throwsters struck once at Ipswich and at least twice at Colchester in attempts to resist further deterioration in wages and working conditions. At Courtaulds' Halstead factory, with its welfare provisions and a wage-scale higher than that in a throwing factory, the female power-loom weavers had hitherto given their philanthropic employers very little trouble, but, when in 1860 wage cuts were imposed, 1,200 of them struck and won.[36] The Commercial Treaty with France had made 1860 a year of crisis for the whole silk industry, now deprived of the partial protection hitherto enjoyed. There was a renewal of trade unionism among handloom weavers at Braintree, Bocking, Halstead, Coggeshall and Sudbury, in association with the powerful East London union.[37] The most unexpected trade to become organised were the Ipswich gardeners who, to secure a 15 per cent wage increase, formed a Gardeners' Mutual Improvement Society.[38] The list of workers involved in trade unionism in 1850-70 is a very long one and those whose actions went unreported may well have been just as numerous.

In these developments former Chartists played a part. Many of them had themselves been strong trade unionists before 1850, so that no gulf lay between them and the unions. Cook, Garrard, Harvey and Orr had been leaders in both politics and trade unionism at Ipswich, as had Dennis, Chapman, Plummer and Barrett at Colchester. During the 1850s Cook was helping his old trade, the shoemakers, while William Barrett, a tailor, seems to have been the spokesman for Colchester trade unionism in general, since it was to him that the engineering workers turned when they needed an experienced man to preside over their Nine Hours Movement in 1872. The service given by the Yarmouth Chartists to their local unions has already been described. At Braintree and Halstead several Chartists had been leaders of the handloom weavers and they continued in that capacity after 1850, James Hunt at Halstead and William Shead, John Cowell, William Potter, Joseph Thorogood and William Russell at Braintree. The man who rallied the dispirited Colchester handloom weavers when they were threatened by the complete closure of their trade was John Castle who belonged to the ex-Chartist group still working for Universal Suffrage in the town.[39] The seamen's movement also drew on the experience of former Chartists both at Yarmouth and at Ipswich where an N.C.A. veteran, Thomas Coe, was the union secretary. Finally, in 1872-4 several former Chartists were able at last to help lead the farm workers. At Halstead James Hunt acted as district secretary to the National Agricultural Labourers' Union, at Colchester Thomas Rawlings gave his support, while at Ipswich Rushbrooke and Cook helped to organise support for Suffolk labourers locked out for membership of the union. Cook became secretary of a trade union committee, which collected money for the labourers from the foundries and other workplaces and held two large rallies in Ipswich, one of which was addressed by Joseph Arch.

The Chartist with the most distinguished record of service to trade unionism was John Howe.[41] Born at Thetford, he attended a Chartist meeting there at the age of twelve and was given the task of snuffing out the candles at its close. After serving his apprenticeship as a carpenter, he went first to Colchester and then moved to London, probably in 1853 when some young carpenters left Colchester during a trade dispute, thus helping those remaining in the town to gain an increase. Joining the new Amalgamated Society of Carpenters and Joiners in Camden Town, he subsequently returned to Colchester, where he started a branch of the Society in 1864. As its secretary, he raised the membership from nine to a hundred and guided the sustained campaign by which the wage rose from 21s. for a 58½ hour week in 1866 to 31s.9d. for a 53½ hour week in 1892; the parallel fall in prices made this an effective doubling of the real value of the wage. He founded a branch of the society in Ipswich, helped to start the Colchester Co-operative Building Society and worked for political and social reform within the radical wing of the Liberal Party. In 1891 he united the dozen or so branches of skilled workers in the town into the Colchester Trades Council, becoming its first chairman. His life of service ended in personal disappointment. Elected to the Borough Council as a radical Liberal, he broke with the Trades Council which had originally supported his candidature but had subsequently transferred its allegiance to the newly formed branch of the Independent Labour Party. He died in one of Colchester's almshouses.

Former Chartists also promoted the growth of the Consumer Co-operative Societies, which were founded at Halstead in 1860, Colchester in 1861, Coggeshall in 1862, Braintree in 1864 and Chelmsford and Ipswich in 1867. These Societies arranged adult classes for their members and helped the youthful trade unions by providing them with meeting places. The Halstead Society was largely the creation of the active group of former Chartists. At Colchester the founder was John Castle, Thomas Rawlings became treasurer and five other one-time N.C.A. members were among the first to join; G. F. Dennis was particularly active at educational meetings.[42] The Society worked hard for the 1867 Reform Act. John Cowell, handloom silk weaver and one of Braintree's last Chartists, was chiefly responsible for the foundation of his local Society, plans for which were made at his house, and William Shead became its chairman. At Ipswich, Rushbrooke and Coe tried unsuccessfully to start a Society in the late 1850s and it was not until the late date of 1867 that the group followed up its campaign for the Reform Act by re-founding the Society, another prominent member of which was Joseph Goody, once Sudbury's leading Chartist and now a resident of Ipswich.

As in politics, so in their work for trade unionism and Co-operation, Chartists had to purchase limited success with some surrender of the independence they had asserted in earlier years. They felt it advisable to recommend trade unions as repositories of Victorian virtues, stressing their avoidance of strikes and their Friendly Society functions. When the Colchester branch of the Amalgamated Society of Carpenters and Joiners entertained the two local Liberal candidates at its annual dinner, its officers drew the visitors' attention to the sickness and unemployment benefits offered by the society and to other evidence of its self-help functions. One of the Liberals commended these arrangements as contributing to the workers' moral welfare, and the other contrasted the Britain of 1839, the year of the Newport Rising, with the Britain of 1879 when workers no longer regarded employers as having interests different from their own.[43] When John Castle persuaded his fellow weavers to ask London silk firms to provide work in Colchester, in order to pay the expenses of the deputation to London, he was obliged to seek subscriptions from Colchester businessmen. This necessitated his first proving the respectability of himself and his fellows to the Mayor who only then endorsed the subscription.[44] Almost any such undertaking, to be successful, needed similar sponsors, as was evident at Braintree in 1860 when the Commercial Treaty with France had led to 40 per cent of the silk weavers being thrown out of work. The workers' leaders, who included several former Chartists, sought a temporary relaxation of the rule that the able-bodied must enter the Workhouse to obtain relief, and they came to the conclusion that their only hope of obtaining this concession was by surrendering the leadership of their cause to the Courtaulds, F. B. Crittall, the brush manufacturer J. West and other sympathetic employers; even so the concession was not forthcoming.[45] Co-operative Societies also courted the patronage of employers and local dignitaries. At Colchester help was given by the editor of the Conservative paper, the Squire of Lexden and the proprietors of the largest mill and the largest foundry. The Terling Society received support from the local squire, the Braintree Society from the second-largest silk firm in the town and the Halstead Society from the owner of a local foundry. In general, working-class leaders felt it advisable to profess current Liberal values, to show deference where it was prudent to do so, to pursue limited sectional interests and eschew grand visions; the former Chartists amongst them mostly followed these trends.

7

Conclusion

Essex and Suffolk Chartism constituted little more than a hundredth part of the movement's national strength. It lacked appreciable support among farm workers, the region's largest occupation, and it usually had to struggle to present its case even in places where it was at its strongest, the country towns and semi-industrial towns. Its direct challenge was easily checked by the local establishment, then dwindled into insignificance and finally died away. It won no local victories, except to establish firmly the formal right of free speech for working people, it engendered no original political initiatives and produced no influential spokesman. It was sustained from outside by the wider movement and the question could be asked whether, without such support, a local Chartism under any name would have enjoyed a long existence.

Viewed as part of the national movement, the region's Chartism was a small affair. Its presence at different times in fifty towns and villages, the sustained work of its branches, their weekly discussions, political campaigning and mass meetings, their leadership of local trade unionism, must be seen as a minute sample of the great volume of similar activity proceeding all over Britain. That very fact serves to illuminate the powerful and pervasive nature of Chartism as a national movement.

Chartists here firmly took the Moral Force side, yet found themselves at variance with British Chartism on few, if any, occasions; even in 1839 they were at one with most of their comrades in regretting the single serious outbreak of insurrection, while refusing to join in the inspired clamour against those who had resorted to it. After 1839 they appear in accord with O'Connor, M'Douall and Ernest Jones and, more importantly, with the policies and tactics of the National Charter Association. William Lovett's admirers here abandoned him as soon as he abandoned the movement. Their views on the Lovett-O'Connor disagreement cast doubt on the very validity of the Moral Force-Physical Force issue, at least in the form in which it has sometimes been presented.

Attention has usefully been given in recent research to Chartism's regional differences, but a striking feature of this region's Chartism is its close similarity to the national movement. That Chartism was a united movement throughout its various localities has been evident enough to those who have studied the Chartist Press and this is emphatically borne out by the firm attachment of its Essex and Suffolk supporters who, in their hundreds, showed an abiding loyalty to their party's leaders and policies. This was due to several political causes, but the more general conditions for this internal harmony may have arisen from the homogeneity of the local leadership throughout the regions, whether those regions were industrial, semi-industrial or largely agricultural. In Essex and Suffolk 79 per cent of known leading members were artisans[1] and, as far as can be estimated, this is very close to the comparable figure for Britain as a whole.[2] The *Northern Star* at one period published the occupations of local N.C.A. branch officers and committees; these lists read much the same, whether they are for industrial or country towns. Of course, at times of popular excitement the tactics of branches in industrial regions were influenced by their hopes of massive support from thousands of industrial workers, but most years between 1838 and 1858, so far from being times of popular excitement, were long periods of hard, patient and usually disappointing organisation by stalwarts of the local branches in all the regions, a majority of whom may well turn out to have been artisans. If this was so, conditions were all the more favourable for the steady development of unity, common loyalties and a consistent outlook, because these men already shared similar economic interests, similar occupational histories and, to some extent, similar religious and political attachments. Comprehensive research into the experience of the artisan trades in 1750-1830 could well illuminate this and other aspects of Chartist history in a far wider setting than Essex and Suffolk.

When seen in the setting of its own society, Essex and Suffolk Chartism had an impact which entitles it to a place in our local history. As a phase in the development of the Essex and Suffolk working-class movement, a movement which by 1982 is over two centuries old, the Chartist period was a distinctive and significant one. It sprang from the local craft unions and from working-class participation in early Reform struggles and, after two decades of existence, it moved back into the mid-Victorian labour world of craft unions, Co-operatives, Friendly Societies and renewed Suffrage struggles. In the meantime it had given rise to a working-class political party some sixty years before its modern equivalent began to take root in the region. This proved a development formidable enough to cause deep anxiety among those controlling local society, who were further concerned that this political independence was being reinforced by an intellectual self-reliance unknown in any quarter here since Civil War times. This independence, in its setting of prolonged poverty and working-class alienation, was a main reason why leading circles, despite their complete success in denying Chartism the smallest democratic concessions, yet went to such painstaking lengths to erect their defensive structure of charitable, religious and educational institutions. A study of their rejection of the Chartist programme cannot fail to call their own standards into consideration. While themselves practising gross electoral corruption and making the crudest calculations of economic advantage in their own party politics, they resolutely and often contemptuously denied elementary democratic rights to a majority of their neighbours. The abuse reserved in local newspapers and on public platforms for Chartist leaders and the workingmen who followed them has much to say about those who uttered it, but it is hard to recognise in these hostile descriptions the able and serious men who refused to be intimidated into the abandonment of democratic reform.

Sources

The most useful source is the Liberal Press (*Essex and Suffolk Times, Essex Herts and Kent Mercury, Suffolk Chronicle*). The most informative of Chartist newspapers are *The Charter*, the *Northern Star*, and the *People's Paper*. Briggs, *Chartist Studies*, 1959, contains a chapter on Chartism in Suffolk, by Hugh Fearn. Extracts from the diary of William Wire and from the memoirs of John Castle are reproduced in Brown, *Essex People*, 1972. For a bibliography of Chartism in general, see Jones, D., *Chartism and the Chartists*, 1975.

Notes and References

Abbreviations used in references

Newspapers

B.B.A.	*Braintree and Bocking Advertiser*	I.J.	*Ipswich Journal*
		L.D.	*London Dispatch*
B.S.	*British Statesman*	N.M.W.	*New Moral World*
C.G.	*Colchester Gazette*	N.S.	*Northern Star*
Ch.Ch.	*Chelmsford Chronicle*	P.M.G.	*Poor Man's Guardian*
E.G.	*Essex and West Suffolk Gazette*	S.C.	*Suffolk Chronicle*
E.H.	*Essex Herald*	**Other**	
E.M.	*Essex, Herts & Kent Mercury*	B.M.	British Museum
E.S.	*Essex Standard*	E.L.L.S.D.	Essex Library Local Studies Dept.
E.S.T.	*Essex and Suffolk Times*		
E.T.	*Essex Telegraph*	E.R.O.	Essex Record Office
Ev.St.	*Evening Star*	P.R.O.	Public Record Office
H.T.	*Halstead Times*	S.R.O.	Suffolk Record Office, Ipswich Branch
I.E.	*Ipswich Express*		

1 The Economic and Political Background

1. Young, A., *General View of the Agriculture of the County of Suffolk*, 1813, p.8.
2. Young, A., *General View of the Agriculture of the County of Essex*, 1807, II, p.270.
3. White, W., *Directory of Essex*, 1848; *Directory of Suffolk*, 1844; E.S. 22.2.1835, 27.1.1843, 15.3.1844, 14.5.1847, 21.10.1853.
4. Raynbird, H., *On the Agriculture of Suffolk*, 1849; White, W., *Directory of Suffolk*, 1844, pp.31.4.
5. Tate, W.E., *Proceedings of Suffolk Institute of Archaeology*, XXV, part 3, 1951, pp.225-63; E.R.O., Folder on Essex Enclosures.
6. E.R.O., D/P 35 (Rate Books, Little Baddow); Census, 1851, Enumerators' Returns for Little Baddow.
7. Rep. Sel. Cttee. on Petitions complaining of Agric. Distress, 1821-2.
8. White, W., *Directory of Essex*, 1848; *Directory of Suffolk*, 1844 (Sections on Chelmsford, Colchester, Bury St. Edmunds, Ipswich).
9. C.G. 19.2.1820.
10. Grace, D.R. and Phillips, D.C., *Ransomes of Ipswich*, 1975; White, W., *Directory of Suffolk*, 1844, p.64; Rep. Sel. Cttee. as in 7 above; Glyde, J., *Moral, Social and Religious Condition of Ipswich*, 1850, p.71.
11. Namier, Sir L., *The Structure of Politics at the Accession of George III*, 2nd. ed., 1957, p.111.
12. Ch.Ch. 22.12.1769, 26.2.1779, 12.2.1779, 5.3.1779.
13. I.J. 3.2.1776, 22.1.1780, 29.1.1780, 19.2.1780, 4.3.1780.
14. I.J. 1.6.1782, 27.3.1784; E.R.O., D/DFg Z1.
15. Ch.Ch. 30.1.1795; I.J. 6.5.1797, 13.5.1797.
16. I.J. 19.1.1793, 2.3.1793.
17. Robinson, H.C., *Diary*, 1869.
18. Ch.Ch. 2.8.1811, 9.8.1811.
19. Ch.Ch. 16.10.1812; C.G. 7.3.1818, 18.9.1819; S.C. 20.11.1819; E.S. 6.3.1863; E.R.O., D/DL 044/3.
20. S.C. 7.10.1820, 9.12.1820, 16.12.1820.
21. Coller, D.W., *The People's History of Essex*, 1861, pp.181-3; E.L.L.S.D., Collection of Press Cuttings.
22. Glyde, J., *New Suffolk Garland*, 1866, pp.435ff.; Ch.Ch. 19.6.1818; C.G. 11.3.1820; S.C. 9.9.1820.
23. Namier, *op.cit.* (Sections on Harwich and Orford); Colchester Poll Book,

24. 1830; S.C. 10.10.1812, 30.12.1848; I.J. 17.7.1830, 2.10.1830.
24. S.C. 8.10.1831.
25. Brown, A.F.J., *Essex People*, 1972, pp.142, 150.
26. I.J. 2.2.1822, 8.2.1823, 15.2.1823, 29.3.1823, 5.4.1823, 13.2.1830; S.C. 27.1.1821, 10.2.1821, 13.2.1830.
27. S.C. 9.1.1830.
28. Ritchie, J.E., *East Anglia*, 1883, p.121; I.J. 13.3.1830; S.C. 26.12.1829, 16.1.1830, 13.2.1830.
29. C.G., E.M., E.S., I.J., S.C. 1831-2, *passim;* Coller, *op.cit.*, pp.183-5.
30. E.M. 21.6.1831.
31. Coller, *op.cit.*, p.184.
32. S.C. 17.7.1830, 4.12.1830.
33. I.J., Ch.Ch. April-May 1772.
34. Census, 1841.
35. Rep. Ryl. Cmsn. on the Poor Laws, 1834, Appendix B1; S.C. 15.6.1844.
36. I.J., S.C., C.G., Ch.Ch. 1815-16, *passim;* Peacock, A.J., *Bread or Blood*, 1965.
37. I.J. Oct.-Nov. 1800.
38. S.C. 13.4.1822.
39. S.C. 8.8.1829, 15.8.1829, 24.10.1829, 13.2.1830, 13.3.1830; Ch.Ch. 30.1.1829, 27.2.1829.
40. Sources for the 'Swing Riots' are too numerous to quote in detail. They include Home Office reports, Quarter Sessions material and references in parish records, but the most convenient single source is the local Press (C.G., Ch.Ch., E.M., E.S., I.J., S.C. Nov. 1830-Jan. 1831).
41. P.R.O., H.O. 52, Box 7 (ii).
42. I.J. 18.12.1830; C.G. 21.12.1887.
43. C.G. 21.6.1834; E.M. 28.10.1834; S.C. 20.9.1834.
44. Tufnell, G., *Address to the Agricultural Labourers*, 1836; C.G., E.S. S.C. June-July 1836.
45. C.G. 23.4.1836; S.C. 22.6.1844.
46. Edsall, *The Anti-Poor Law Movement*, 1971, pp.34-5; Brown, *op.cit.*, p.76; E.R.O., G/DM 1; C.G. 31.1.1835, 17.10.1835; Ch.Ch. 12.6.1835; E.S. 22.7.1836; S.C. 16.5.1835, 10.10.1835.
47. Glyde, J., *Autobiography of a Suffolk Labourer*, III, Ch.4; C.G. 19.12.1835, 26.12.1835, 2.4.1836, 30.4.1836; S.C. 16.5.1835, 28.11.1835, 19.12.1835.
48. S.R.O., HA11/B5/25; S.C. 30.5.1835.
49. C.G. 1.7.1837, 8.7.1837.
50. C.G. 6.8.1836, 1.4.1837; Ch.Ch. 26.10.1838.
51. I.J. Jan-Feb. 1831; E.M. 2.8.1831; Ch.Ch. 13.3.1835; P.M.G. 18.3.1831.
52. I.J. 16.11.1833, 30.11.1833; S.C. 22.11.1834.
53. C.G. 4.4.1835, 18.4.1835; S.C. 15.8.1835.
54. E.S. 1.2.1834, 29.10.1837.
55. E.R.O., Borough of Colchester, Alehouse Recognizances.
56. I.J. 30.9.1758; E.R.O., Q/SO 3, 5.
57. I.J. 2.12.1758; Brown, *op.cit.*, p.43.
58. Brown, *op.cit.*, pp.88-9.
59. Ch.Ch. 12.4.1765, 17.5.1765, 31.5.1765, 30.9.1785; I.J. 27.6.1752, 23.5.1772.
60. I.J. 10.11.1792.
61. Brown, *op.cit.*, p.110.
62. E.R.O., Q/RSf2.
63. Kiddier, W., *The Old Trade Unions*, 2nd ed., 1931, pp.16,31,94,164; *Returns relative to the expenses of the poor*, 1815; S.C. 9.9.1826.
64. E.S. 24.5.1834; E.M. 27.5.1834; S.C. 19.9.1834.
65. S.C. 5.4.1834, 12.4.1834, 12.12.1835, 16.6.1838.
66. S.C. 12.4.1834.
67. E.S. 19.9.1834.
68. Ch.Ch. 30.5.1794; I.J. 8.12.1792, 15.12.1792, 19.1.1793, 23.2.1793, 2.3.1793, 7.12.1793; S.R.O., Notice to innholders in the Hundred of Mutford.
69. Brown, *op.cit.*, pp.108-9; Glyde, J., *New Suffolk Garland*, 1866, p.439.
70. E.L.L.S.D., Wiles, Diary and Notebook.
71. Cobbett, W., *Rural Rides*, (Everyman ed.), II p.221; S.C. 13.3.1830, 20.3.1830; E.S. 9.6.1832.
72. E.M. 8.11.1831, 26.6.1832; E.S. 4.3.1831, 15.4.1831, 9.6.1832; I.J. 8.9.1832.
73. S.C. 30.12.1848.
74. Ev.St. 20.10.1842.
75. C.G. 5.11.1836.
76. E.S. 23.10.1840.
77. S.C. 21.11.1840.
78. Glyde, J., *Autobiography of a Suffolk Labourer*, III, Ch.4; Ch.Ch. 28.4.1837.
79. E.S.T. 2.2.1838, 18.8.1838.
80. E.S.T. 15.12.1838.
81. C.G. July 1835-Jan. 1836.
82. S.C. 20.8.1836.
83. Ch.Ch. 21.8.1835.
84. Ch.Ch. 5.4.1839; C.G. 8.4.1837.
85. E.S. 25.12.1835.
86. P.M.G. 20.4.1833, 25.1.1834; S.C. 8.8.1835.
87. I.J. 23.6.1832.
88. S.C. 29.11.1834.
89. S.C. 4.7.1835, 10.9.1836.
90. C.G. 19.12.1835, 30.4.1836; S.C. 15.11.1834, 22.11.1834, 19.12.1835, 1.7.1837.

2 Chartism, 1838-9

1. C.G. 1.4.1837; L.D. 13.8.1837; Lovett Collection in Birmingham Central Reference Library.
2. E.S.T. 9.2.1838; L.D. 11.2.1838, 22.4.1838.
3. S.C. Dec. 1837-Mar. 1838, *passim*.
4. S.C. 3.2.1838, 3.3.1838.
5. E.S.T. Jan.-March 1838, *passim*.
6. E.S. 9.2.1838; E.S.T. 15.9.1838.
7. E.R.O., D/P268/18/1,2.
8. Ch.Ch. 7.10.1836.
9. Coleman, *Courtaulds*, 1969, pp.103-4; Ch.Ch. 28.3.1837, 11.1.1839, 5.4.1839.
10. E.M. 26.6.1832; E.S. 30.6.1832.
11. Ch.Ch. 13.2.1835; B.B.A. 27.1.1864.
12. B.B.A. 17.5.1871; Ev.St. 23.12.1842.
13. E.L.L.S.D., Poem, 'The State Chair', by Lister Smith; B.B.A. 27.1.1864.
14. Ch.Ch. 22.4.1836, 28.4.1837.
15. B.M., Place Collection, Add. MSS. 37.773.
16. E.S.T. 9.2.1838, 26.5.1838, 28.7.1838, 1.9.1838.
17. E.S.T. 14.4.1838.
18. Rules of a Friendly Society of the Silk Workers of Great Coggeshall (in private custody).
19. C.G. 8.4.1837; Ch.Ch. 13.10.1837.
20. E.S.T. 5.1.1838, 14.7.1838, 15.12.1838.
21. E.S.T. 5.5.1838.
22. S.C. 16.6.1838; E.S.T., I.J., S.C. Aug. 1838.
23. S.C. 25.8.1838.
24. S.C. 3.11.1838, 10.11.1838, 19.1.1839; E.M. 4.12.1838; L.D. 23.9.1838.
25. S.C. 3.11.1838, 4.5.1839; E.S.T. 8.9.1838; B.M., Place Collection, Add. MSS. 34,245A, 1.5.1839, 2.5.1839.
26. B.M., Place Collection, Add. MSS. 37,773; E.S., E.S.T., Ch.Ch., S.C. Sept. 1838.
27. B.M., Place Collection, Add. MSS. 27,820; E.S.T. Nov. 1838-Feb. 1839.
28. E.M. 18.12.1838, 25.12.1838; Ch.Ch. 14.12.1838; B.M., Place Collection, Add. MSS. 34,245A, 17.4.1839.
29. E.S.T. 17.11.1838, 8.12.1838; E.M. 11.12.1838; E.S. 16.11.1838.
30. E.S. 21.12.1838; E.S.T. 8.9.1838, 15.9.1838; B.M., Place Collection, Add. MSS. 37,773, 18.12.1838.
31. E.S.T. 1.12.1838, 8.12.1838, 29.12.1838; I.J. 1.12.1838; L.D. 25.11.1838; S.C. 9.3.1839.
32. E.M. 11.12.1838, 18.12.1838; E.S.T. 6.7.1839; S.C. 27.4.1839.
33. E.M. 2.4.1838, 20.8.1839; E.S.T. 22.6.1839, 6.7.1839; L.D. 13.1.1839, 15.6.1839; I.J. 6.4.1839; N.S. 1.2.1840; S.C. 9.2.1839, 18.5.1839; B.M., Place Collection, Add. MSS. 34,245A, 11.3.1839.
34. *The Charter*, 6.10.1839; E.M. 27.11.1838, 4.12.1838; I.J. 1.12.1838, 8.12.1838.
35. E.M. 1.1.1839; I.J. 29.12.1838.
36. Lovett Collection, 16.11.1838; B.M., Place Collection, Add. MSS. 34,245B; E.S.T. 12.1.1839; I.E. 15.10.1839.
37. Frost, T., *Forty Years Recollections*, 1880, pp.56-7; Lovett Collection, 13.10.1839; S.R.O., Letter from Barmby to John Glyde, 1841; S.C. 3.8.1839, 21.9.1839, 12.10.1839; *The Charter* 5.1.1840.
38. *The Charter* 6.10.1839, 13.10.1839; S.C. 19.10.1839.
39. B.M., Place Collection, Add. MSS. 34,245B, 17.7.1839.
40. *The Charter* 10.2.1839; E.S.T. 15.12.1838; L.D. 29.10.1837.
41. E.S. 21.6.1839; E.S.T. 22.6.1839.
42. E.S. 22.11.1839, 29.11.1839, 20.12.1839.
453. B.M., Place Collection, Add. MSS. 34,245A, 30.4.1839.
44. E.S.T. 2.2.1839, 16.2.1839, 27.4.1839.
45. *The Charter* 31.3.1839; I.J. 9.3.1839; S.C. 9.3.1839, 23.3.1839.
46. E.S.T. 8.12.1838; I.J. 24.5.1839; S.C. 25.5.1839.
47. Ch.Ch. 22.2.1839; E.S.T. 1.6.1839; I.J. 1.6.1839; S.C. 18.5.1839.
48. B.M., Place Collection, Add. MSS. 34,245A, 5.3.1839.
49. E.S.T. 16.3.1839; N.S. 12.10.1839.
50. E.S.T. 29.12.1838, 1.6.1839.
51. E.S.T. 22.12.1838, 5.1.1839, 12.1.1839.
52. E.S.T. 6.7.1839; S.C. 13.7.1839.
53. E.S. 16.8.1839; E.S.T. 10.8.1839, 17.8.1839.
54. B.M., Place Collection, Add. MSS. 34,245B, 17.7.1839, 30.7.1839.
55. E.M. 25.6.1839; E.S.T. 16.3.1839, 22.6.1839, 14.9.1839.
56. E.S.T. 6.4.1839.
57. N.S. 20.7.1839, 12.10.1839.
58. Lovett Collection; E.S.T. Nov. 1839-Jan. 1840; N.S. Jan.March 1840.
59. *The Charter* 15.12.1839; E.M. 26.11.1839; E.S. 29.11.1839, 6.12.1839; S.C. 9.11.1839, 30.11.1839, 4.1.1840, 18.1.1840, 1.2.1840.
60. E.M. 26.11.1839, 24.3.1840; E.S.T. 9.11.1839; I.E. 8.10.1839.

3 Years of Maturity, 1841-5

1. S.C. 18.1.1840.
2. *The Charter* 5.1.1840; *Southern Star* 19.1.1840.

3. *The Charter* 24.11.1839, 5,1,1840; S.C. 16.11.1839, 29.2.1840.
4. S.C. 11.7.1840, 15.8.1840, 28.11.1840.
5. S.C. 19.12.1840.
6. S.C. 29.2.1840, 7.3.1840, 2.1.1841, 27.2.1841.
7. S.C. 13.3.1841.
2. N.S. 23.1.1841; I.E. 25.5.1841.
9. I.E. 22.6.1841.
10. B.S. 8.5.1842, 30.7.1842, 15.10.1842; I.J. 9.4.1842; N.S. 27.11.1841, 4.12.1841, 11.12.1841, 8.10.1842.
11. S.C. 28.1.1843.
12. B.S. 30.7.1842.
13. N.S. 17.4.1842, 22.8.1841, 18.12.1841.
14. N.S. 18.12.1841, 8.1.1842.
15. E.S. 21.4.1843; N.S. 29.7.1843.
16. N.S. 5.6.1841, 11.12.1841, 8.1.1842, 5.3.1842, 9.4.1842, 6.8.1842.
17. I.E. 27.4.1841; N.S. 17.12.1842.
18. Ev.St. 14.10.1842.
19. I.E. 12.4.1842; N.M.W. 25.9.1841; N.S. 12.2.1842.
20. N.S. 9.4.1842.
21. N.S. 30.4.1842.
22. B.S. 8.5.1842.
23. S.C. 29.1.1842.
24. S.C. 14.5.1842, 4.6.1842, 11.6.1842.
25. B.S. 30.7.1842; S.C. 9.3.1844.
26. I.E. 28.12.1841; N.S. 5.6.1841, 24.12.1841, 25.6.1842; S.C. 24.12.1841.
27. B.S. 30.7.1842; Ev.St. 30.10.1842; N.S. 25.6.1842, 6.8.1842; S.C. 30.7.1842.
28. N.S. 26.3.1842, 17.12.1842.
29. I.E., I.J., S.C. Aug. 1842, *passim*.
30. *The Cambrian* 26.4.1839.
31. S.C. 20.8.1842, 21.1.1843, 25.2.1843.
32. Ev.St. 15.12.1842; I.J. 26.11.1842; S.C. 19.11.1842, 26.11.1842.
33. Ev.St. 19.11.1842.
34. Ev.St. 15.12.1842.
35. E.S. 30.6.1843; N.S. 29.4.1843; S.C. 21.1.1843.
36. E.S. 21.4.1843; N.S. 29.4.1843, 6.5.1843, 9.7.1843.
37. N.S. 25.1.1845.
38. S.C. 12.2.1848.
39. Ch.Ch. 22.2.1839; E.S.T. 15.12.1838; I.E. 15.10.1839.
40. Ev.St. 21.1.1843; E.S. 30.6.1843; S.C. 15.4.1843, 24.10.1846.
41. S.C. 30.3.1844, 4.5.1844, 2.11.1844.
42. N.S. 11.5.1844, 8.6.1844.
43. N.S. 2.3.1844, 13.4.1844, 20.4.1844, 2.8.1845.
44. E.S. 9.10.1846.
45. Western, *Letter to Chelmsford Agricultural Society*, 1843.
46. S.C. 11.5.1844.
47. E.S.T. 22.12.1838.
48. S.C. 6.4.1844.

4 Recovery and Final Decline, 1846-58

1. N.S. 25.12.1847.
2. N.S. Dec. 1845-Nov. 1846.
3. E.S. 30.7.1847; N.S. July-Aug. 1847; S.C. 30.10.1847.
4. I.E., I.J., S.C. June-Aug. 1847; I.E. 25.4.1848.
5. S.C. 29.4.1848.
6. S.C. 30.10.1847.
7. S.C. 30.10.1847, 6.11.1847.
8. S.C. 30.10.1847, 6.11.1847; N.S. 4.12.1847.
9. N.S. 19.2.1848, 18.3.1848; S.C. 5.2.1848, 19.2.1848, 11.3.1848, 18.3.1848, 25.3.1848.
10. I.E., I.J., S.C. March 1848.
11. E.S. 14.7.1848.
12. E.H. 25.4.1848; N.S. 1.4.1848, 8.4.1848.
13. E.H. 25.4.1848; E.S. 21.4.1848, 28.4.1848.
14. E.H. 25.4.1848; I.E. 11.4.1848; N.S. 29.4.1848; S.C. 15.4.1848, 22.4.1848.
15. S.C. 22.4.1848.
16. Ch.Ch. 5.5.1848; N.S. 29.4.1848, 6.5.1848.
17. E.S. 23.6.1848; S.C. 10.6.1848.
18. E.H. 25.4.1848, 13.6.1848; E.S. 28.4.1848, 11.8.1848; I.E. 18.4.1848; N.S. 6.5.1848, 13.5.1848; S.C. 29.4.1848.
19. N.S. 16.9.1848.
20. S.C. 1853-5 (Letters from J. Cook).
21. *People's Paper* 15.5.1852, 22.10.1852, 10.12.1853, 20.5.1854, 5.12.1857; N.S. 10.5.1851, 20.12.1851; S.C. 22.2.1851, 1.3.1851, 15.3.1851.
22. E.T. 12.3.1859.

5 Assessment

1. E.S. 6.7.1847.
2. S.C. 31.7.1847.
3. N.S. 8.4.1848.
4. E.M. 2.4.1839, 18.6.1839; E.S. 22.9.1843; E.S.T. 22.6.1839; S.C. 30.11.1839.
5. E.S.T. 9.11.1839.
6. E.M. 29.1.1839; S.C. 16.11.1839.
7. S.C. 3.8.1839.
8. E.S.T. 15.12.1838.
9. E.S.T. 18.8.1838; S.C. 3.11.1838.
10. E.S.T. 15.12.1838; Lovett Collection, 29.7.1838.
11. E.M. 27.11.1838; E.S.T. 15.9.1838, 15.12.1838, 9.11.1839; I.E. 17.9.1839; I.J. 18.8.1838; S.C. 5.5.1838, 24.7.1847, 6.11.1847,

8.1.1848, 5.2.1848.
12. *Educational Journal and Communist Apostle* Nov. 1841; E.S.T. 15.12.1838; I.J. 6.4.1839, 11,5,1839, 24.5.1839; N.M.W. 29.5.1841; N.S. 2.3.1844.
13. E.S.T. 9.2.1838, 5.5.1838, 1.9.1838, 15.9.1838, 3.11.1838, 26.1.1839; I.E. 15.10.1839; S.C. 9.10.1830, 18.5.1839,12.10.1839, 19.10.1839, 30.10.1847, 6.11.1847, 2.4.1859.
14. E.S.T. 22.12.1838; S.C. 19.2.1848.
15. E.S.T. 15.9.1838; S.C. 16.11.1839, 27.4.1844.
16. E.S.T. 8.12.1838; I.E. 17.9.1839; S.C. 14.9.1839.
17. E.S.T. 1.12.1838.
18. E.M. 3.12.1839; E.S.T. 3.8.1839; S.C. 30.10.1847.
19. E.S.T. 15.9.1838; E.M. 12.1.1839.
20. S.C. 1.9.1838.
21. E.S.T. 26.1.1839; S.C. 3.3.1838, 19.12.1840.
22. E.S.T. 15.12.1838; B.M., Place Collection, Add. MSS. 34,245A, 23.4.1839.
23. S.C. 7.4.1855.
24. N.S. 6.6.1840; B.M., Place Collection, Add. MSS. 34,245B, 17.7.1839, Add. MSS. 27.820.
25. E.S.T. 15.9.1838.
26. S.C. 10.6.1848.
27. E.M. 11.12.1838; N.S. 25.1.1845.
28. *The Charter* 5.1.1840.
29. P.R.O. B.T. 41/474-6 (This source has provided all the information about Land Co. membership).
30. E.L.L.S.D., *Public Men of Ipswich*, 1875, pp.139-40.
31. E.S. 11.8.1848; I.J. 6.4.1839; N.S. 20.7.1839.
32. I am indebted to Janet Gyford for most of the information about Witham Land Co. members.
33. E.S.T. 8.12.1838.
34. E.T. 16.8.1890.
35. E.S. 8.2.1839.
36. Glyde, *Condition of Ipswich, op.cit.*
37. E.S. 22.9.1843, 16.6.1848; E.S.T. 18.1.1840; Cromwell, *History of Colchester*, 1825, pp.386-7.
38. E.S. 17.5.1839.
39. E.S. 6.10.1843; I.J. 29.12.1838.
40. E.S. 16.6.1843.
41. I.J. 8.12.1838.
42. E.S. 15.5.1839; E.S.T. 20.10.1838; I.J. 24.8.1839.
43. E.S. 3.9.1841; S.C. 24.8.1839.
44. National Society for Education, *Annual Reports*, 1812, 1818.
45. E.S. 16.4.1847.
46. E.S. 26.8.1842, 14.7.1848; E.S.T. 16.2.1839.
47. E.S. 6.12.1839.
48. E.S. 23.10.1846.
49. E.S. 1.9.1848; S.C. 1.2.1840, 16.12.1848, 26.1.1855.
50. S.C. 27.5.1843.
51. S.C. 4.2.1843.

6 The Legacy of Essex and Suffolk Chartism

1. E.G. 16.7.1852, 30.7.1852.
2. E.G. 15.10.1852.
3. S.C. Jan.-May 1859.
4. E.L.L.S.D., *Public Men of Ipswich*, p.245.
5. I.J. 29.1.1859.
6. E.T. 12.3.1859; E.S. 30.5.1860, 29.3.1861.
7. S.C. 9.6.1860.
8. Ch.Ch., E.S., E.T., H.T., S.C. April 1866-June 1867.
9. H.T. 1865-1884, *passim*.
10. Ch.Ch., E.H., E.T., H.T., S.C. July-Sept. 1884 (for the 1884 Reform Act movement in Essex and Suffolk).
11. S.C. Dec. 1875.
12. S.C. 19.7.1884, 26.7.1884, 29.7.1884, 6.9.1884.
13. S.C. 26.9.1884.
14. E.T. 20.8.1859.
15. E.S. 27.4.1860.
16. H.T. 7.2.1874.
17. I.J. 14.4.1866.
18. E.S. 21.3.1866, 6.4.1866.
19. H.T. 14.4.1866.
20. E.H. 12.2.1867.
21. S.C. 14.4.1866.
22. E.T. 18.3.1893.
23. Br.St. 30.7.1842; S.C. 17.4.1841, 24.5.1850.
24. S.C. 19.6.1841.
25. S.C. 11.10.1851.
26. S.C. 26.1.1850.
27. Glyde, *Condition of Ipswich, op.cit.*, pp.65,68,236-7; N.M.W. 15.10.1842, 11.2.1843; N.S. 3.2.1849; S.C. Jan-March 1850, Feb-June 1853.
28. N.M.W., especially 1838-40, *passim*.
29. N.M.W., *passim*.
30. E.G. July-Aug. 1853; S.C. 12.11.1853, 14.2.1857, 29.10.1859.
31. S.C. 5.4.1856, 31.5.1856; Amalgamated Society of Tailors, *Annual Reports* (for Bury St. Edmunds, Colchester, Ipswich).
32. E.G. 22.4.1853, 6.5.1853; S.C. 31.5.1856, 4.10.1856.
33. S.C. 20.3.1847, 10.1.1852.
34. S.C. 6.7.1850, Feb.-March 1851, April-Nov. 1853, Jan.-March 1854, 8.3.1856, 5.4.1856.
35. E.G. 1.4.1853.
36. E.G. 30.9.1853; E.S. 14.6.1861; E.T. 19.5.1860, 26.5.1860; H.T. 16.2.1867; S.C. 4.10.1856.
37. E.S. 31.8.1860, 7.12.1860, 14.6.1861;

       B.B.A. 13.7.1860, 20.7.1860.
38. S.C. 12.5.1866.
39. Brown, *op.cit.*, pp.122-28.
40. S.C. 5.5.1874, 6.6.1874.
41. Brown, *Colchester 1815-1914*, 1980, pp.137-9.
42. Brown, *Essex People*, pp.128-30.
43. *Colchester Mercury* 20.3.1879.
44. Brown, *Essex People*, pp.122-3.
45. E.S. June 1860.

7 Conclusion

1. Including weavers.
2. Jones, D., *Chartism and the Chartists*, 1975, pp.30-32.

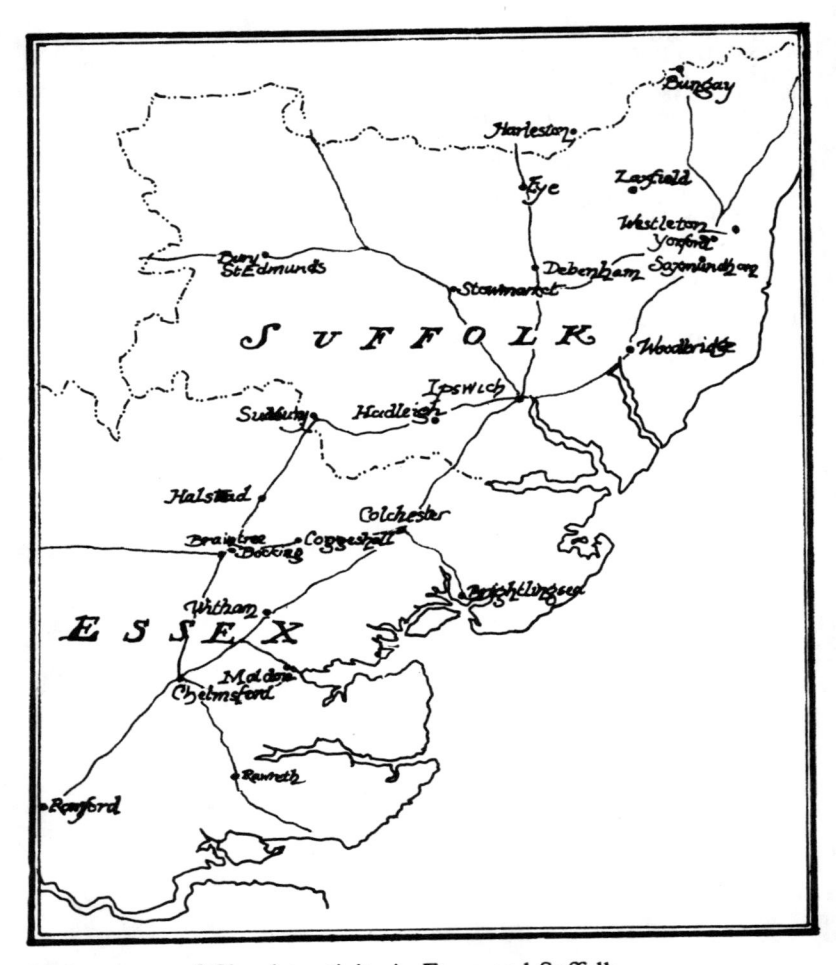

Major scenes of Chartist activity in Essex and Suffolk.

Indexes

(i) General

Adult education, 107-9. *See also* Mechanics' Institutes
Agriculture, 9, 14; depression, 10-11, 12, 14, 19, 22; rent, 11, 12, 18-19; societies, 11, 12, 27; technical progress, 10, 11, 13. *See also* Corn Laws, Farmers, Landowners
Aldeburgh, 11, 17, 21
Aldham, 105
America, 15, 91
Apprenticeship, 31, 41
Ardleigh, 28
Arkesden, 25
Artisans, 13-14, 32, 119; masters, 17, 21; Nonconformity, 32; politics, 16, 32, 34. *See also individual trades*
Baddow, Gt., 25, 105, 106
Baddow, Lt., 12, 25
Ballot, Open/Secret, 21, 34, 37, 38, 41, 43, 58, 111, 114
Baptists, 86, 94
Basildon, 29
Beccles, 29, 102; Owenism, 118; Reform politics, 15, 20
Bedfield, 29
Benacre, 11
Bentall family, 13, 14
Bentley, Gt., 27
Bergholt, West, 29, 75
Berkshire, 24
Bildeston, 21, 119
Blacksmiths, 51, 97
Boreham, 29
Boxford, 21
Bradfield (Suff.), 26
Bradwell-on-Sea, 25, 33
Braintree/Bocking, 10, 17, 21, 34, 36, 102, 111; agricultural society, 11; incendiarism, 25; New Poor Law, 36; Reform politics, 15; silk, 9, 42-3; trade unionism, 31, 32, 42, 120; woollen cloth, 9
Brandon, 102; riot, 23
Brentwood, 29, 102, 112
Bricklayers, 34, 37; trade unionism, 31, 32
Bright, John, 111, 114
Brightlingsea, 25-6, 119
Brome, 26
Bromley, Lt., 27
Brushmakers, 34, 101; trade unionism, 32, 48
Bumpstead, Steeple, 25
Bunbury, Sir H., 16-17
Bungay, 15, 20, 102
Bures, 29, 33
Bury St. Edmunds, 13, 102; Parliamentary representation, 11, 15, 17, 21; Reform politics, 15, 16, 18, 19-21; trade unionism, 31, 32, 34, 119

Canada, 49, 91
Caroline, Queen, 16, 18
Carpenters, 34, 54, 101, 116, 119; trade unionism, 31, 32, 116, 119, 120, 121; wages, 32, 116
Charities, 37, 38, 68, 89, 103-5
Chelmsford, 13, 21, 24, 25, 28, 102, 115; Church Rates, 36; Co-operative Society, 121; Reform politics, 14, 15, 16, 19, 21, 33, 34, 36; trade unionism, 31, 32
Church of England, 11, 86, 94, 105-6; clergy, 12, 20, 21, 26, 60, 83, 118
Church Rates, 35, 36, 37, 40, 45
Clacton, Gt., 25, 26
·Clacton, Lt., 25, 26
Clare, 23
Clavering, 25
Coachmakers, 37, 39
Cobbett, William, 33, 34, 37, 40, 48, 118
Cobden, Richard, 73
Coggeshall, 9, 102, 106; Co-operative Society, 121; silk, 9, 31, 120; trade unionism, 31; woollen cloth, 9, 31
Colchester, 23, 25, 31, 34, 102, 104, 107, 114; agricultural influence, 13; artisans, 32; church building, 106; Church Rate, 36; Corporation, 16; economy, 13, 14; Parliamentary representation, 11, 15, 16, 17, 21, 33; political clubs, 16, 36; Reform politics, 15-21, 30, 33-34; silk, 9, 13; tailoring, 13, 31; trade unionism, 31, 32, 35, 119-21
Colchester Gazette, 20, 28
Colne, Earls, 11
Combination Acts, 23, 31
Congregationalists, 81, 82, 86
Co-operative Societies, 31, 120, 121-2, 124
Coopers, 41, 57
Corn Laws, 11, 17, 41; Repeal, 11, 35
Courtaulds, 9, 17, 21, 36, 43, 44, 50, 60, 82, 83, 99, 112, 119, 121
Cressing, 27
Danbury, 25
Dedham, 28
Dengie, 23
Donyland, East, 80
Dovercourt, 25
Drinkstone, 23
Dunmow, Gt., 11, 28, 31, 102
Dunwich, 11, 17, 20, 21
Education, 41; Monitorial System, 106-7; purpose of, 106-8. *See also* Adult Education, Mechanics' Institutes
Ellough, 26
Elmswell, 26
Engineers, 32, 97, 101, 119
Epping, 102
Essex: county constituencies, 11, 17, 19 20, 78; population, 13-14, 22. *See also*

133

Agriculture
Essex Mercury, 17, 93
Essex Standard, 14, 20, 42, 49, 58, 83, 89, 98, 105, 114
Essex Times, 59, 93, 108
Eye, 20, 27, 29, 102; Parliamentary representation, 11, 17, 21
Farm workers, 22-30, 35, 110-11; protest movements, 11, 22-30; trade unionism, 23, 27, 110, 120; unemployment, 18, 22, 24; wages, 22, 23, 24-6, 27, 29. *See also* Incendiarism
Farmers: complicity in Swing riots, 12, 26; control of villages, 11-12, 50-1; politics, 12, 15, 16-17, 18-19, 68, 98, 101; rents, 11, 12, 18-19, 26; size of farms, 12; technical progress, 10, 11, 12; tenant farmers, 11, 18, 19, 21; tithe, 12, 18, 19, 26; urban influence, 12, 13. *See also* Agriculture
Felstead, 29
Finchingfield, 23, 25
Fisheries/fishermen, 13, 97
Flatford, 97
Foundries, 12-14, 97. *See also* Leiston: Garretts; Ransomes
Framlingham, 16, 102
France: French Revolutions, 31, 33, 80, 88, 90-1, 108
Friendly Societies, 30, 31, 32, 45, 100, 115, 124
Gedding, 23
Gestingthorpe, 97
Gladstone, W. E., 113, 116
Glemham, Gt., 21
Glyde, J., 104, 105
Gooch, Sir Thos., 11, 19, 27
Grafton, Duke of, 17, 20
Greensted, 55
Hadleigh (Suff.), 23, 26, 102
Halesworth, 10, 20, 102, 118
Halstead, 9, 15, 25, 28, 102; Co-operative Society, 121-2; farm workers' protests, 23, 30; Poor Law protests, 28, 29; silk, 9, 119-20
Hampshire, 24
Harlow, 102
Harvey, D. W., 16, 18-19, 33-4, 36, 47
Harwich, 60, 97, 102; Parliamentary representation, 17, 20, 21; Reform movements, 15, 20, 34; trade unionism, 31, 119
Hatfield Peverel, 80
Haverhill, 21, 102
Hedinghams, 23, 28, 102; workhouse damaged, 28-9
Henham, 23, 25
Henny, Gt., 22
Heybridge, 10, 13, 114
Holland, Gt., 25, 28
Hornchurch, 102
Hundon, 23
Huntingfield, Lord, 20, 26
Incendiarism, 11, 18, 22, 23, 25-6, 27, 29-30, 74-6; approval by labourers, 30, 75

Inns/beershops/publicans, 13-14, 18, 30; political clubs, 33, 34, 44
Ipswich, 10, 13-14, 26, 102, 116; artisans, 32; charities, 104; Co-operative Society, 121; Mechanics' Institute, 108, 109; Parliamentary representation, 11, 16, 17, 20, 21, 33, 38, 40; Reform politics, 16, 18, 20, 21, 33, 34; trade unionism, 31-3, 37, 113, 119, 120; workhouses attacked, 28, 37
Ipswich Journal, 24, 46, 51, 111, 114
Justice, 22, 94; Assizes, 27; Petty Sessions, 11, 28; punishment, 25-6, 27, 29, 42; Quarter Sessions, 11, 31, 60
Justices of the Peace, 11, 21, 24, 25, 27, 28, 29, 37, 42, 74, 80, 82, 90
Kelvedon, 16, 112
Kent, 24, 25
Kenton, 23
Kettlebaston, 23
Kirby, 25
Landowners, 10, 11, 25, 80, 98, 104-5; political influence, 11, 17, 20, 21, 50; rents, 11, 18, 26; urban influence, 11, 12, 13, 103
Langham, 21, 23
Lavenham, 102
Lawford, 23
Laxfield, 20, 28
Layer Breton, 23
Layer-de-la-Haye, 27
Leiston: Garretts, 10, 13, 17, 21, 97
Leighs, Gt./Lt., 29
Letheringham, 28
Liberals, 36, 37, 38, 40, 44, 56, 57, 70-1, 79-80, 82, 84, 85, 98, 103, 112-3; fear of Chartism, 103, 113-5; Reform clubs, 34, 36; working-class support, 111-6, 120-1. *See also* Whigs
London, 33, 106; economic connections with Essex and Suffolk, 9, 10, 12, 22, 42
Lowestoft, 30, 58, 97, 102, 118
Maldon, 10, 104, 105, 114; Parliamentary representation, 11, 14, 17, 21, 33, 34; Reform politics, 14, 20, trade unionism, 31
Manningtree, 102, 108, 119
Martlesham, 23
Mechanics' Institutes, 40, 41, 60, 74; political bias, 107-8
Melford, Long, 9, 102
Mellis, 26
Middle class, 17-19, 21, 79-80. *See also* Professions, Shops
Mildenhall, 20, 102
Mile End, Colchester, 23, 25
Military, use of, 23, 25, 27, 31, 37, 80
Mistley, 102, 119
Municipal reform, 34, 37, 40
Nayland, 21
Needham Market, 32
Netherlands, 10, 12
Newmarket, 102
Nonconformity, 17, 35, 39-40, 41; Church Rates resented, 35, 36; ministers,

134

18, 118; politics, 15, 16, 36, 81. *See also* Baptists; Congregationalists; Peculiar People; Quakers; Wesleyans
Norfolk, 9, 10, 24
North Cove, 26
Norwich, 40, 106
Oakley (Suff.), 26
Oakleys (Essex), 11
O'Connell, Dan., 91
Orford, 11, 17, 21
Osyth, St., 25
Owen, Robert/Owenism/Socialism, 33, 37, 40, 118
Paine, Thos., 15, 33, 37, 118
Paper making, 14; trade unionism, 32
Parish: officers, 12, 21; vestry, 12, 22, 25
Peasenhall, 13, 97
Peculiar People, 54
Peldon, 25, 27
"Peterloo", 16
Police: County, 55, 64, 82; Parish, 23, 28; Specials, 16, 25, 26, 80, 82
Polstead, 21, 29
Poor Law, New, 11, 12, 22, 32, 35, 45, 121; effect on wages, 28, 32, 35; Guardians, 12, 28, 29, 36; opposition to, 28-9, 35, 37-8, 40, 42, 43, 45, 73; workers elect sympathetic Guardians, 36, 42-3, 45, 47, 110; workhouses attacked, 28-9, 36-7
Poor Law, Old, 12, 19, 22; economies, 22, 27; Labour Rate, 26, 28; Speenhamland, 22
Population, 14; economic distribution, 13; urban, 13-14, 102
Press: Conservative, 34, 83, 93; Liberal, 17, 34, 42, 57, 83, 93. *See also individual newspapers*
Professions, 13, 16, 17, 18; politics, 17-18, 20
Printers, 32, 34
Prittlewell, 102
Quakers, 78, 80, 86, 99-100
Ramsey, 25, 27
Ransomes, 10, 13-14, 58, 59-60, 70, 79, 97; Corn Laws supported, 35; trade unionism, 119
Rattlesden, 23
Rawreth, 29
Rayleigh, 25, 29
Rebecca Riots, 105
Rebow family, 35, 107-8
Reform, Parliamentary: Acts, 11, 19-21, 110, 112-5; clubs, 16, 34; disillusion with, 34-6, 43; movements, 11, 14-21
Religion: *See* Baptists, Church of England, Congregationalists, Nonconformity, Peculiar People, Quakers, Wesleyans
Ridgewell, 25
Ringsfield, 26
Riots, 11, 23-30, 33; machine-breaking, 22-5; Riot Act, 23, 28, 37
Rochford, 24
Romford, 24, 102

Round, G. C., 104, 105
Roxwell, 25
Royalty, 14-15, 16, 18, 33, 41, 116
Rushbrooke, 26
Rushmere, 25, 56
Saffron Walden, 33, 102, 112; trade unionism, 31; workhouse attacked, 36-7
Sailors, 37, 84, 97; trade unionism, 31-2, 84, 119, 120
Sawyers, 32
Saxmundham, 119
Scotland, 56, 92
Semer, 28
Sheering, 21
Shipbuilding, 14; trade unionism, 31-2
Shoemakers, 32, 37; trade unionism, 31, 32, 74, 83, 116, 119, 120
Shops/shopkeepers/commerce, 13-14, 17, 21, 53, 79; politics, 17-18, 20, 34, 98, 100, 101; shop assistants, 44, 74
Silk industry, 9, 12, 13, 14, 32, 34, 79, 82; depressions, unemployment, 42, 65, 79, 98; handloom weavers, 9, 32, 36, 42, 43, 100, 115, 120, 121; power loom weavers, 9, 119; throwing mills, 9, 74; trade unionism, strikes, 31, 32, 119, 120; wages, 32, 42, 98
Soham, Earl, 29
Soham, Monk's, 23
Southwold, 20
Spexhall, 30
Stanford Rivers, 24
Stanningfield, 23
Stansted Mountfitchet, 27
Stapleford Tawney, 24
Stebbing, 28
Stonedredgers, 32, 74, 119
Stonham, Earl, 19, 29
Stortford, Bishop's, 10
Stowmarket, 10, 18, 102
Stradbroke, 28
Strikes: carpenters, 119; engineers, 119; farmworkers, 11, 22, 24-7; sailors, 31, 119; shoemakers, 119; silk workers, 74, 119; woollen weavers, 31
Sudbury, 9, 10, 102, 105; Parliamentary representation, 17, 20, 30, 33, 34; Reform politics, 15, 20; silk industry, 9, 120
Suffolk: county constituency, 11, 17, 20; population, 13-14, 22. *See also* Agriculture
Suffolk Chronicle, 17, 19-20, 37, 46, 60, 63, 64, 70, 75, 79, 82, 91
Surrey, 24
Sussex, 24
Tailoring/tailors, 13, 33; trade unionism, 31, 32, 34, 73-4, 90, 119
Tendring, 25, 29
Terling, 29, 122
Thaxted, 25, 28, 102; Reform politics, 21
The Times, 28, 81
Thetford, 120
Thorndon (Suff.), 28
Tithe, 12, 18, 19, 26, 35
Toft, 26
"Tolpuddle Martyrs", 32-3, 35, 46, 85

Toppesfield, 24, 29
Tories/Conservatives, 11, 18, 20, 36, 55, 56, 57, 78, 103, 114; Tory-Whig coalitions, 15, 19, 68, 69, 79, 103. *See also* Press
Trade unionism, 30-2, 42, 62, 119-20; Combination Acts, 23, 31; G.N.C.T.U., 32, 37, 40. *See also* individual trades
Unemployment/unemployed, 18, 26, 28, 35, 74, 79; Labour Rate, 26, 28; silk industry, 35, 42, 79; work schemes, 29. *See also* Farm workers
Wages, 14; artisans, 32, 116, 120; wool weavers, 31. *See also* Farm workers, Silk industry
Waldringfield, Gt., 106
Wales, 44, 56, 57, 59, 92, 97
Walpole, 26
Waltham Abbey, 102
Waltham, Gt./Lt., 22, 29
Walton, 25
Wars: American, 15; Napoleonic, 9, 10, 15. *See also* Peace movements
Wattisham, 23
Wellington, Duke of, 16, 19, 21
Wesleyans, 40, 86
Western family, 16, 35, 75
Weston, 26
Wetheringsett, 118
Whelnetham, 26

Whepstead, 26
Whigs, 11, 14-21, 36, 37, 55, 64, 78, 79; Church Rates supported, 35; Corn Laws supported, 11, 35; Tory-Whig coalitions, 15, 19, 68, 69, 79, 103
Wickford, 29
Wickham Market, 29, 73
Wickham St. Pauls, 83
Wickhambrook, 23
Wilkes, John, 14
Willingham, 26
Wiltshire, 24
Witham, 11, 16, 31, 36, 102, 106; incendiarism, 24; trade unionism, 32; Vestry dispute, 110-11
Women: employment, 9, 22, 32, 42; wages, 22
Woodbridge, 102; Reform politics, 21, 33; trade unionism, 31
Woollen cloth, 9, 12, 31, 34; clothiers, 9, 15, 18, 33; friendly society, 30; fullers, 9, 31; trade unionism, 30-31; weavers, 9, 30-1, 33; woolcombers, 9, 30
Wormingford, 27
Wortham, 29
Writtle, 25, 28, 29
Yarmouth, 14, 37, 102; trade unionism, 31, 119
Yaxley, 118
Young, Arthur, 10, 23

(ii) Chartism

(a) The Essex and Suffolk Movement

Adult education, 42, 43, 44, 45, 48, 62, 65, 69, 89, 93, 108-9, 117, 118
Ages of local leaders, 41, 101, 117
Aims, 41-2, 44, 46, 47, 48, 51, 55, 63, 80, 85-92
Anti-Corn Law League, 56, 57, 60, 62-3, 66, 72-3, 87, 98
Artisans, 41, 43, 45, 46, 53, 54, 58, 65, 73, 92, 97, 100, 101, 102, 123
Chartist families, 65, 67, 81, 101
Class-relations, views on, 48, 54-5, 56, 66, 93, 94, 95
Coffee-houses, 67, 77, 118
Complete Suffrage Union, 66, 68, 69, 70-1, 99, 111
Corn Laws, 47, 48, 51, 59, 60, 63, 72, 85, 87, 98
Education, 41-2, 44, 59, 85, 86, 88-9
Elections, 57, 68, 69-70, 78-9
Farm workers, 45, 50-6, 58, 62, 64-5, 68, 74-6, 79, 83, 87, 92, 94, 97, 101, 105, 118, 120
General Strike, 46, 48, 58, 67, 68-9, 97
Incendiarism, 54, 65, 74-6
Industrial workers, 97-8, 101
Inns/innkeepers/beerhouses, 52, 55, 56, 67, 71, 100, 101, 118

Ireland, 91
Labour theories of value, 46, 48, 49, 89-90
Land Scheme, 77-8, 79, 90, 96, 98, 101, 117
Liberals/Whigs, 41, 46, 47, 57, 58, 66, 70-1, 78, 82, 85, 93-4
Libraries, 43, 45, 118
London Working Men's Association, 39, 45, 47, 49, 56, 62, 85, 90, 91, 92
Middle-class support, 43, 98-9
"Moral Force", 41, 44, 47, 58, 60, 66, 92, 93, 94, 123
New Poor Law, 29, 40, 42, 48, 51, 52, 54, 55, 56, 63, 64, 72, 73, 85, 86, 87-8
National Charter Association, 63-84 *passim*, 93, 117, 123
National Chartist movement, 47, 55, 56, 58, 66, 67, 69, 81-2, 85, 86, 92-3, 96
Newport Rising, 59, 62, 93, 107, 121, 123
News rooms, 63, 67, 77
Nonconformity, 39-40, 41, 45, 46, 52, 70, 86-7, 92, 94, 100
Northern Star, 65, 67, 72, 73, 109, 123
O'Connor, Feargus, attitudes to, 41, 49, 58, 65, 67, 69, 72, 82, 84, 93-4, 112, 123

Organisations, 39, 66, 68
Owenism/Socialism, 40, 53, 63, 64, 67, 73, 84, 90, 96, 109, 118
Peace policies/pacifism, 44, 49, 53, 66, 79, 80-1, 90-1
Petitions, 45, 46, 47, 48, 59, 65, 68, 81-2
"Physical Force", 57, 58, 60, 92
Press, Chartist, 55, 67, 77, 83, 84, 96, 117-8. *See also Northern Star*
Reform Act of 1867, 112-3
Religious influences, 46, 48, 52
Royalty, attitudes to, 41, 44, 48, 63, 80-1, 85, 86

Shoemakers, 40, 41, 83, 97, 100, 101
Silk workers, 42, 45, 50, 97-8
Social activities, 67, 77
Tailors, 40, 41, 44, 54, 73-4, 97, 100
Temperance, 41, 42, 63, 64, 66, 67, 69, 73
Trade unionism, 66-7, 68-9, 73-4, 83, 84, 94-5, 120, 123
Unemployed/unemployment, 79, 80, 86, 90, 98
Victimisation, 49-50, 52, 65, 117
"Victims", 60, 67, 82, 83, 84, 90
Women, 47, 50, 67, 74, 90, 97-8, 101

(b) *The local Chartist leaders and some national leaders*

Barmby, J., 53, 62, 64, 72, 88, 90, 91, 99
Barrett, W., 73-4, 84, 120
Bearman, G., 43, 98
Bedlow, T., 54-5
Bird, C., 40, 58
Bird, J., 33, 37, 38, 40, 58, 62, 68, 79
Blatch, W., 42, 48, 65, 84, 116, 118
Booley, R., 39-40, 46, 52, 57, 62, 66, 70, 72, 79, 80, 82, 88-9, 90, 90, 91, 92, 93
Bugg, F., 100, 111, 113, 116
Castle, J., 120, 121
Chapman (Colchester), 74, 120
Chapman (Yarmouth), 84
Cleave, J., 47, 48-9, 50, 56
Clubb family, 65, 78, 81, 118
Coe, T., 111, 120, 121
Cook, J., 38, 40, 66, 67, 79, 80, 83, 91, 94, 100, 113, 117, 118, 120
Cowell, J., 120, 121
Dennis, G., 72, 74, 78, 90, 118, 120, 121
Fisher, T., 84
Francies, S., 79, 81, 82
Frost, J., 77, 78
Gammage, R., 65, 71
Garrard, W., 40, 50, 52-3, 57, 58, 62, 63, 66, 67, 71, 72, 73, 76, 79, 83, 90, 91, 95-6, 99, 117, 118, 120
Goody, J., 67, 77, 121
Goslin, J., 37-8, 40, 46, 48, 53, 57, 58, 63, 64, 66, 79, 80, 88, 91, 93, 95, 117
Gould, J., 51, 62, 63, 75-6, 92
Harvey, C., 40, 62, 120

Hearn, Friston, 52, 53, 64, 98
Howe, J., 113, 116, 120-1
Hull, R., 49, 88-9
Hunt, J., 44, 120
Jones, Ernest, 84, 96, 113, 123
Lovett, W., 44, 56, 62, 65, 66, 93, 123
Lovewell, H., 40, 66, 70, 79, 91, 92
Mason, W., 68
M'Douall, P., 68-9, 73, 94-5, 123
M'Pherson, D., 37, 40, 41, 46, 49, 52, 57, 58, 62, 63, 64, 68, 70, 71, 72-3, 79, 80, 86-7, 88, 89, 90, 91, 94, 98, 99, 111, 117, 118
Newman, T., 100, 116
Orr, R., 40, 57, 62, 120
Parker, B., 42, 65, 90, 98
Parmenter, W., 44, 71
Pearce, J., 79
Plummer, T., 73-4, 78, 80, 90, 91, 120
Potter, W., 115, 120
Rawlings, T., 65, 84, 116, 120, 121
Royall, J., 73, 84, 112
Rushbrooke, W., 40, 79, 100, 111, 112-3, 120, 121
Shead, W., 43, 120, 121
Smith, B., 44, 99
Smith, L., 43-4, 50, 65, 71, 82, 89, 99
Thorogood, J., 49, 86-7
Vincent, H., 40, 49, 69-71, 78-9
Whimper, N., 40, 41, 46, 73, 83-4
White, J., 37, 40, 47
Wire, W., 36, 41, 42, 47, 78, 85

(c) *The main centres*

Assington, 97
Benhall, 53, 62, 64
Bildeston, 51, 119
Boxford, 51
Braintree/Bocking, 39, 44, 48, 50, 57, 59, 60, 65, 66, 67, 71, 72, 82, 83, 84, 97, 112; adult education, 43-4; Anti-Corn Law League, 60, 87; Co-operatives, 89, 121; inns, beerhouses, 66, 67, 71; internationalism, 91; Land Branch, 77; meeting condemned by Justices, 82-3; middle-class support, 44, 98; "Moral Force" views, 39, 44, 60; New Poor Law opposed, 87; petition, 81; silk workers' support, 50, 65, 66, 71, 97-8; trade unionism, 73, 120; women Chartists, 67

Brandon, 80
Brightlingsea, 66, 72; fishermen, 97; Land Branch, 77; women Chartists, 67
Bulmer, 97
Bungay, 55, 118
Bury St. Edmunds, 51-2, 59, 60, 72; election, 78; Land Branch, 77; N.C.A. branch, 64, 66; Owenism, 118; public meetings, 69, 83; Reform Act of 1867, 112
Chelmsford, 45, 49-50, 54, 60, 69, 82; Church Rates opposed, 86; desire for Chartist unity, 66; London demonstrations, 49, 81; Land Branch, 77; N.C.A. Branch formed, 65; Operatives' Reform Association, 39, 45, 49; Reform Act of 1867, 112; village meeting, 55; women Chartists, 67
Coggeshall, 39, 45, 60, 67, 72, 82; Church Rate opposed, 45, 86; Land Branch, 77; N.C.A. branch, 65-6; New Poor Law opposed, 87; silk weavers, 65, 97
Colchester, 39-42, 60, 65, 67, 72, 81, 84, 91, 94, 97, 102, 112, 117; aims, 85; artisans prominent, 100; ban on meeting, 81; Co-operative Society, 121-2; Corn Laws, 47, 73; divergence of views, 48-9, 57; General Strike rejected, 58; internationalism, 91; Land Branch, 77; London demonstration, 81; militants, 49; "Moral Force", 41-2; N.C.A. branch, 65, 78; Nonconformity, 41; O'Connor supported, 49, 69; pacifism, 79, 80, 91; petitions, 47-8, 67-8; pro-Liberal views, 41, 57, 78; Reform Act of 1867, 112, 113; support from Liberals, 82; Temperance, 66; trade unionism, 68, 73-4, 120-1; use of opponents' meetings, 56-7
Cornard, 97
Darsham, 53
Debenham, 51, 100
Diss, 52
Epping, 55, 58
Exning, 77
Eye, 51, 60, 62, 64, 68, 84
Flatford, 97
Framlingham, 64, 100
Fressingfield, 98
Friston, 52, 58, 62, 64
Gestingthorpe, 97
Hadleigh, 51, 75-6, 87, 96
Halstead, 39, 50, 57, 60, 65, 82, 83, 112, 113; Co-operative Society, 113, 121; Land Branch, 77; library, 45; middle-class support, 98; N.C.A., 78; Nonconformity, 44; Reform Act of 1867, 112; silk workers, 44, 50, 65, 78, 97, 120
Harleston, 52, 58, 64-5, 68
Harlow, 55
Harwich, 66
Hatfield Broad Oak, 55
Hatfield Peverel, 97
Hedinghams, 66, 98
Ipswich, 39-41, 48, 50, 51, 52, 53, 56, 59, 60, 62, 66, 68, 72, 82, 83-4, 97, 111-4; Address to the People of Paris, 80-1; aims, 86; Anti-Corn Law League opposed, 62-3, 72-3; coffee-house, 63; Complete Suffrage Union, 70-1, 111; delegate sent to Convention, 81; discussion group, 118; diversity of views, 39-41, 66; elections, 57-8, 59, 62, 63-4, 68, 70, 78-9; internationalism, 80-1; Ipswich Chartist Association, 58, 63; Land Branch, 77-8; London demonstration, 81; middle-class support, 98, 99-100; N.C.A., 63, 66, 78, 79; New Poor Law, 46, 47, 63, 87-8; Parliamentary voters, 57, 98; petitions, 46, 47, 59-60; Ransomes workers, 59, 97; Reform Acts of 1867 and 1884, 112-3; rural campaign, 50-6; women Chartists, 67
Kersey, 97
Lavenham, 72
Laxfield, 53, 62
Leighs, Lt., 97
Long Melford, 97
Maldon, 55, 60, 66, 84, 97; Land Branch, 77; trade unionism, 74
Manningtree, 66
Middleton (Suff.), 53
Newton, 97
Ongars, 55
Rawreth, 39, 50, 54-5, 97; New Poor Law opposed, 39, 55, 87
Rayleigh, 55, 60
Romford, 50, 55, 56-7, 60; Anti-Corn Law League opposed, 72; Land Branch, 77
Roothings, 55
Saxmundham, 52, 53, 60, 64, 100; Owenism, 118
Silver End, 97
Stowmarket, 51, 60, 62, 63, 64, 72; N.C.A., 78
Sudbourne, 53
Sudbury, 51, 57, 59, 60, 67, 72, 84, 97; artisans prominent, 100; Land Branch, 77; N.C.A., 64, 78; petition, 81; reading-room, 67; silk-workers, 64, 97; Temperance, 67; trade unionism, 73; village meeting, 83
Thetford, 52
Totham, Gt., 97
Waltham Abbey, 55
Walthamstow, 55, 72
Wenhaston, 53
Westleton, 53, 58
Wickford, 55, 97
Witham, 55, 60, 66, 67, 72, 82, 94, 97, 101-2, 111; Land Branch, 77, 78
Wivenhoe, 66
Woodbridge, 52, 53, 64, 65, 73
Woodford, 55
Yarmouth, 64, 68, 83, 84, 94, 112; Land Branch, 77; Owenism, 118; Reform Act of 1867, 112; sailors, 84, 97; trade unionism, 73, 84
Yoxford, 53, 99; Owenism, 118